For Jonathan Paul King
and
In Memory of
Luther Waddington King
Alba Iregui King
Maria Luisa Iregui

Religious satire and polemic constitute an elusive presence in *Paradise Lost*. In this important new book, John N. King shows how Milton's poem takes on new meaning when understood as part of a strategy of protest against ecclesiastical formalism and clericalism. The experience of Adam and Eve before the Fall recalls many Puritan devotional habits. After the Fall, they are prone to "idolatrous" ritual and ceremony that anticipate the religious "error" of Milton's own age. Vituperative sermons, broadsides, and pamphlets, notably Milton's own tracts, afford a valuable context for recovering the poem's engagement with the violent history of the Civil Wars, Commonwealth, and Restoration, while contemporary visual satires help to clarify Miltonic practice. Eighteenth-century critics who attacked breaches of decorum and sublimity in *Paradise Lost* alternately deplored and ignored a literary and polemical tradition deployed by Milton's contemporaries. This important study sheds new light on Milton's epic and its literary and religious contexts.

John N. King is Professor of English at the Ohio State University. His books include *English Reformation Literature: The Tudor Origins of the Protestant Tradition* (1982), *Tudor Royal Iconography: Literature and Art in an Age of Religious Crisis* (1989), and *Spenser's Poetry and the Reformation Tradition* (1990). He is co-editor of *Literature and History*, and Literature Editor of *Reformation*.

MILTON AND RELIGIOUS CONTROVERSY

MILTON AND RELIGIOUS CONTROVERSY

SATIRE AND POLEMIC IN
PARADISE LOST

JOHN N. KI

The Ohio

CAMBRIDGE
UNIVERSITY PRESS

PUBLISHED BY THE PRESS SYNDICATE OF THE UNIVERSITY OF CAMBRIDGE
The Pitt Building, Trumpington Street, Cambridge United Kingdom

CAMBRIDGE UNIVERSITY PRESS
The Edinburgh Building, Cambridge, CB2 2RU, UK http://www.cup.cam.ac.uk
40 West 20th Street, New York, NY 10011–4211, USA http://www.cup.org
10 Stamford Road, Oakleigh, Melbourne 3166, Australia

First published 2000

Printed in the United Kingdom at the University Press, Cambridge

Typeset in Baskerville 11/12.5pt [VN]

A catalogue record for this book is available from the British Library

Library of Congress Cataloguing in Publication data
King, John N., 1945–
Milton and religious controversy: satire and polemic in Paradise lost / John N. King
p.   cm.
Includes bibliographical references and index.
ISBN 0 521 77198 6 (hardback)
1. Milton, John, 1608–1674.   Paradise lost.   2. Christianity and literature – England – History
– 17th century.   3. Christian poetry. English – History and criticism.   4. Verse satire. English –
History and criticism.   5. Milton, John, 1608–1674 – Religion.   6. Polemics in literature.   I.
Title.
PR3562.K45   2000
821'.4–dc21   99–15847 CIP

ISBN 0 521 77198 6 hardback

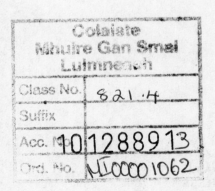

Contents

Illustrations

Preface

This study aims to recover an all but forgotten dimension of *Paradise Lost*. That John Milton had a corrosively bitter and astringent wit will come as no surprise to readers of his polemical tracts. His fondness for what Samuel Johnson condemned as "controversial merriment" constitutes a more elusive presence in the biblical epic, one recovered by teasing out sly hints, sarcastic innuendoes, and deeply embedded typological patterns. Ardent sermons, fiery broadsheets, and belligerent pamphlets of the mid-seventeenth century, notably Milton's own antiprelatical tracts, afford a rich context for recovering the poem's engagement with the violent history of the era of the Civil Wars, Commonwealth, and Restoration. The iconography of visual satire affords a fertile field of analogies to Miltonic practice.

Details of *Paradise Lost*, some familiar and some overlooked, take on new meaning when seen as part of a strategy of antiformalistic polemic against the Church of Rome, High Church Protestantism, and clericalism of all creeds. The vituperative context of religious satire and polemic illuminates elements of the poem such as the "communion" meal shared by Adam and Raphael in the Garden of Eden and the way in which Cain's murder of Abel typifies the origin of conflict between "true" and "false" churches. Indeed, recovery of the discourse of ecclesiastical satire should enable readers to reinterpret attacks on breaches of decorum and sublimity in the epic that are traceable to the neoclassical canons of critics such as Joseph Addison and Dr. Johnson. Among the chief instances are responses to the much maligned allegory of Sin and Death and to the War in Heaven.

This book results furthermore from a consideration of *Paradise Lost* from the vantage point of the native tradition of religious controversy and satire. Like Spenser, Milton apprehended works attributed to John Wycliffe, Geoffrey Chaucer, and the author known as William Langland as proto-Protestant texts. The argument takes their writings, and verse by Spenser and the Spenserian poets, Phineas Fletcher in particular, not as sources or influences, but as notable instances of cultural practices associated with religious polemic and satire. Fully aware of manifest differences between sixteenth- and seventeenth-century English poetry, politics, and religion, this book also perceives important points of continuity.

Intellectual debts have compounded during the course of this project. I am indebted to friends and colleagues whose readings of the entire book, at different points during its progress, have provided many important suggestions for improvement. Standing by the project from its inception, John T. Shawcross and Stephen Honeygosky generously commented on early drafts. For many valuable suggestions, I am grateful to Luke Wilson, John G. Norman, Annabel Patterson, and Blair Worden. I owe special thanks to Robert Entzminger for a probing critique of the penultimate draft, one that pointed the way toward resolution of some stubborn problems. For their very helpful readings as evaluators for Cambridge University Press, I extend warm thanks to Stephen Fallon and John Morrill. For constructive readings of particular parts of the book, I am grateful to Gale H. Carrithers, Jr., Raymond Frontain, James D. Hardy, Jr., David Loewenstein, Gregory Machachek, Katharine Narveson, Thomas G. Olsen, Carla Pestana, Janet Spencer, and Jeffrey Wheeler. I also acknowledge very helpful assistance in research afforded by Nancy W. Miller, Thomas G. Olsen, and Kevin Lindberg. I am grateful to Mark A. Bayer for his gracious assistance with verifying citations, proof-reading, and compilation of the index. Many friends and colleagues at The Ohio State University have offered generous assistance, encouragement, and wise counsel. Among them I count Morris Beja, James Bracken, Deborah Burks, David Frantz, Kermit Hall, Christopher Highley, Nicholas Howe, Lisa Kiser, Ethan Knapp, Vassilios Lambropoulos, Eve Levin, Isaac Mowoe, James Phelan, Phoebe Spinrad, and Christian Zacher. Their extramural counterparts are John Ackerman, James Bednarz, Patrick Cheney, Mary Thomas Crane, Darryl Gless, Peter Kaufman, Gordon Kipling, Albert Labriola, Lucy and Mark Le Fanu, Barbara Kiefer Lewalski, Arthur Marotti, Janel Mueller, David Norbrook, Anne Lake Prescott, and Glynn Redworth. I thank Josie Dixon, my resourceful editor at Cambridge University Press, for furthering publication of this book. I am grateful to Jane Wheare for meticulous copyediting. All remaining errors of fact or interpretation are my own.

More general obligations are to undergraduate and graduate students in courses and seminars taught at Bates College and The Ohio State University. The first inklings of the way that I think about Books 11 and 12 of *Paradise Lost* date back to my participation in Barbara Lewalski's National Endowment for the Humanities Residential Seminar on "Renaissance Genres and Genre Theory" at Brown University (1981–82). Participants in my National Endowment for the Humanities Summer Seminar for College Teachers on "The English Reformation: Literature, History, and Art" (1997) helped me to think through a variety of issues. Responses of colleagues who attended presentations at the following gatherings were most helpful: Newberry Library Milton Seminar (1995); Oxford University Seminar on Language, Culture, and History: 1500–1800 (1996); "*The Faerie Queene* in the World, 1596–1996," an interdisciplinary symposium at Yale University (1996); and the International Congress of Medieval Studies at Kalamazoo, Michigan (1997).

Completion of this project owes much to librarians and keepers at collections and archives that gave access to important records. They include the British Library, Bodleian Library, Department of Prints and Drawings at the British Museum, Folger Shakespeare Library, Henry E. Huntington Library, Library of Congress, Ohio State University Libraries, Saint Andrews University Library, and Warburg Institute.

Generous funding and released time for this project have come from many sources. I thank the National Endowment for the Humanities for a fellowship for university professors and a travel-to-collections grant. Different entities at The Ohio State University have supported this project through faculty professional leave and other forms of assistance. For matching funds and grants in aid, I am grateful to the College of Humanities and Department of English. The Center for Medieval and Renaissance Studies has provided grants in support of travel to collections and photography. An Andrew W. Mellon Foundation Fellowship supported research at the Henry E. Huntington Library. The National Humanities Center provided the haven where I finished this book as Lilly Fellow in Religion and the Humanities, funded by the Lilly Endowment. I am grateful to the Center's administrators, librarians, and fellows in the Class of 1998 for their unflagging support.

A number of editors and publishers have granted permission for the inclusion of previously published work in revised and expanded form. Essays upon which Chapter 4 is based are "Milton's Cave of Error: A Rewriting of Spenserian Satire," forthcoming in *Worldly Relations: Exploring Selves and Others in Spenser and the Early Modern Age*, ed. Patrick Cheney and Lauren Silberman (Lexington: University of Kentucky

Press, 1999); and "Milton's Sin and Death: A Rewriting of Spenser's Den of Error," forthcoming in *Form and Reform in Renaissance England: Essays in Honor of Barbara Kiefer Lewalski*, ed. Mary Crane and Amy Boesky (Newark: University of Delaware Press, 2000). Chapter 5 assimilates material from "Milton's Paradise of Fools: Ecclesiastical Satire in *Paradise Lost*," in *Catholicism and Anti-Catholicism in Early Modern English Texts*, ed. Arthur Marotti (London: Macmillan, 1999), pp. 198–217. The bulk of Chapter 7 comes from "Miltonic Transubstantiation," *Milton Studies* 36 (1998), pp. 41–58.

Spelling is modernized in quotations from pre-1800 texts, with the exception of passages from Middle English and poems written in an archaic style by Edmund Spenser and Spenserian poets such as Phineas Fletcher. Italicization and capitalization that depart from modern usage are ignored unless retention is essential to convey the sense of the document. Changes in punctuation are introduced only if they are essential to clarify the sense of textual passages. Contractions are expanded, and roman numerals are spelled out. The abbreviation sig. is omitted from signature references. I have used bold type to supply special emphasis. All dates are in New Style. Unless otherwise noted, London is the place of publication in pre-1900 book titles and reference is to first editions.

My greatest obligation is to Pauline and Jonathan, my wife and son, and to my late father, Luther, who have sustained this project for many years.

Abbreviations

BCP	John E. Booty, *The Book of Common Prayer 1559: The Elizabethan Prayer Book* (Charlottesville: University Press of Virginia, 1976).
B.L.	British Library.
Bodl.	Bodleian Library.
Carey	Poems other than *PL* in *Poems of John Milton*, ed. Carey and Fowler.
CD	Milton (attrib.), *De Doctrina Christiana* (*On Christian Doctrine*).
Columbia	Milton, *The Works of John Milton*, ed. Frank Allen Patterson, 18 vols. (New York: Columbia University Press, 1931–8).
Comus	Milton, *A Mask at Ludlow*.
CPW	John Milton, *Complete Prose Works of John Milton*, ed. Don M. Wolfe, et al., 8 vols. (New Haven: Yale University Press, 1953–1982).
CVT	Giles Fletcher, *Christs Victory and Triumph*, in Giles and Phineas Fletcher, *Poetical Works*, 2 vols. (Cambridge University Press, 1908–1909).
DNB	Leslie Stephen and Sidney Lee, *Dictionary of National Biography*, 63 vols. (London, 1885–1900).
ELR	*English Literary Renaissance*.
ERL	John N. King, *English Reformation Literature: The Tudor Origins of the Protestant Tradition* (Princeton University Press, 1982).
Flannagan	*PL*, ed. Roy Flannagan (New York: Macmillan, 1993).
Folger	Folger Shakespeare Library.
Fowler	*PL* in *Poems of John Milton*, ed. Carey and Fowler.
FQ	Edmund Spenser, *The Faerie Queene*, ed. A. C. Hamilton (London: Longman, 1979).

George	*Catalogue of Political and Personal Satires Preserved in the Department of Prints and Drawings in the British Museum,* prepared by Frederic G. Stephens and M. Dorothy George, 11 vols. in 12 (London: British Museum, 1870–1954).
Hill, *MER*	Christopher Hill, *Milton and the English Revolution,* 2nd ed. (Harmondsworth: Penguin, 1979).
Hind	Arthur M. Hind, *Engraving in England in the Sixteenth and Seventeenth Centuries,* 3 vols. (Cambridge University Press, 1953–1964).
HLQ	*Huntington Library Quarterly.*
Hughes	John Milton, *Complete Poems and Major Prose,* ed. Merritt Y. Hughes (Indianapolis and New York: Odyssey Press, 1957).
Hume	P[atrick] H[ume], *Annotations on Milton's "Paradise Lost"* (1695).
L&H	*Literature and History.*
Luther	Martin Luther, *Works,* ed. Jaroslav Pelikan, et al., 55 vols. (St. Louis: Concordia Publishing House, 1959).
ME	William B. Hunter, Jr., John T. Shawcross, John M. Steadman, et al., *A Milton Encyclopedia,* 9 vols. (Lewisburg: Bucknell University Press, 1978–83).
Milton, Poems, ed. Warton	Milton, *Poems Upon Several Occasions, English, Italian and Latin, with Translations, by John Milton. Viz. Lycidas, l'Allegro, Il penseroso, Arcades, Comus, Odes, Sonnets, Miscellanies, English Psalms, Elegiarum Liber, Epigrammatum Liber, Sylvarum Liber,* ed. Thomas Warton (1785).
MiltonQ	*Milton Quarterly.*
MiltonS	*Milton Studies.*
MRTS	Medieval & Renaissance Texts & Studies.
Ode	Milton, *On the Morning of Christ's Nativity.*
OED	J. A. H. Murray, et al., *A New English Dictionary on Historical Principles,* 11 vols. (Oxford University Press, 1884–1933).
OER	Hans Hillerbrand, et al., *The Oxford Encyclopedia of the Reformation,* 4 vols. (Oxford University Press, 1996).
Orgel and Goldberg	*John Milton,* ed. Stephen Orgel and Jonathan Goldberg (Oxford University Press, 1990).
Parker	William Riley Parker, *Milton: A Biography,* 2 vols. (Oxford: Clarendon Press, 1968).
PL	Milton, *Paradise Lost.*
PR	Milton, *Paradise Regained.*

SPART	John N. King, *Spenser's Poetry and the Reformation Tradition* (Princeton University Press, 1990).
STC	A. W. Pollard, et al., *A Short-Title Catalogue of Books Printed in England, Scotland, and Ireland, and of English Books Printed Abroad, 1475–1640*, 2nd ed., rev. and enlarged, 3 vols. (London: Bibliographical Society, 1976–86).
TRI	John N. King, *Tudor Royal Iconography: Literature and Art in an Age of Religious Crisis*, Princeton Essays on the Arts (Princeton: Princeton University Press, 1989).
Wing	Donald Wing, *Short Title Catalogue of Books Printed in England, Scotland, Ireland, Wales and British America and of English Books Printed in Other Countries 1641–1700*, 2nd ed. rev. and enlarged, 3 vols. (New York: MLA, 1972).

Note on texts

Except for biblical passages quoted in early printed books, scriptural texts are from *The Geneva Bible*, facsimile of the 1560 edition with introduction by Lloyd E. Berry (Madison: University of Wisconsin Press, 1969). Miltonic texts are from *The Poems of John Milton*, ed. John Carey and Alastair Fowler (London: Longman, 1968) and *Complete Prose Works of John Milton*, ed. Don M. Wolfe, et al., 8 vols. (New Haven: Yale University Press, 1953–1982). Spenserian quotations are from Edmund Spenser, *The Faerie Queene*, ed. A. C. Hamilton (London: Longman, 1977); and *The Yale Edition of the Shorter Poems of Edmund Spenser*, ed. William Oram, et al. (New Haven: Yale University Press, 1989). Unless otherwise noted, silent reference is made to the following sources: *DNB*; *OED*; *STC*; Wing; David Lyle Jeffrey, ed., *A Dictionary of Biblical Tradition in English Literature* (Grand Rapids, MI: William B. Eerdmans, 1992); Edward Le Comte, *A Dictionary of Puns in Milton's English Poetry* (New York: Columbia University Press, 1981); and John T. Shawcross, *Milton: A Bibliography for the Years 1624–1700* (Binghamton, NY: MRTS, 1984).

CHAPTER I

Controversial merriment

Paradise Lost is deeply engaged with bitter religious strife that dominated seventeenth-century British public life. Nevertheless, critics from the time of Samuel Johnson until the present day have failed to apprehend the fundamental importance of ecclesiastical controversy, indeed of levity and satire, in John Milton's great epic of the Fall. Although Dr. Johnson contemptuously dismisses the "controversial merriment" that he discerns throughout Milton's antiprelatical and antimonarchical tracts, he claims that topical reference is virtually absent from *Paradise Lost*.[1] Scholars have amply acknowledged the overt critique of the Roman Catholic church and the established Church of England in the harsh allegations of Milton's revolutionary pamphlets as well as the more subtle infusion of polemical concerns into *A Mask at Ludlow* (hereafter cited as *Comus*).[2] Fully a generation after Christopher Hill published his massively influential, and contested, thesis concerning Milton's engagement with religio-political radicalism,[3] however, readers have recognized only disconnected instances of religious controversy and satire in the epic.[4]

The present study seeks to amend that deficiency by disclosing the deep engagement of *Paradise Lost* with religious controversy colored by what the poet perceived as the massive setback of the Restoration. This book employs *Lycidas* as a point of entry into analysis of the integral role played by anti-Catholic and antiprelatical complaint and satire in Mil-

---

[1] Johnson, "Life of Milton" (1779), in J.P. Hardy, ed., *Johnson's "Lives of the Poets": A Selection* (Oxford: Clarendon Press, 1971), p. 61.

[2] See Thomas N. Corns, *Uncloistered Virtue: English Political Literature, 1640-1660* (Oxford: Clarendon Press, 1992), ch. 2; Leah S. Marcus, *The Politics of Mirth: Jonson, Herrick, Milton, Marvell, and the Defense of Old Holiday Pastimes* (University of Chicago Press, 1986), ch. 6; Achsah Guibbory, *Ceremony and Community from Herbert to Milton: Literature, Religion, and Cultural Conflict in Seventeenth-Century England* (Cambridge University Press, 1998), ch. 6.

[3] Hill, *Milton and the English Revolution*, 2nd ed. (Harmondsworth: Penguin, 1979); hereafter cited as *MER*.

[4] Achsah Guibbory comes closest to the mark in *Ceremony and Community*, pp. 191, 196, 201.

ton's biblical epic. Examination of the early reception of *Paradise Lost* will demonstrate how readers including Joseph Addison and other neoclassical critics suppressed a polemical and satirical side deeply embedded within a text that they revered, despite partial disclaimers, as a sublime masterpiece divorced from contemporary history. His declaration that "Milton's chief talent, and indeed his distinguishing excellence, lies in the sublimity of his thoughts" exemplifies the imposition of a critical fiction that dominated thinking during the eighteenth, nineteenth, and first three quarters of the twentieth century.[5] Retrieval of the epic's forgotten engagement with religious polemics complements recent political readings of the poem.[6] Like such studies, this book recovers contemporary, topical, and polemical concerns in order to counter an older view that the text stands sublimely above the fray. It complicates and enriches the more recent view of *Paradise Lost* as a Puritan poem colored by the experience of the English Revolution and Restoration.[7]

Recovery of the pugnaciously sardonic side of Milton's poem qualifies the findings of scholars who have demonstrated its timeless concern with Christian faith and worship.[8] Recovery of the forgotten engagement of *Paradise Lost* with invective, mockery, surly insult, parody, and satire, even at some of its more sublime moments, demonstrates how thoroughly the text is embedded in contemporary affairs during an age of revolution and reaction. The argument adds to our knowledge of the profound multigenericity of *Paradise Lost* by demonstrating how a satirical mode, which long ago fell into oblivion, infuses many of the poem's genres and sub-genres.[9] The epic's polemical dimension is not simply a layer of meaning superimposed upon other elements, but an inextricable part of those elements, and one whose recognition changes our perceptions of the poem in a fundamental way.

Milton's *Of Reformation* (May 1641) affords a useful index for defining

[5] Joseph Addison and Richard Steele, *The Spectator*, ed. Donald F. Bond, 5 vols. (Oxford: Clarendon Press, 1965), no. 279. See Leslie E. Moore, *Beautiful Sublime: The Making of* Paradise Lost, *1701–1734* (Stanford University Press, 1990), p. 2, et seq.

[6] For example, Mary Ann Radzinowicz, "The Politics of *Paradise Lost*," in *Politics of Discourse: The Literature and History of Seventeenth-Century England*, ed. Kevin Sharpe and Steven N. Zwicker (Berkeley and Los Angeles: University of California Press, 1987), pp. 204–29; *Milton and Republicanism*, ed. David Armitage, et al. (Cambridge University Press, 1995).

[7] See Sharon Achinstein, *Milton and the Revolutionary Reader* (Princeton University Press, 1994), ch. 5; Laura L. Knoppers, *Historicizing Milton: Spectacle, Power, and Poetry in Restoration England* (Athens, GA: University of Georgia Press, 1994), ch. 3.

[8] e.g. Michael Lieb, *Poetics of the Holy: A Reading of* Paradise Lost (Chapel Hill, NC: University of North Carolina Press, 1981), passim; Regina M. Schwartz, *Remembering and Repeating: On Milton's Theology and Poetics* (Cambridge University Press, 1988), pp. 72–74.

[9] Although satire is absent even from Barbara K. Lewalski's magisterial study, *"Paradise Lost" and the Rhetoric of Literary Forms* (Princeton University Press, 1985), she does consider the Father's irony and wrath (pp. 125–26).

polemical matrices in *Paradise Lost.* The tract's flamboyant invective vilifies ecclesiastical ceremonialism and reservation of the power of ordination by diocesan bishops as "pomp of prelatism" and "popedom" (*CPW* 1: 527–28). Although the pamphlet supports the Presbyterian effort to overthrow episcopacy, Milton would abandon the Presbyterian cause by 1644. We must remember that he engaged in lifelong exploration of ever-changing formalistic, Puritan, Presbyterian, Independent, and antiformalistic religious ideas. I employ **formalism** and **formalist(ic)** rather than the anachronistic terms **Anglicanism** and **Anglican**. Although a character named **Anglican** appears nowhere in John Bunyan's *Pilgrim's Progress* (1678), for example, **Formalist** does. Equally well, I employ the term **antiformalism** or **antiformalist(ic)** in place of **nonconformist** to define Milton's varied stances during the 1640s, 1650s, 1660s, and 1670s. To align him with **nonconformity**, a slippery subcategory of **antiformalism**, would indicate that he failed to attend worship in parish churches. Although it is possible that he avoided all contact with the "state" church, we cannot rule out the alternative possibility that he worshipped in parish churches that observed an **antiformalistic** style. No evidence exists that Milton ever attended a Sunday service other than in a parish church. **Puritan** remains viable as a term for the reformist minority committed to strict spirituality that went beyond the set worship of the *Book of Common Prayer*.[10]

Publication of Milton's *Of Reformation* coincided with the introduction before the House of Commons of the Root and Branch Bill to abolish episcopal prerogatives. On that highly charged occasion, Milton's tract appealed for completion of ecclesiastical reforms left unfinished at the time of England's 1530s schism from Rome, which marked the beginning of "fourscore years" during which the episcopal "viper of sedition . . . hath been breeding to eat through the entrails of our peace." By contrast, the revolutionary ferment of the early 1640s allegedly revives an abortive Reformation inspired during the fourteenth century by John Wycliffe, whose "short blaze [was] soon damped and stifled by the Pope and prelates."[11] Milton attacks the Elizabethan Compromise of 1559 for

---

[10] See J.C. Davis, "Against Formality: One Aspect of the English Revolution," *Transactions of the Royal Historical Society* 6th ser., 3 (1993), pp. 265–88; J.C. Davis, "Religion and the Struggle for Freedom in the English Revolution," *Historical Journal* 35 (1992), pp. 526–30; and Patrick Collinson, *The Religion of Protestants: The Church in English Society, 1559–1625* (Oxford: Clarendon Press, 1982), pp. 107–111, 138.

[11] *CPW* 1: 525–26, 531–32, 538–39, 614. *Animadversions Upon the Remonstrant's Defence, Against Smectymnuus* (1641) and *Reason of Church Government* (1641) echo *Of Reformation* in attacking "this fourscore years and so long we have been your slaves to serve it up for you, much against our wills" and "this fourscore years vexation of his church under your Egyptian [i.e. prelatical] tyranny" (*CPW* 1: 733, 793).

mingling Protestant theology with Roman Catholic ceremonialism and imposing the wearing of clerical vestments, prelatical governance of the church, and a liturgy based upon the medieval Latin rite.

Collapsing distinctions between "papistry" and episcopacy, *Of Reformation* attributes failures in the Church of England to William Laud, appointed Archbishop of Canterbury in 1633, who presided over a perceived swerve toward Roman Catholicism.[12] Of course, Laud executed policies initiated and approved by Charles I (1625–49). Despite its official Protestant theology, the Church of England harbored many resemblances to papal Catholicism, by contrast to the thoroughly Reformed churches of Holland and Geneva. Antiformalists like Milton rejected a national Church that retained enrobed prelates, vested priests, and iconic symbols such as the royal coat of arms. For Protestant nationalists, the marriages of Charles I, Charles II, and James II to foreign Catholic queens conjured up the specter of a Roman Catholic succession. Only parliament remained committed to a Protestant religious settlement. Catholic veneration of relics and religious images fueled Protestant fears of "idolatry." Because English Protestantism had never totally eradicated the "Roman Other," outlandish panics concerning papist "peril" periodically engulfed the country.

By reversing key Protestant beliefs and practices, Archbishop Laud blocked Puritans from pursuing clerical careers. *Lycidas* bitterly attacks Laudian "innovations," which included opposition to Puritan lectureships dedicated to Bible-based preaching. A few years later, Milton declared that he had been "church-outed by the prelates."[13] Laud elevated religious uniformity above the Protestant doctrine of *sola scriptura* ("scripture alone"). The High Churchman's advocacy of ceremony and gravity is well known, but he placed sacramentalism, anathema to Puritans, at the top of his theological agenda. Almost a century earlier, Protestant opposition to the Roman-rite Mass had led to the dismantling of altars and erection of freestanding communion tables in church naves. Coupled with the pulling down of chancel screens that bore outsized roods, or crosses, Protestant emphasis upon Bible reading in the vernacular and pulpit preaching had bridged the gulf between clergy and laity that yawned by the end of the Middle Ages.

Laudian sacerdotalism (assertion of priestly prerogatives) restored the role of the established clergy as formalistic intercessors between human and divine, rather than preachers of the Word. De-emphasizing Bible

---

[12] The pamphlet does not attack Laud by name, but references at *CPW* 1:594 ("the chief of them") and elsewhere clearly refer to him.   [13] Milton, *The Reason of Church Government*; *CPW* 1: 823.

interpretation and sermons, Laud restored high altars screened off by railings that excluded laity from sacred enclosures accessible only to clergy (Figure 24). The Laudian view that communicants receive the body and blood of Jesus Christ during the communion service outraged militant Protestants, who dreaded reestablishment of the alleged "magic" of transubstantiation and the highly theatrical Roman-rite Mass. Many Protestants were willing to die for their belief in the Lord's Supper as a memorial celebration of Jesus Christ's sacrifice on the Cross, as opposed to the actual recreation of his physical body at a repeated priestly celebration at a high altar. Puritans like Milton perceived clerical genuflection and bowing to the altar as marks of idolatry. The Laudian ideal of the "beauty of holiness" complemented heightened sacramentalism with a revival of church ornamentation, stained glass, and neo-Gothic ecclesiastical architecture.[14] We must not forget that Milton hated Presbyterian formalism in matters of church government and discipline almost as much as he hated Catholicism and Episcopalianism. In 1649, for example, he believed that the threat to the infant republic from Presbyterian Scotland was graver than the threat from Catholic Ireland. Miltonic invective goes beyond the association of "popish" and Episcopalian clergy with superstition to vilify sacerdotalism of all clergies.

In contrast to the explicit attacks of *Lycidas* and Milton's polemical tracts, *Paradise Lost* encodes highly allusive antipathy toward a more vaguely defined Catholic "Other." In doing so, it responds to the imposition of censorship and stringent penalties upon religious dissent. The present argument draws continually upon interconnections between Milton's early poetry and prose and an epic that participates in a reengagement with revolutionary issues of the mid-century. *Paradise Lost* reflects upon an era that witnessed the unprecedented executions of both Archbishop Laud and Charles I. It also considers and responds to the persecution of antiformalists during the Restoration, a time when Charles II presided over the reestablishment of Laudian ecclesiastical innovations.

Milton's writings participated in and shaped the mindset of militant Protestants who believed that apocalyptic conflict with the Church of Rome endangered the cause of "true" religion. Fears concerning Romanist plots organized by a fifth column of Jesuit missionaries or crypto-

[14] See Derek Hirst, *Authority and Conflict: England, 1603–1658* (Cambridge, MA: Harvard University Press, 1986), pp. 165–66.

Catholic bishops were pervasive throughout the seventeenth century.[15] Protestants perceived threats from foreign Catholic powers, notably the Hapsburgs, the Holy Roman Empire, and, increasingly, the regime of Louis XIV of France. Even *Areopagitica* (1644), a text commonly regarded as a libertarian call for freedom of the press, excludes Catholics from Milton's appeal for relaxation of prior censorship: "I mean not tolerated popery and open superstition, which, as it extirpates all religions and civil supremacies, so itself should be extirpate."[16]

Affording a turbulent context for Milton's career, deep-seated Protestant fears of "papistry" inspired street demonstrations, burnings in effigy, satirical broadsheets, and other outbursts at moments of perceived national peril such as the Gunpowder Plot (1605), the proposed marriage between Prince Charles and the Infanta of Spain (1623), the breakdown in royal and episcopal authority (1640s), the Irish Rebellion (1640s), the Great Fire of London (1666), the Popish Plot (1678), and the Glorious Revolution (1688). Enshrining chronic fear and hatred of "popery," an emergent nationalistic calendar focused upon celebration of those "miraculous and providential deliverances" with bonfires, bells, and pope-burning processions (see Figures 9, 19).[17] Lurid tales of persecution in Foxe's *Book of Martyrs*, which underwent continuous posthumous expansion, contributed to local panics over alleged Roman Catholic plots. Catholics had launched assassination plots against Elizabeth I and James I, and Charles I hid for several days after the slaying of the Duke of Buckingham. Although English recusants represented a small minority, the Protestant establishment felt potentially outnumbered by resistant Catholics at home and their powerful allies abroad.

By proposing extension of the right to worship to dissenters in public and Roman Catholics in private, Charles II's second Declaration of Indulgence (1672) triggered a religio-political crisis during the years following publication of *Paradise Lost* (1667). Blocking that decree, parliament instead passed the first Test Act (12 March 1673). It attempted to

[15] See N. H. Keeble, *The Literary Culture of Nonconformity in Later Seventeenth-Century England* (Athens, GA: University of Georgia Press, 1987), pp. 1–17; Caroline M. Hibbard, *Charles I and the Popish Plot* (Chapel Hill, NC: University of North Carolina Press, 1983).

[16] *CPW* 2: 565. See Stanley E. Fish, "Driving from the Letter: Truth and Indeterminacy in Milton's *Areopagitica*," in *Re-Membering Milton: Essays on the Texts and Traditions*, ed. Mary Nyquist and Margaret W. Ferguson (New York: Methuen, 1988), pp. 234–35, 250.

[17] See Robin Clifton, "Fear of Popery," in *The Origins of the English Civil War*, ed. Conrad Russell (London: Macmillan, 1973), pp. 144–67; Peter Lake, "Anti-popery: The Structure of a Prejudice," in *Conflict in Early Stuart England*, ed. R. Cust and Ann Hughes (New York: Longman, 1989), pp. 72–106; David Cressy, *Bonfires and Bells: National Memory and the Protestant Calendar in Elizabethan and Stuart England* (Berkeley and Los Angeles: University of California Press, 1989), pp. 90–92, and passim.

eliminate crypto-Catholic officeholders by requiring them to attend the service of holy communion and subscribe to an antitransubstantiation oath. Soon afterward, Milton returned to the arena of religious controversy with *Of True Religion, Heresy, Schism, Toleration, and What Best Means May Be Used Against the Growth of Popery* (c. May 1673), his final religio-political pamphlet. It came out not long before the "revised and augmented" second edition of *Paradise Lost* (summer 1674).

Milton's tract appeals for toleration of all Protestant sects including Anabaptists, Socinians, and Arminians, as part of an effort to forge a united Protestant front "against the growth of popery." The exclusion of Roman Catholics from any relaxation of the harshly punitive measures imposed upon nonconformists by the Clarendon Code (1661–65) shows that Milton's fierce hostility to "papistry" had survived unabated since his prior appeal for Roman Catholic exclusion in *Areopagitica*.[18] If *Christian Doctrine* has provided a useful vehicle for interpreting *Paradise Lost*, despite Milton's public veiling of heretical positions (e.g. antitrinitarianism and mortalism), it seems all the more likely that we may use *Of True Religion* as a tool for analyzing the biblical epic.[19]

The present investigation of antisacerdotal traces in *Paradise Lost* pursues the goal of exploring the terra incognita of the poem's involvement with religious complaint, satire, and invective.[20] That side of the text has received virtually no attention.[21] Responding to Mikhail Bakhtin's caution that "in world literature there are probably many works whose parodic nature has not even been suspected,"[22] this book challenges the prevalent opinion that Satan is "never ridiculous" and that "no one would argue that the satiric is a dominant mode" in *Paradise Lost*.[23] This study proposes to alter the way in which we read Milton's

---

[18] On the terms of the Clarendon Code and the Second Declaration of Indulgence, see Keeble, *Culture*, pp. 45–60.   [19] *CPW* 8: 408–12, 429.

[20] The following studies of Milton's satirical prose exclude *PL* from consideration: J. M. French, "Milton as a Satirist," *PMLA* 51 (1936): pp. 414–29; George W. Whiting, "The Satire in *Eikonoklastes*" *N&Q* 170 (1936), pp. 435–38; D. M. Rosenberg, "Satirical Technique in Milton's Polemical Prose," *Satire Newsletter* 5 (1971): pp. 91–97; Irene Samuel, "Milton on Comedy and Satire," *HLQ* 35 (1972): pp. 107–30; Raymond A. Anselment, *"Betwixt Jest and Earnest": Marprelate, Milton, Marvell, Swift and the Decorum of Religious Ridicule* (University of Toronto Press, 1979), ch. 4.

[21] Although the following studies address satire in *PL*, they avoid religious polemicism: John Wooten, "Satan, Satire, and Burlesque Fables," *MiltonQ* 12 (1978), pp. 51–58; and Robert A. Kantra, *All Things Vain: Religious Satirists and Their Art* (University Park, PA: Pennsylvania State University Press, 1984), pp. 75–83.

[22] Bakhtin, *The Dialogic Imagination: Four Essays*, ed. Michael Holquist, trans. Caryl Emerson and Michael Holquist (Austin: University of Texas Press [Slavic Series], 1981), p. 374.

[23] Leon Guilhamet, *Satire and the Transformation of Genre* (Philadelphia: University of Pennsylvania Press, 1987), p. 9. For an apprehension of the narrator's ironically detached and "darkly comic" view of Satan, see John P. Rumrich, *Milton Unbound: Controversy and Reinterpretation* (Cambridge University Press, 1996), p. 22.

account of the Fall by indicating how hints at religious complaint and satire permeate a work not avowedly satiric or polemical.

Satire is a problematic mode, because it has never corresponded to any particular genre. Because satire can assume an extraordinary variety of external formal characteristics, "diversity of form is paradoxically the 'fixed' form of satire."[24] Dr. Johnson defines it as a mode "employed in the writing of invective,"[25] thus excluding uses of irony and parody that fail to attack. Recognizing that nomenclature related to genres and modes lacks consistency, the present study identifies individual genres with a range of external, formal features. Unrelated to external form, literary modes employ a variable range of features that modify genres as adjectives modify nouns. The satirical mode thus infuses examples of different genres to produce, for example, the attenuated satire on epic convention during the War in Heaven. The remote family resemblances associated with the satirical mode may link texts like distant cousins within a far-flung clan.

Milton's reflections on satire are little known by contrast to our familiarity with his theorizing about tragedy and epic.[26] Attack is the essence of satire according to *An Apology for Smectymnuus* (c. April 1642), and it bears a particular burden in the cause of ecclesiastical reform. In the course of defending Milton's personal character against ad hominem attack in *A Modest Confutation of a Slanderous and Scurrilous Libel* (1642), a tract generally attributed to Bishop Joseph Hall, Milton's *Apology* insists that satire must possess teeth and bite. It does so in the course of mocking Hall's claim to have originated English satire in *Virgidemiarium . . . [or] Toothless Satires* (1597):

But that such a poem should be toothless, I still affirm it to be a bull, taking away the essence of that which it calls itself. For if it bite neither the persons nor the vices, how is it a satire, and if it bite either, how is it toothless, so that toothless satires are as much as if he had said toothless teeth.

Milton ridicules the aged bishop's composition of formal verse satire on the model of "the Latin, and Italian satirists" (*CPW* I: 915–16).

The amusingly punning and oxymoronic vein of the *Apology* exemp-

---

[24] Alastair Fowler, *Kinds of Literature: An Introduction to the Theory of Genres and Modes* (Cambridge, MA: Harvard University Press, 1982), pp. 106–07, 110.

[25] Samuel Johnson, *A Dictionary of the English Language* (1755), "satire."

[26] See Edward Le Comte's "Milton as Satirist and Wit," in *Th'Upright Heart and Pure: Essays on John Milton Commemorating the Tercentenary of the Publication of "Paradise Lost,"* ed. Amadeus P. Fiore, vol. X (Pittsburgh, PA: Duquesne University Press, 1967), pp. 45–59; Joel Morkan, "Wrath and Laughter: Milton's Ideas on Satire," *Studies in Philology* 69 (1972), pp. 475–95; John M. Steadman, " 'Teeth Will Be Provided': Satire and Religious or Ecclesiastical Humor," *Thalia* 6 (1984): pp. 23–31.

lifies wry etymological wordplay and vernacular quibbling that also permeate religious complaint and satire in *Paradise Lost*. Milton's insistence that satire must bite aligns it with **sarcasm**, whose meaning reflects its derivation from σαρκάζειν (Greek for "to tear flesh, gnash the teeth, speak bitterly"). Even the word **bull** suggests a slur, in line with wordplay in Milton's *Of True Religion* (1673), which declares that the term **Roman Catholic** is a paradoxical usage based upon a ludicrous contradiction in terms: "Whereas the papist boasts himself to be a Roman Catholic, it is a mere contradiction, one of the Pope's bulls." False etymology grounds **bull**, a vernacular expression for fraudulent trickery, upon scornful reference to papal bulls (i.e. decrees).[27]

Milton defends satire from the charge that it is a trivial mode akin to low comedy and farce. Witty puns accordingly function as a serious component of a mode that approaches the elevated genres of tragedy and epic:

A satire, as it was borne out of a tragedy, so ought to resemble his parentage, to strike high, and adventure dangerously at the most eminent vices among the greatest persons, and not to creep into every blind tap-house that fears a constable more than a satire.

The *Apology* thus reorders the hierarchy of literary genres and modes propounded by theorists such as Francesco Sansovino, whose *Discorso in materia della satira* (1560) insists that satire joins comedy in the lowliness of its style, subject matter, characterization, and mode of imitation.[28] Early modern critics agreed that epic and tragic are the highest modes, but it is worthy of note that the revision of Nicolas Boileau's *Art of Poetry* (1683) by Milton's contemporary, John Dryden, elevates satiric to a place immediately beneath them.[29]

It is true that Milton disapproves of "mere jesting about the abuses of religion," but it is inappropriate to conclude that the "high-minded disposition" of Miltonic satire excludes "mockery."[30] On didactic grounds, his *Apology* defends satirists who are "tart against the prelates" and condones style that is "rough and dangerous . . . trivial or boisterous." Acknowledging the need to justify "this vein of laughing," Milton's *Animadversions Upon the Remonstrant's Defence, Against Smectymnuus* (July? 1641) advocates "grim laughter" and "zeal of truth" as vehicles for "teaching and confuting" religious error. Sarcastic raillery is as appropriate to topically charged passages in *Paradise Lost* that allude to ecclesi-

---

[27] *CPW* 8: 422; *OED* "bull" sb⁴ 1–2.   [28] Guilhamet, *Satire*, pp. 2–3.
[29] Fowler, *Kinds of Literature*, p. 220. Sir William Soames translated Boileau's *Ars poétique*.
[30] Kantra, *All Things Vain*, pp. 75–76.

astical affairs as it is to the sardonic assault on "pomp of prelatism" and "popedom" in *Of Reformation*. Indeed, *De Doctrina Christiana* claims that "parables, hyperboles, fables, and the various uses of irony are not falsehoods since they are calculated not to deceive but instruct."[31]

Milton's earliest biographers commend his sardonic habit of mind. By 1681 John Aubrey noted in manuscript that he was 'Extreme[ly] pleasant in his conversation, and at dinner, supper, etc." Aubrey added in pencil: "but satirical. He pronounced the letter R very hard." A marginal gloss on *Litera canina* (i.e. the canine letter) clarifies that remark because the hard pronunciation of **r**, presumably in the manner of a growl, produces a sneering expression that resembles a snarling dog. Aubrey may also reflect upon the derivation of **cynical** from κυνικός ("dog-like, churlish").[32] Attributed to John Dryden, a notation on the facing page explains that Milton's pronunciation was "A certain sign of a satirical wit."[33] Dryden knew him and his writings, and his recollection throws light on his own imitation of *Paradise Lost* in caustic satires that move from the sublime to the ridiculous: *Absalom and Achitophel* and *Mac Flecknoe*. The latter poem brings to mind Milton's attack on Bishop Hall's "toothless satires" when it taxes Thomas Shadwell for writing bad poetry: "With whate'er gall thou sett'st thyself to write / Thy inoffensive satires never bite" (lines 199–200).

Dryden's testimony accords with Milton's reputation for teasing and raillery. Edward Phillips recalls that his uncle, who tutored him during the early 1640s, indulged in raffish merrymaking that stopped short of ribaldry: "He would drop into the society of some young sparks of his acquaintance . . . the beaux of those times, but nothing near so bad as those now-a-days; with these gentlemen he would so far make bold with his body, as now and then to keep a gaudy-day." Phillips' memory that Milton's first wife, Mary Powell, yearned for "joviality" seems to suggest that his uncle's cynical wit passed over her head. Independently of Aubrey and Phillips, the anonymous "Life of Mr. John Milton" (Bodl. MS Wood D. 4) records that "he had a sharp wit, and steady judgment." The report of John Toland, the nonconformist controversialist,

---

[31] *CPW* 1: 663–64, 914, 916; 6: 761. *De Doctrina Christiana* is cited hereafter as *Christian Doctrine* or *CD*. Milton's authorship has been questioned by William B. Hunter, with replies by Barbara Lewalski and John T. Shawcross, in "The Provenance of the *Christian Doctrine*," *Studies in English Literature 1500-1900* 32 (1992), pp. 129–66. I subscribe to the consensus that ascribes the manuscript of *CD* (London, Public Record Office, SP 9/61) to Milton, even though that text may be a redaction of an earlier, non-Miltonic document.   [32] *OED* "canine" adj. 1c and 3.

[33] From "Minutes of the Life of Mr. John Milton" (Bodl. MS Aubrey 8), in Helen Darbishire, ed., *The Early Lives of Milton* (London: Constable, 1932), p. 6.

that Milton was a person "of wonderful parts, of a very sharp, biting, and satirical wit" might have amused him, given his views on Joseph Hall's "toothless satires." Having no illusions about the good taste of Milton's derisive insults, Toland jokingly admires "flowers" of satirical wit in the antiprelatical tracts.[34]

In accordance with the shift to neoclassical canons of taste, most Restoration and eighteenth-century critics experienced difficulty in reconciling the spiteful scurrility of Milton's prose tracts with the achievement of *Paradise Lost*. Not only did they disagree with his pre-Enlightenment decorum of invective satire, but many of them detested Milton's politics and religion. Thus George Bate, physician to Charles I and II, censures Milton's "satires and libels" as the work of a "livid and malicious wit."[35]

Joseph Addison exerted a profound influence upon generations of critics through papers on *Paradise Lost* that appeared in *The Spectator* (1711–12), the widely read collection of essays that influenced the re-fashioning of literary taste along neoclassical lines. In accordance with his prescriptive views on epic decorum, Addison decries the intrusion into the epic of both puns and burlesque (see Chapters 4–5). His position accords with that of Thomas Hobbes, a philosopher contemporary to Milton, who articulated the neoclassical rule that it is improper for a heroic poet "to represent scurrility or any action or language that moveth much to laughter. The delight of an epic poem consisteth not in mirth, but admiration. Mirth and laughter is proper to comedy and satire."[36] In more general terms, Horace Walpole, the eighteenth-century man of letters, condemns the "controversial ribaldry" of six-teenth- and seventeenth-century religious complaint and satire: "All the subjects were religious; all the conduct, farcical."[37]

A combination of Tory political principles and neoclassical rules more stringent than Addison's provoked Dr. Johnson's withering disap-proval of the "peevish" temperament of "an acrimonious and surly republican." Condemning the stylistic roughness of Milton's religious polemics, Johnson also censures "controversial merriment" resulting from his effort "to be humorous." Even "more offensive" than "contro-

---

[34] Darbishire, ed., *Early Lives*, pp. viii–ix, 29, 39, 62, 64, 115, and 195. Toland's "Life of John Milton" was the preface to: *A Complete Collection of the Historical, Political, and Miscellaneous Works of John Milton, Both English and Latin* (1698). See also Parker, p. 579.

[35] Bate, George, *Elenchi Motuum Nuperorum in Anglia*, rev. ed. (1663), pp. 237–38.

[36] Hobbes, "Answer to Davenant's Preface to *Gondibert*," (c. 1650) in *Critical Essays of the Seventeenth Century*, ed. J. E. Spingarn (Oxford: Clarendon Press, 1908-1909), vol. II, p. 64.

[37] Walpole, *A Catalogue of the Royal and Noble Authors of England* (Strawberry Hill, 1758), vol. I, p. 17.

versial merriment," however, is Milton's "gloomy seriousness: 'Such is his malignity that hell grows darker at his frown.'" The quotation comes from the encounter between Satan and Death, which Johnson regards as a profound flaw in *Paradise Lost*. He makes light of Miltonic quibbling: "Those who are not convinced by his reasons may be perhaps delighted with his wit." Understatement enhances his charge that the use of wit and humor in religious controversy may "to some men perhaps . . . seem offensive."[38]

Although Dr. Johnson has a keen eye for identifying raillery in Milton's prose pamphlets, despite his distaste for it, he subscribes to the prevailing view that *Paradise Lost* lacks a topical and polemical dimension. Other than the references to Milton's blindness and the "evil days though fallen, and evil tongues" of the Restoration (3.23–26, 7.26), he discovers "no other internal notes of time" in the epic. Johnson sees Milton's complaint about slander by "evil tongues" as a mark of churlishness, moreover, one that "required impudence at least equal to his other powers—Milton, whose warmest advocates must allow that he never spared any asperity of reproach or brutality of insolence."[39]

Aversion to Milton's religion, politics, and character has encouraged twentieth-century critics such as T. S. Eliot and F. R. Leavis to attempt to dislodge him from the literary canon.[40] Repeating strictures that originated with Addison and Johnson, interpreters including William Empson have failed to comprehend that satire, invective, divine laughter, and parody play an essential role in *Paradise Lost*. An editor of *An Apology for Smectymnuus* accordingly explains that Milton's biographers have found it difficult, "even while admiring the loftiness and fluency of the autobiographical passages, to accept the less flattering portions: Milton's dealing in personalities, his anger, his plain bad manners." He explains that the tract "displays a side of Milton not shown in the poetry. What is revealed, however, is not always pleasant: sharp sarcasm, bitter wrangling, unreasoning and even indecent vituperation, pettiness – all these aspects of Milton are made clear."[41] Even readers sympathetic with Milton's religious beliefs experience distress in trying to reconcile malicious diatribe in the antiprelatical tracts with the finesse of *Paradise Lost*.

Challenging widespread distaste for Milton's polemicism, the present

---

[38] Johnson, "Life of Milton" in *Lives of the Poets*, pp. 61, 87, 91. *PL* 2.719–20 reads "that hell/Grew darker at their frown."   [39] Ibid., p. 99.

[40] David G. Norbrook, *Poetry and Politics in the English Renaissance* (London: Routledge and Kegan Paul, 1984), pp. 1–2.   [41] Preface by Frederick L. Taft in *CPW* I: 866.

study argues that a sardonic habit of mind represents an essential component of his creative impulse. Taking seriously instances of "controversial merriment" that Dr. Johnson deplored, this book makes no effort to turn *Paradise Lost* into a religious tract, anticlerical allegory, or roman à clef, or to flatten its rich diversity into one-dimensional satire on idle bishops or clandestine Jesuit priests. Nonetheless, we should recognize that a dazzling multiplicity of polemical gestures, polemical hints, jarring glimpses, and defamatory innuendoes represents not a nonessential superimposition upon the poem but a functional part of the text, and one whose presence alters interpretation of *Paradise Lost* in an essential way. Recognition of the poem's controversial side rewards Milton's readers by complicating and enriching our understanding of an encyclopedic poem that critics prior to Christopher Hill understood as a sublime masterpiece standing above the fray of history. Like the *Aeneid*, *Commedia*, and *Gerusalemme liberata*, *Paradise Lost* is enmeshed inextricably in the religious context and worship practices of its own age.

In analyzing the engagement of *Paradise Lost* with religious controversy, I argue for a sweeping definition of the satiric as a mode that involves debasement, vilification, or ridicule of recognizable historical targets. Attack by means of more or less laughable instances of linguistic appropriation, imitation, or innuendo is an essential component of Milton's ecclesiastical satire. It encompasses puns and quibbles; fables that veil allegorical attack; parody, burlesque, or travesty of recognizable literary styles, devices, and forms; and startling instances of indecorous polemical vocabulary or sustained invective complaint. We may think in terms of a satirical spectrum that ranges from polemical abuse colored by rhetorical figures that stop short of fictiveness, to constructions that are more or less fictive, to a point where satire shades into comedy unconcerned with discernible historical particulars.[42] Puns are not always humorous, but they often highlight sardonic attacks on religious "error." The interpretative indeterminacy and ambiguity inherent in punning and verbal irony complicate the act of reading in ways compatible with Stanley Fish's pioneering thesis concerning *Paradise Lost* as a minefield of verbal traps designed to ensnare the reader in deceptive rhetoric as a means of dramatizing the fallen condition and engaging the right reader in a corrective process of spiritual education.[43]

We should be mindful of Dr. Johnson's distinction between "the

[42] Edward W. Rosenheim, *Swift and the Satirist's Art* (University of Chicago Press, 1963), p. 31.
[43] Fish, *Surprised by Sin: The Reader in "Paradise Lost"* (Berkeley and Los Angeles: University of California Press, 1971), pp. 4 et seq.

generality of the reflections" in satire as opposed to lampoon, "which is aimed against a particular person."[44] The open-ended generality of *Paradise Lost* accords with the Johnsonian definition of satire. We cannot identify lampoons on specific individuals, but identification of historical occasions and polemical contexts for anticlerical complaint and satire is possible. Roman Catholicism always constituted a safe target for militant Protestants like Milton, because "popery" versus Protestantism represented a "false" choice to the majority of early modern British readers. Vestiges of Romanism may appear to taint the established Church of England or "Jesuitical" Presbyterianism. Intrusions of indecorous terminology appropriate to polemical broadsheets, pamphlets, and theological tracts may signal satirical shifts in Miltonic verse. The jarring rupture caused by the satirical segment in *Lycidas*, in which St. Peter vilifies the failures of "false" shepherd-pastors, corresponds to the heavy presence of satirical passages in *Paradise Lost*. The epic narrator frequently employs contemporaneous polemical vocabulary to stigmatize Satan as a "false" cleric associated with the "trumpery" of the futuristic monastics of the Paradise of Fools, or the Pope, or high-ranking bishops or archbishops.

Long-standing attention to epic decorum in *Paradise Lost* has veiled Milton's recourse to the Bible for models of invective complaint and mockery. Nonetheless, Milton's *Apology for Smectymnuus* cites scriptural precedent for using 'tart rhetoric in the church's cause." In particular, Proverbs 3:34 justifies being "'froward with the froward . . . [and throwing] scorn upon the scorner, whom if anything, nothing else will heal.'" "Baiting" of one's opponent may seem "trivial and boisterous," but a "rough and dangerous" manner is appropriate to satire.[45] Indeed, Milton is in touch with the "ecstatic fury" of the Hebrew prophets as satirists who employ "derision, scorn, and ridicule" to attack the unrighteous.[46] The harshness of Jesus' invective attack on the hypocrisy of the Pharisees and Scribes as a "generation of vipers" (Matt. 23:13–33) affords a precedent for Christian satire. Milton claims that Jesus' naming of "the dunghill and the jakes [i.e. privy]" when "speaking of unsavory traditions" sanctions "bitter and ireful rebukes."[47] Such pre-

---

[44] Johnson, *Dictionary*, "satire."   [45] *CPW* I: 875, 901, 914.

[46] Thomas Jemielity, "Divine Derision and Scorn: The Hebrew Prophets as Satirists," *Cithara* 25 (1985), p. 47; Herbert Marks, "The Twelve Prophets," in *The Literary Guide to the Bible*, ed. Robert Alter and Frank Kermode (Cambridge, MA: Harvard University Press, 1987), p. 223.

[47] *CPW* I: 895, 899, 903, 909.

cedents accord with Martin Luther's position that one ought "to jeer and flout [the Devil], for he cannot bear scorn."[48]

A further need exists to complicate the traditional view of *Paradise Lost* as a hexameral poem (concerning the creation of the world in six days according to Genesis) in a Latinate and Italianate manner by recognizing the text's engagement with cultural practices associated with the native tradition of anticlerical complaint and satire. Avoiding Roman satirists including Martial and Juvenal, who came into vogue during the 1590s, Milton's *Apology* cites medieval English prototypes such as *Piers Plowman* as precedents for truly corrective satire (*CPW* I: 915–16). Milton accordingly advocates the rough style and subject matter of an old-fashioned mode that Tudor theorists wrongly derived from ancient Greek satyr plays.[49] Like many contemporaries, he identifies satire with prophecies against wrongdoing uttered by blunt-spoken visionary radicals. By convention, a plainspeaking vernacular truth-teller appeals for restoration of Christian ideals.

It is unnecessary to seek sublimity in Milton's "controversial merriment" or to confine analogies in sexual and scatological innuendoes to the ancient world or Italy when we encounter the disorderly sexuality of Sin and Death, or the malodorous Paradise of Fools associated with the "backside of the world" (3.494),[50] or the alimentary and anal aggression of the fallen angels during the War in Heaven. John Toland perceives no conflict between raillery of that kind and "the unparalleled sublimity and force of the expression, with the delicacy of his thoughts."[51] Emphasis on sexual abandon and gross bodily functions is a familiar element of anticlerical satire composed by Geoffrey Chaucer, the anonymous author known as William Langland, Edmund Spenser, and the Marprelate pamphleteers. In *Paradise Lost*, therefore, the transgressiveness of Satan and his offspring, Sin and Death, may recall the frenzied onslaught of the Blatant Beast as a vehicle for open-ended anti-monastic satire in Spenser's *Faerie Queene*:

---

[48] As quoted in C. S. Lewis, *The Screwtape Letters* (New York: Macmillan, 1948), p. 7; *CPW* I: 878.

[49] E.g. George Puttenham, *The Art of English Poesy* (1589), in G. Gregory Smith, ed., *Elizabethan Critical Essays*, 2 vols. (London: Oxford University Press, 1904), vol. II, pp. 27, 32. See Alvin Kernan, *The Cankered Muse: Satire of the English Renaissance* (New Haven: Yale University Press, 1959), pp. 41, 45, 54–56, 59.

[50] See Michael Lieb, *The Dialectics of Creation: Patterns of Birth and Regeneration in "Paradise Lost"* (Amherst, MA: University of Massachusetts Press, 1970), p. 32; John Wooten, "The Comic Milton and Italian Burlesque Poets." *Cithara* 22 (1982): pp. 3–12.

[51] "Life of Milton," in Darbishire, ed., *Early Lives*, p. 179.

> Into their cloysters now he broken had,
>   Through which the Monckes he chaced here and there,
> And them pursu'd into their dortours sad,
> And searched all their cels and secrets neare;
> In which what filth and ordure did appeare,
> Were yrkesome to report. (6.12.24)

A Spenserian poem well known to Milton, Phineas Fletcher's *The Locusts, or Appollyonists* (1627) imitates that scene:

> Down cloysters fall: the Monkes chac't from their sty
> Lie ope, and all their loathsome company;
> Hypocrisie, rape, blood, theft, whooredome, Sodomy. (2.23)[52]

Although the scurrility of polemical moments in *Paradise Lost* deeply troubled Addison, Johnson, and other readers, *Gargantua and Pantagruel*, *The Faerie Queene*, and *The Locusts* afford rich precedents for bodily disorderliness and grotesque sexual misconduct associated with Satan's encounter with Sin and Death, the Paradise of Fools, War in Heaven, and other episodes. Sensual appetites, bodily emission, and dismemberment are found, for example, in Rabelaisian satire on Scholasticism. In a lurid parody of transubstantiation and the Mass, Spenser's representation of Error and her brood encompasses disfigurement, suckling with both poison and blood, vomiting, decapitation, and explosive engorgement. Bakhtin's work on the carnivalesque aspect of Rabelaisian humor illuminates how pre-Enlightenment religious satirists exploited degrading ridicule for the sake of corrective attack. In his view, grotesque bodily humor has a "positive, assertive character" that balances the pronounced downward movement of satirical debasement with uplifting spiritual ideals. Often identifying Satan and the rebel angels with the lower body (belly, genitals, and backside), Milton's epic recalls medieval laughter at the Devil's involvement with the "material bodily stratum."[53] During the German Reformation, propagandists exploited carnivalesque humor to degrade the papacy.[54] Martin Luther's scatological invective is notorious. Earthy humor and misrule characteristic of popular culture similarly inform ludicrous allusions to clerical

---

[52] An expansion of Fletcher's Gunpowder Plot poem, *Locustae, vel Pietas Iesuitica*, published in the same volume.

[53] Mikhail Bakhtin, *Rabelais and His World*, trans. Hélène Iswolsky (Bloomington: Indiana University Press, 1984), pp. 5, 19, 41, 109, 311.

[54] Peter Stallybrass and Allon White, *The Politics and Poetics of Transgression* (Ithaca, NY: Cornell University Press, 1986), p. 15. For analysis and qualification of Bakhtin, see pp. 1–26. See also R. W. Scribner, *For the Sake of the Simple Folk: Popular Propaganda for the German Reformation* (Cambridge University Press, 1981).

misconduct and religious turmoil in *Paradise Lost*. Grotesque inversions of Roman Catholic or Laudian sacramentalism, in particular, pervade Satan's institution of parodic worship in both hell and Eden.

Any investigation of the polemical and satirical dimension of *Paradise Lost* must come to terms with Milton's relationship to Spenser, his self-declared master, who affords a looming poetic model for antipapal satire and criticism of vestiges of Catholicism within the Church of England. The present study questions findings that link them as members of an uncomplicated and apolitical Christian humanistic tradition.[55] Transcending "shared mythological commonplaces," the connection between Spenser and Milton is "predominantly political, polemical, and full of hostilities."[56] Indeed, Puritans contemporary to Milton appropriated Spenser as a fellow traveler. Spenserian poets of Milton's age emulated Spenser's praise of Queen Elizabeth, despite her own lack of religious zeal, in order to provide a counterbalance to Stuart efforts to achieve rapprochement with Continental Catholicism. Little-known compositions by seventeenth-century Spenserian poets (Giles and Phineas Fletcher, William Browne, and George Wither) function as a bridge between Spenser and Milton.[57] Milton followed Spenser's lead in modeling antiprelatical attacks in both *Lycidas* and his revolutionary pamphlets on religious eclogues in Spenser's *Shepheardes Calender* ("May," "July," and "September"), the May Eclogue in particular. Books One and Five of *The Faerie Queene* leave an imprint upon satirical episodes in *Paradise Lost*, notably Satan's encounter with Sin and Death.

Milton's invocation of "our sage and serious poet Spenser, whom I dare be known to think a better teacher than Scotus or Aquinas" in *Areopagitica* is deservedly famous. John Dryden further reports that "Milton has acknowledged to me, that Spenser was his original."[58] Defining the precise nature of Milton's relationship to Spenser has been a vexed issue in English literary history. Most recently, Harold Bloom and critics whom he has influenced have applied the insights of poststructuralist theory and feminist scholarship to their discovery of acts of mimetic rivalry or transumptive (i.e. self-reflexive) allusion in Milton's

---

[55] e.g. E. M. W. Tillyard, *Studies in Milton* (London: Chatto & Windus, 1951) and A. S. P. Woodhouse, *The Heavenly Muse: A Preface to Milton*, ed. Hugh MacCallum (University of Toronto Press, 1972).

[56] Annabel Patterson, *Reading Between the Lines* (Madison, WI: University of Wisconsin Press, 1993), pp. 36–56, citing pp. 41 and 45.

[57] Norbrook, *Poetry*, chs. 3, 8, 10. See also Corns, *Uncloistered Virtue*, p. 63.

[58] *CPW* 2: 516. Dryden, preface to *The Fables* (1700), in *The Best of Dryden*, ed. Louis I. Bredvold (New York: Ronald Press, 1933), p. 503.

misreading of *The Faerie Queene* in *Areopagitica*.[59] Like earlier efforts, their attempts to link the two poets have ignored the common commitment of Spenser and Milton to militantly Protestant politics and poetics. Of course, it is important to acknowledge that Milton differs from Spenser in taking the radical step of renouncing episcopal and monarchical governance.

Milton discovered in Spenser a poet who, refusing to be bound by strict classical and Continental precedents, espoused the pseudo-Chaucerian spirit of native Protestant religious complaint and satire.[60] Milton's own reading encompassed anticlerical satires that many contemporaries understood as militantly Protestant tracts. In addition to *Piers Plowman*, they include Chaucerian tales and the pseudo-Chaucerian *Plowman's Tale*. *Of Reformation* thus cites Chaucer's portrayal of the "merry Friar" and quotes from *The Plowman's Tale*, fancifully attributed to "our Chaucer's Plowman," as a prophetic "caution to England to beware her bishops in time."[61] Puritans read that relentless attack on lordly prelates as a prefiguration of the assault on Laudian churchmen.[62] Polemical annotations in a seventeenth-century reprint, *The Plowman's Tale. Showing by the Doctrine and Lives of the Romish Clergy, that the Pope is Antichrist and they His Ministers* (1606), afford a foundation for their interpretation. The editor presents the tale as a "complaint against the pride and covetousness of the clergy: made no doubt by Chaucer, with the test of the [Canterbury] Tales" (A4).[63]

In addition to pseudo-Chaucerian tales, examination of rare instances of seventeenth-century visual satire enables us to situate *Paradise Lost* within a broad framework of Reformation cultural and polemical practices. Although much has been written on Milton and the visual arts, the relationship between his poem and scurrilous contemporary caricature, a pictorial equivalent of burlesque, has gone without notice. The poem's critique of clerical transgression recalls vilification of the Roman Other

---

[59] Harold Bloom, "Milton and His Precursors," in *A Map of Misreading* (New York: Oxford University Press, 1975); John Guillory, *Poetic Authority: Spenser, Milton, and Literary History* (New York: Columbia University Press, 1983), pp. 130–38; Maureen Quilligan, *Milton's Spenser: The Politics of Reading* (Ithaca, NY: Cornell University Press, 1983), pp. 50–72.

[60] See *SPART*, pp. 14–109, passim.

[61] *CPW* 1: 570, 560, 579, 916. See *ERL*, pp. 323–25, 330–39.

[62] Laud's predecessor as Archbishop of Canterbury, George Abbot, cited *The Plowmans Tale* in opposition to Arminian innovations, just as John Gee's *Foot Out of the Snare* (1624) took Chaucer's portrayal of the Friar as a prototype for anti-Jesuit satire (p. 20). See also Anthony Low, *The Georgic Revolution* (Princeton University Press, 1985), pp. 180–95.

[63] Milton's own copy of the 1602 edition of Thomas Speght's edition of Chaucer's *Works* (Jackson Boswell, *Milton's Library* [New York: Garland, 1975] no. 330) positions the apocryphal *Plowman's Tale* as a companion piece to *The Parson's Tale*. See *SPART*, pp. 26–27.

both as a target in itself and as a screen for attacking Laudian prelates or Presbyterians in illustrated broadsheets and pamphlets of the revolutionary era. For example, explanatory verses in *Time Carrying the Pope from England to Rome* assimilate attack on English episcopacy into a defamatory broadside against the papacy (Figure 18). It might seem facetious to claim that a blind poet negotiates within an iconographical world, but recent critical studies demonstrate that he participates in the profound internalization of pictorialism and iconoclasm during the Reformation.[64]

Rather than draw analogies with isolated visual images, the present study grounds its iconographical claims upon a broad survey of sixteenth- and seventeenth-century English visual satires. Visual counterparts for controversial moments in *Paradise Lost* are drawn from illustrated copies of rare or unique broadsheets, polemical ballads, and tracts in the Thomason Collection of the British Library and the holdings of the Department of Prints and Drawings of the British Museum, the Folger Shakespeare Library, and the Henry E. Huntington Library. Most of this visual material is cited and reproduced for the first time in the present study.

Just as caricatures in polemical broadsheets and tracts afford keys to interpretation, early modern habits of annotation and editing document ways in which some early readers perceived controversial hints and innuendoes in Miltonic texts. Accordingly we need to take seriously the first extended commentaries on Milton's youthful poetry and *Paradise Lost*, compiled by Thomas Warton the Younger and Patrick Hume respectively.[65] Annotating connections between Milton's prose pamphlets and his verse, Hume and Warton set the poetry within the context of contemporary religious and political polemics. Building upon them, this study draws continuously upon Milton's polemical prose to situate *Paradise Lost* within the complicated matrix of religio-political controversy across the middle decades of the seventeenth century. The work of early editors, notably the anti-Jacobite scholars who included polemical engravings in their first folio edition of *Paradise Lost* (1688), offers further insight into Milton's critique of alleged failures in the Christian church (see Chapter 3).

---

[64] See Ernest Gilman, *Iconoclasm and Poetry in the English Reformation: "Down Went Dagon"* (University of Chicago Press, 1986), ch. 6.

[65] Warton, ed., *Poems Upon Several Occasions, English, Italian, and Latin, with Translations, by John Milton* (1785); P. H., *Annotations on Milton's "Paradise Lost"* (1695). I refer to P. H. as Patrick Hume in accordance with standard practice. Hereafter cited as Warton or Hume.

By investigating the interrelationship of literature, history, politics, and ideology, I share in the endeavor of a new generation of literary, ecclesiastical, social, and political historians. This study contributes to the current reevaluation of literature with reference to neglected areas of religious strife, parliamentary politics, and local historical circumstances.[66] It grounds interpretation in historical context; considers the interaction between literary texts and historical process; examines the interaction of literary and extra-literary texts within culture at large; and analyzes the dynamic force of literature in politics and society. At the same time, my method is highly inductive because it defines large cultural patterns on the basis of archival scholarship, diachronic history, and terms of analysis in use in early modern times, rather than a reconfiguration of those categories in terms of postmodern analysis.

Arguing further for the centrality of religion in early modern culture, I embrace the view that "religion is back in the angle of vision in literary studies."[67] By contrast, religion has tended to drop out of new historicist studies, except as it receives treatment as an ideology that serves as a front for political power.[68] Although Fredric Jameson notes that "Marxists can no longer afford the luxury of assigning the problem of religion to the ashcan of history" and that early modern religion "is the master-code in which issues are conceived and debated," his approach to *Paradise Lost* illustrates how ideologically driven critics tend to collapse religion and politics together in such a way as to privilege class conflict at the expense of theological doctrine and religious polity.[69] Furthermore, I question any unproblematic identification of "dominant culture" with the formalistic theology of Lancelot Andrewes, Richard Hooker, and

---

[66] In addition to work cited above by Achinstein, Hill, Marcus, Norbrook, and Patterson, see Stephen Greenblatt, *Renaissance Self-Fashioning: From More to Shakespeare* (University of Chicago Press, 1980); Jean E. Howard, "The New Historicism in Renaissance Studies," *ELR* 16 (1986), pp. 13–43; Michael Wilding, *Dragons Teeth: Literature in the English Revolution* (Oxford: Clarendon Press, 1987); David Loewenstein, *Milton and the Drama of History: The Historical Vision, Iconoclasm, and the Literary Imagination* (Cambridge University Press, 1990); Steven N. Zwicker, *Lines of Authority: Politics and English Literary Culture, 1649–1689* (Ithaca, NY: Cornell University Press, 1993).

[67] Annabel Patterson, "Still Reading Spenser After All These Years?," *ELR* 25 (1995), p. 433. For recent historicist investigation of literature and religion, see *ERL*; *SPART*; Barbara K. Lewalski, *Protestant Poetics and the Seventeenth-Century Religious Lyric* (Princeton University Press, 1979); Richard Helgerson, *Forms of Nationhood: The Elizabethan Writing of England* (University of Chicago Press, 1992), ch. 6; and Paul Whitfield White, *Theatre and Reformation: Protestantism, Patronage, and Playing in Tudor England* (Cambridge University Press, 1993).

[68] See Debora K. Shuger, *Habits of Thought in the English Renaissance: Religion, Politics, and the Dominant Culture* (Berkeley and Los Angeles: University of California Press, 1990), pp. 1–16 et passim.

[69] Fredric Jameson, "Religion and Ideology: A Political Reading of *Paradise Lost*," in *Literature, Politics, and Theory*, ed. Francis Barker, et al. (London: Methuen, 1986), 35–56, citing pp. 35, 37.

John Donne.[70] That position marginalizes figures such as Foxe, John Bale, John Jewel, and Spenser, whose ideas afforded a foundation for Elizabethan "orthodoxy" before they underwent retrospective "radicalization" in the seventeenth century, and successors such as the Spenserian poets, Milton, and Marvell, who stand in a problematic relationship to a formalistic center.

Taking *Lycidas* as its starting point, this study considers ways in which St. Peter's jeremiad (i.e., sustained invective) against "false" shepherd-pastors who fail to feed the "flock" of Christian believers accords with polemical outbursts by the epic narrator in *Paradise Lost*. Milton's youthful adaptation of Spenserian pastoral satire during an age of festering Puritan discontent anticipates the importance of Spenserian allegory as a vehicle for religious controversy in the biblical epic.

Prominent textual loci in *Paradise Lost* take on new meaning when read in the light of bitter seventeenth-century controversies concerning religious formalism, transubstantiation, the relative merits of the Roman-rite Mass versus the Protestant communion service, priestly vestments, and related religious issues. Recognition of the poem's polemical matrices enables us to recover a gritty, pugnacious, and sarcastic side of an epic that continued to harry advocates of "false" religion during the Restoration. Before the Fall, polemical innuendoes focus heavily, but not exclusively, on Satan in the demonic world of hell and chaos. Proleptic (i.e. anticipatory) parodies satirize corruption that steals into the church during human history following the Fall rather than Adam and Eve in their unfallen state.

Recognition of Milton's appropriation of vituperative rhetoric reminiscent of 1640s and 1650s controversial broadsheets, sermons, and pamphlets enriches, and complicates, our understanding of tensions, ambiguities, and contradictions built into *Paradise Lost*. This study thus investigates the antipapal coloration of the gathering of fallen angels that converges on the "secret conclave" at Pandaemonium in the epic's opening books. Scriptural parodies underpin intimations concerning Satanic leadership of a "false" church in hell. The conclave in hell prepares the way for the problematic intrusion of Spenserian allegory in episodes involving Sin and Death, whose twisted nature conjures up images of perverse sexuality, rape, and monstrous birth often associated with ecclesiastical disorder in seventeenth-century propaganda. Tangled relationships among members of different generations descended

---

[70] Shuger, *Habits*, pp. 6, 8.

from Satan represent the ramification of evil in terms of a sinister family tree. Satan's sojourn at the Paradise of Fools affords the occasion for the epic's most extended outburst of explicit religious satire. His ensuing encounter with Archangel Uriel hinges upon an epistemological confusion between disguising and fantasy, which Spenser and other Protestant artists had identified with formalistic and ceremonial religion. The mock-heroic debasement of the rebel angels during the War in Heaven bears a relationship to the iconography of Fifth of November celebrations of Gunpowder Day as a nationalistic victory against the forces of international Catholicism.

As an anticipation of corruption in the Christian church, Satan's invasion of Eden prepares the way for the Edenic meal shared by Adam and Raphael. Their repast hints at Protestant anxieties concerning transubstantiation and the Roman-rite Mass. In related episodes, sacramental concerns underlie some surprising theological connections between Holy Communion and marriage. The discovery of idolatry by Eve and Adam, at the time of the invasion of Eden by Sin and Death, associates theological controversy with life in the fallen world. It may be that we hear disrespectful parodies of Roman Catholic devotional formulae and hymns to the Virgin Mary in Eve's temptation and fall. Antiformalist suffering and spiritual fortitude are inscribed upon Archangel Michael's prophetic history of the world in Books 11 and 12 of *Paradise Lost*. Foretelling the invasion of the Christian church by ravening clerical "wolves," those closing books commend patient obedience, suffering, and faith as a complement to the predominantly negative and destructive character of the text's earlier polemical moments.

The present argument lodges no claim to evaluate Milton's poem in its totality. Nor does it advance an argument for religious allegory in Milton's representation of the demonic and human worlds. Neither consistent nor ever-present, Milton's polemicism constitutes an allusive network of intimations, hints, echoes, and innuendoes within a polysemous interplay of narrative and dramatic voices. The present study resists the widespread presumption that *Paradise Lost* is unrelated to contemporary polemics concerning the state of the church. Contributing to the epic goal of justifying "the ways of God to man," "controversial merriment" affords a human complement to mordant laughter that rings out in heaven at the antics of Satan and his cohorts.

CHAPTER 2

Milton reads Spenser's May Eclogue

A retrospective addition to the headnote for *Lycidas* in *The Poems of Mr. John Milton* (1645) claims prophetic status for a pastoral elegy that "by occasion foretells the ruin of our corrupted clergy then in their height." Milton's Trinity Manuscript and the poem's first edition in 1638 had simply stated: "In this monody the author bewails a learned friend, unfortunately drowned in his passage from Chester on the Irish Seas, 1637." The 1645 collection appeared late in a year during which the House of Commons ordered the decapitation of Archbishop William Laud and edged toward abolition of episcopacy. The revised headnote therefore sharpens the threat that false churchmen would fall victim to the "two-handed engine at the door" (line 130). Scholars have ignored the interchange among *Lycidas*, Milton's reading of Spenser's May Eclogue as a prophecy of the downfall of Laudian prelates, and a long-standing tradition of anticlerical complaint and satire.[1] Ways in which Milton's poem anticipates more subtle instances of anticlerical attack in *Paradise Lost* have therefore gone without notice.

The revised headnote invites investigation of Milton's religious radicalism before the breakdown of episcopal authority in the early 1640s. In pursuing that inquiry, we need to guard against anachronistic reading of the radicalism of Milton's antiprelatical tracts backward into his pre-1640 verse.[2] The debate concerning the nature and degree of his

---

[1] Thomas Warton is the sole exception (see below). In *Visionary Poetics: Milton's Tradition and his Legacy* (San Marino: Huntington Library, 1979), Joseph A. Wittreich, Jr., understands the May Eclogue and *Lycidas* in terms of apocalyptic prophecy, but he is not concerned with the historical circumstances of seventeenth-century religious disputes or the polemics that they generated (pp. 105, 121, 132–35, 257–58).

[2] David Loewenstein, " 'Fair Offspring Nurs't in Princely Lore': On the Question of Milton's Early Radicalism," *MiltonS* 28 (1992), p. 38; Annabel Patterson, " 'Forc'd Fingers': Milton's Early Poems and Ideological Constraint," in *"The muses common-weale": Poetry and Politics in the Seventeenth Century*, ed. Claude Summers and Ted-Larry Pebworth (Columbia, MO: University of Missouri Press, 1988), pp. 9–22. See also Norbrook, *Poetry*, ch. 10; Thomas N. Corns, "Ideology in the *Poemata*," *MiltonS* 19 (1984), pp. 195–203.

youthful political radicalism continues, but his religious radicalism (as distinct from the socially inflected radicalism assumed by Marxist critics)[3] is overdue for reassessment. Even though Milton had a deeply conservative strain unconnected to the kind of radicalism that we see in John Lilburne, for example, his identification of ecclesiastical reform with the values of a learned Protestant aristocracy constituted a "radical" position during the 1620s and 1630s.[4]

During the eighteenth century, two critical poles existed concerning Milton's use of pastoral elegy as a vehicle for satire on ecclesiastical affairs. Designating Edmund Spenser as the chief English model "for mixing religious disputes with pagan and pastoral ideas," Thomas Warton the Younger concludes that Milton "no doubt" composed *Lycidas* with Spenser's May Eclogue in mind. Warton is in touch with pre-Enlightenment ideas when he commends Milton's emulation of one of three religious satires among the twelve eclogues in Spenser's *Shepheardes Calender*.[5] Since Warton's time, that connection to Spenserian religious satire has received virtually no attention. By contrast, Dr. Johnson's "Life of Milton" censures Milton for ruining a poem already flawed by violation of pastoral decorum:

With these trifling fictions are mingled the most awful and sacred truths, such as ought never to be polluted with irreverent combinations. The shepherd likewise is now a feeder of sheep, and afterwards an ecclesiastical pastor, a superintendent of a Christian flock. Such equivocations are always unskillful, but here they are indecent and at least approach to impiety.[6]

Adherence to neoclassical decorum prevents Dr. Johnson from giving credence to Milton's use of pastoral elegy as a vehicle for allegory concerning the vocation of Milton and his drowned friend, Edward King, as shepherd-preachers.

Although *Lycidas* pays homage to Virgil's *Eclogues* as **the** model for stylized verse about life among shepherds, St. Peter's outburst against false shepherds aligns Milton's poem with an alternative tradition of anticlerical satire that includes Spenser's May Eclogue. It dates back to Peter's fierce prophecy of retribution against the corrupt usurpation of Pope Boniface VIII in Dante's *Paradiso*:

---

[3] E.g. Hill, *MER*, pp. 29–30; Wilding, *Dragons Teeth*, pp. 7–9.

[4] Barbara K. Lewalski, "How Radical Was the Young Milton?" in *Milton and Heresy*, ed. John Rumrich and Steven Dobranski (Cambridge University Press, 1998), pp. 49–72.

[5] Edmund Spenser, *The Yale Edition of the Shorter Poems of Edmund Spenser*, ed. William A. Oram, et al. (New Haven and London: Yale University Press, 1989), p. 23. On religious satire in Spensers eclogues, see *SPART*, pp. 14–46.   [6] Warton, pp. 21, 35; Johnson, *Lives of the Poets*, p. 95.

Rapacious wolves in shepherds' garb behold
In every pasture! Lord, why dost Thou blink
Such slaughter of the lambs within Thy fold?   (27.19–66).

Petrarch introduced the innovation of doubling of the roles of shepherds as figures for poets and clerics in eclogues that rail against the Avignon papacy. Baptista Mantuanus Spagnuoli (Mantuan) then elaborated upon both Virgilian and Petrarchan precedent in *Adolescentia seu Bucolica* (Mantua, 1498), a collection of neo-Latin eclogues that became a staple of the English grammar-school curriculum. His standing as leader of the Carmelite order lent credence to his satires on clerical ignorance, greed, and corruption. Many English readers regarded Dante, Petrarch, and Mantuan as proto-Protestant predecessors of both Spenser and Milton.[7] In *Of Reformation*, Milton himself cites Petrarch's Sonnet 108 as an attack against the Church of Rome as the Whore of Babylon (*CPW* I: 559).

In *Animadversions*, Milton clearly appropriates Spenser's May Eclogue as antiprelatical prophecy. The tract indicates that Piers, a namesake of Piers Plowman and militant defender of ministerial calling, attacks a worldly rival who neglects his clerical vocation, the

false shepherd Palinode in the eclogue of May, under whom the poet lively personates our prelates, whose whole life is a recantation of their pastoral vow, and whose profession to forsake the world, as they use the matter, bogs them deeper into the world: Those our admired Spenser inveighs against, not without some presage of these reforming times.

Quoting Piers's diatribe against hireling shepherds and nonresident holders of benefices ("May," lines 103–31) in its entirety, that passage leads Warton to conclude that Milton "copied the sentiments of Piers, a Protestant controversial shepherd" when he composed *Lycidas*.[8] Indeed, a Latin translation of *The Shepheardes Calender* that circulated in manuscript during Milton's years at Cambridge University substitutes the name Lycidas for Piers; it was published during the Commonwealth (Figure 1).[9] Claiming to expose "the doctrine and lives of the Romish clergy," a 1606 edition of *The Plowman's Tale* makes it clear that contemporaries of Milton saw Spenser as a Protestant radical. Accompanied by a declaration that "the Pope is Antichrist and they His Ministers," an annotation explains: "Of such shepherds speaks Master Spenser in his *Calender*" (A1r, 3v).

In actual fact, *Animadversions* distorts Piers's appeal for reform within

---

[7] *SPART*, pp. 14–15.   [8] *CPW* I: 722; Milton, *Poems*, ed Warton, p. 21.
[9] Theodore Bathurst, trans., *Calendarium Pastorale* (comp. c. 1608, publ. 1653). Theocritus originates use of **Lycidas** as a pastoral name (*Idyll* 7.27).

46   **MAY.**

With Hawthorne-buds,and sweet Eglantine
And girlonds of Roses,and sops in wine.
Such merry-make holy Saints doth queme:
But we here sitten as drownd in a dreme.
       PIERS.
For yonkers *Palinode* such follies fit,
But we tway been men of elder wit.
       PALINODE.
Siker,this morrow,no longer ago,
I saw a shole of shepheards out-go,
With singing and shooting,and jolly cheere:
Before them yode a lusty tabrere,
That to the meynie a horne-pipe plaid,
Whereto they dauncen each one with his maid,
To see these folks make such jovisaunce,
Made my heart after the pipe to daunce.
Tho to the green-wood they speeden them all
To fetchen home May with their musicall:
And home they bringen in a royal throne,
Crowned as King:and his Queen attone
Was Lady *Flora*,on whom did attend
A faire flock of Faeries,and a fresh bend
Of lovely Nymphs. (O that I were there,
To helpen the Ladies their May-bush bear!)
Ah *Piers*,been thy teeth on edge,to think,
How great sport they gaynen with little swinke?
       PIERS.
Perdie,so farre am I from envie,
That their fondness inly I pitty:
Those faytours little regarden their charge,
While they letting their sheep runne at large,
Passen their time, that should be sparely spent,
In lustlines and wanton merriment.
Thilke same been shepheards for the divels sted,
That playen while their flocks be unfed.
              Well

            MAIUS.   47

Congrege quas spinâ violaria lucida texunt,
Alterneque rosis intersita candida bellis.
Talia Sylvano frontem Satyrisque serenant,
Nos consopiti stupido torpore sedemus.
       LYCIDAS.
Hæc (Doryla) teneris infantia convenit annis,
Altius at sapere nostra hæc maturior ætas.
       DORYLAS.
Hac equidem aurorâ (nuper transacta renarro)
Egressos vidi denso agmine ruris alumnos,
Solenni streperos plausû, festisque choreis;
Cornicen his etiam succosus prævius ibat,
Qui tremulum raucis diverberat aera bombis:
Dum (latus unicuique suâ stipante puellâ)
Hi peronato gaudent pede plaudere terram.
Hanc dum lætitiam stupui, fremitusque secundos,
Æmula subsultant parili præcordia gestu.
Inde petunt virides glomerato examine sylvas,
Ut primùm verni carpant libamina Maii.
Tum Faunum folio fultum, cinctumque corollis
Arborum gestant, huic conjux, assidet unâ
Flora novo peplo solito conspectior, illam
Stipant densato famulantes agmine Nymphæ.
(O hujus partem esse chori, si fata dedissent,
Cum Nymphis Floram ut sociâ cervice subirem!)
O Lycida, potis es non intabescere, tantas
Delicias recolens nullo conamine partas?
       LYCIDAS.
His ut ego invideam? (Doryla) quin semper eorum
Et miror miserorque imo deliria corde:
Insanæ quòd nullâ obeant sua munia curâ,
Sed pecudes passi passim sine lege vagari,
Decurrunt vitam parcè cantèque terendam
Ebria turba jocis, lascivo diffluarisu.
Tartareum genus hæc pastorum emersit ab orco,
Qui inanni dum grex ag os jejunus oberrat;
            Apparet

Figure 1   Translation of Piers as Lycidas. Edmund Spenser, *Calendarium Pastorale*, translated by Theodore Bathurst (1653), pp. 46-47.

the church by interpreting it as antiprelatical satire in tune with the revolutionary world of the early 1640s. E.K.'s original commentary on the May Eclogue explains that Piers attacks "the Pope, and his Anti-Christian prelates, which usurp a tyrannical dominion in the Church, and with Peter's counterfeit keys, open a wide gate to all wickedness and insolent government." Spenser's first commentator goes on to uphold the episcopal hierarchy, however, thus undercutting Milton's prophetic reading:

Nought here spoken, as of purpose to deny fatherly rule and godly governaunce (as some malitiously of late have done to the greate unreste and hinderaunce of the Churche) but to display the pride and disorder of such, as in steede of feeding their sheepe, indeed feede of theyr sheepe. (Gloss on line 121)

Milton composed *Lycidas* in honor of the late Edward King during the aftermath of the 1637 incident when William Prynne (who had lost the tips of his ears in 1633 for libeling Queen Henrietta Maria) joined John Bastwick and Henry Burton in having his ears savagely sliced off on a scaffold at New Palace Yard, Westminster. This was for publishing a tract against Laud and his fellow prelates. That cause célèbre affords an historical occasion for St. Peter's attack on "false" shepherds (lines 108–31). It may be that the alignment between "th'abhorred shears" of the Fury and the anxiously "trembling ears" of Milton's swain (lines 75–77) suggests an allusion to ear-cropping. Written after Milton's falling out with Prynne and the Presbyterians, the original draft of "On the New Forcers of Conscience Under the Long Parliament" (1646) employs the only other example of the "shears"/"ears" rhyme to mock the clipping of "marginal P——'s ears."[10] (That nickname refers to Prynne's habit of crowding the margins of his books with notes.) Following the relaxation of censorship after Laud's downfall, the punishment of Bastwick, Prynne, and Burton would inspire venomous attacks such as Richard Overton's *A New Play Called Canterbury, His Change of Diet* (1641), which satirizes Laud for feasting upon his victims' ears (Figure 2). His maimed victims flank the caricature of Laud as he feasts upon a severed ear.

Given Milton's construction of *Lycidas* as an allegory concerning the vocation of poet-priest that he shared with Edward King, St. Peter's attack on false shepherds would seem to reflect upon the poet's recent renunciation of his own clerical calling in favor of a poetic career.[11] In

[10] Lines 14–15 and n. on line 17. John Leonard, " 'Trembling Ear': The Historical Moment of *Lycidas*," *Journal of Medieval and Renaissance Studies* 21 (1991), pp. 63, 69–70.

[11] John T. Shawcross, *John Milton: The Self and the World* (Lexington, KY: University of Kentucky Press, 1993), pp. 68–69.

THE FIRST ACT.

*Enter the Bishop of Canterbury, and with him a Doctor of Physicke, a
Lawyer, and a Divine; who being set downt, they bring him variety
of Dishes to his Table,*

C *Anterbury*, is here all the dishes, that are provided?
Doct. My Lord, there is all : and 'tis enough, wert for a Princes table,
Ther's 24. severall dainty dishes, and all rare.

B, *Cant.* Are these rare : no, no, they please me not,
Give me a Carbinadoed cheek, or a tippet of a Cocks combe :
None of all this, here is meate for my Pallet.

Lawyer. My Lord, here is both Cocke and Phesant,
Quaile and Partridge, and the best varieties the shambles yeeld.

A 2

Cant.

Figure 2   Archbishop Laud Dining on the Ears of Prynne, Bastwick, and Burton.
Richard Overton, *A New Play Called Canterbury, His Change of Diet* (1641), A2^r.

an embittered account of how Milton was "church-outed by the prelates," *The Reason of Church Government* explains that "coming to some
maturity of years and perceiving what tyranny had invaded the Church
. . . I thought it better to prefer a blameless silence before the sacred
office of speaking bought, and begun with servitude and foreswearing"
(*CPW* I: 822–23). Milton shared the restiveness of Prynne, Bastwick, and
Burton concerning Laudian ecclesiastical innovations.

St. Peter's jeremiad signals a brusque tonal shift from the poem's
modulated pastoral opening, which concludes with Phoebus' consolation that heavenly reward compensates for the untimely death of
Lycidas (i.e. Edward King). Arriving at the rear of the procession of
mourners, following "sage Hippotades" and "Camus, reverend sire,"
Peter addresses the problem of the faithful shepherd-priest in a world of
religious corruption:

> Last came, and last did go,
> The pilot of the Galilean lake,
> Two massy keys he bore of metals twain,
> (The golden opes, the iron shuts amain)
> He shook his mitred locks and stern bespake.   (lines 108–12)

Anticipating similar moments in *Paradise Lost* (e.g., the narrator's outbursts against "trumpery" and "hypocrisy" in Book 3), his harsh vernacular voice signals an abrupt semantic shift from the swain's sonorous
phrases, such as "Without the meed of some melodious tear" (line 14).
The Bible affords precedents for the apostle's harsh invective, notably
Ezekiel's prophecy against "the shepherds of Israel" that "feed not the
sheep" (Ezek. 34:2–3). Annotation in the Geneva Bible interprets them
typologically as "shepherds that despised the flock of Christ." In a
similar outburst, Jesus juxtaposes himself as the Good Shepherd, who
"giveth his life for his sheep" with the hireling who abandons them
(John 10:11–14).

By invoking the vexed issue of ecclesiastical authority, the speaker's
paired keys constitute a problematic touch because they bring to mind a
distinctive feature in papal heraldry, the crossed keys of St. Peter.[12]
Although some debate exists concerning whether the "pilot of the
Galilean Lake"(1.109) represents Jesus or Simon Peter, the allusion to
the "keys of the kingdom of heaven" (Matt. 16:19) conferred upon Peter
by Jesus seems conclusive. Protestants accepted Peter's apostolic status,
but they rejected the papal claim to apostolic succession based upon

---

[12] See George H. McLoone, "*Lycidas*: Hurled Bones and the Noble Mind of Reformed Congregations," *MiltonS* 26 (1990), pp. 63, 66–67.

Jesus' commission: "Thou art Peter, and upon this rock I will build my church" (Matt. 16:18). Although the Catholic appropriation of Peter as the prototypical Pope is little different from the Protestant typology of England as a New Israel, Milton and his co-religionists rejected the Pope as an illegitimate authority for whom no scriptural warrant exists. The speaker's "mitred locks" combines oblique wordplay upon **keys** and **locks** with an explicit reference to episcopal headgear anachronistically associated with St. Peter as the first Bishop of Rome. Prominence of his **miter** suggests that Milton has not yet abandoned episcopacy *per se*.

It may be that St. Peter functions as a voice for the "invisible church" identified with the body of Christian believers as opposed to the clerical establishment. Protestants accepted the Augustinian belief in a "true" church that came into being with Adam and Eve, an idea that informs *Paradise Lost*. By contrast, the pilot attacks corruption in the hierarchical establishment of the "visible church," whose leadership is claimed both by the Pope and Archbishop Laud. Interpretation of the Petrine keys as an unproblematic symbol for the papacy cuts against the grain of Milton's identification of "the right use of the keys" with true ministry and Bible preaching in *The Reason of Church Government* (*CPW* 1: 832–33). By contrast, "Peters counterfet keyes" symbolize the papal claim to primacy over other bishops according to E.K.'s commentary on Spenser's May Eclogue (line 121).

St. Peter's long-standing association with episcopacy problematizes any understanding that *Lycidas* anticipates Milton's call for extirpation of prelacy in his 1640s pamphlets. The poem's apparent sympathy for "true" episcopacy suggests that it may be anachronistic to discover a call to abolish episcopacy years before 15,000 Londoners endorsed the Root and Branch Petition of 1640. By 1641 *Of Prelatical Episcopacy* would argue that "Peter's being at Rome as bishop cannot stand with concordance of scripture" (*CPW* 1: 635), but *Lycidas* stops short of calling for the outright abolition of episcopacy at the same time that it attacks prelatical abuses. Prynne adopted a similar position in 1637.[13]

The pilot's harangue directs an oxymoronic attack at "Blind mouths" that neglect preaching to feed upon ecclesiastical wealth. John Ruskin's renowned explication of the following passage posits a binary opposition between "true" and "false" prelates:

> Blind mouths! that scarce themselves know how to hold
> A sheep-hook, or have learned aught else the least
> That to the faithful herdman's art belongs! (lines 119–21)

---

[13] Norbrook, *Poetry*, p. 280.

Based on the etymological sense of **bishop** as "overseer" and **pastor** as "shepherd," Ruskin declares: "The most unbishoply character . . . is therefore to be blind. The most unpastoral is, instead of feeding, to want to be fed, to be a Mouth."[14] Even the wooden "sheep-hook" is charged with significance, because the humble shepherd's crook is an attribute of Christ as the Good Shepherd rather than the Pope, patriarchs, and archbishops, whose gilded and bejeweled crosiers signify hierarchical status. Indeed, *Of Reformation* attacks the Pope for rejecting "the pastorly rod and sheep-hook of Christ" (*CPW* 1: 605). Thomas Warton interprets the passage as the first overt instance of Milton's hostility to a professional clergy paid through tithes: "He here animadverts on the endowments of the church, at the same time insinuating that they were shared by those only who sought the emoluments of the sacred office, to the exclusion of a learned and conscientious clergy" (Milton, *Poems*, ed. Warton, p. 20).

The carnivalesque engorgement of grotesquely overfed churchmen results in the starvation of their flocks for want of spiritual fodder. The speaker attacks

> such as for their **bellies'** sake
> Creep and intrude, and climb into the fold,
> Of other care they little reckoning make,
> Than how to scramble at the shearers' **feast**,
> And shove away the worthy bidden **guest**;
>   . . .
> And when they list, their lean and flashy songs
> Grate on their scrannel pipes of wretched straw,
> The **hungry** sheep look up, and are not **fed**,
> But **swoll'n with wind**, and the rank mist they draw,
> **Rot** inwardly, and foul contagion spread.
>
> (lines 114–18, 123–27)

An anticarnival spirit informs the striking metaphor of famished "sheep" (i.e. congregants), whose swelling with **wind** ridicules counterfeit pastors for preaching empty sermons that make their flocks suffer from flatulence. John Aubrey's reminder about Milton's pronunciation of "the letter R very hard" accords with the satirical edge of the harsh

---

[14] Ruskin's *Sesame and Lilies* (1891), as quoted in Merritt Y. Hughes, et al., *A Variorum Commentary on the Poems of John Milton*, 6 vols. (New York: Columbia University Press, 1970–), vol. II, p. 675. In *A Sermon Preached to the Honourable House of Commons Assembled in Parliament. At Their Public Feast, November 17. 1640*, 3rd ed. (1641), Cornelius Burges attacks "blind guides and idle shepherds [who] care not to erect preaching where there is none" (p. 52).

alliteration of "**Gr**ate on their sc**r**annel pipes of w**r**etched st**r**aw." It appears that Peter's denunciation of gluttonous pastors goes beyond their abandonment of preaching to indict Archbishop Laud's imposition of a Mass-like celebration at a high altar in place of the Lord's Supper ("the shearers' feast") shared by the communicant ("the worthy bidden guest") at a communion table. The language anticipates the grotesque alimentary imagery in _Of Reformation_, which colorfully attacks the "canary-sucking, and swan-eating palate" of the prelate who gobbles up "a plump endowment" with a "many-benefice-gaping mouth."[15] In _Paradise Lost_, ravenous appetite, indigestion, and flatulence also hint at attack on religious corruption.

Despite the claim that Milton had already rejected episcopacy and that the relative moderation of _Lycidas_ reflects "caution rather than conciliation" at a time when strict censorship was in force,[16] even tracts that he composed after the lapsing of censorship in 1640 argue in favor of nonceremonial, evangelical episcopacy that eschews wealth and fulfills the ideals of pastoral ministry.[17] He subverts the orthodox sense of **bishop** in _Of Reformation_, for example, which reverts to the trope of "Blind mouths" to contrast the "true apostolic bishop" who "feeds his parochial flock" with "a tyrannical crew and corporation of impostors, that have blinded and abused the world" under the name of "prelatism." Milton finished that pamphlet prior to the 27 May introduction of the unsuccessful Root and Branch Bill by Sir Edward Dering, another defender of "primitive episcopacy."[18] Claiming that "false" bishops are "blind judges of things before their eyes," _Of Prelatical Episcopacy_ (1641) articulates an ideal of pastoral episcopacy favored by William Tyndale, John Bale, and other low-church Protestants.[19] In a related vein, an anonymous pamphlet entitled _Triple Episcopacy: or, a Threefold Order of Bishops_ (1641), published in the same year as _Of Reformation_, satirizes two examples of "false" prelacy, one "of Men, and another of the Devil," both of whom have the recognizable features of Archbishop Laud. The title-page woodcut mocks Laud's advocacy of the prayer book and superstition, whereas the Bible in the hand of the "true" bishop iden-

---

[15] _CPW_ 1: 549; Parker, p. 162.   [16] Leonard, "Trembling Ear," pp. 76–79.

[17] On the "hermeneutics of censorship," see Annabel Patterson, _Censorship and Interpretation: The Conditions of Writing and Reading in Early Modern England_, (Madison, Wis: University of Wisconsin Press, 1984), pp. 113–15, and passim.

[18] _CPW_ 1: 537–38. On Dering's personal copy of _Of Reformation_, see Jason Rosenblatt, "Sir Edward Dering's Milton," _Modern Philology_ 79 (1982), pp. 376–85.

[19] _CPW_ 1: 629. See the Prologue on 1 Timothy, in _The Work of William Tyndale_, ed. G. E. Duffield (Appleford: Sutton Courtenay Press, 1964), p. 154.

tifies him with Protestant belief in the sufficiency of the scriptures (Figure 3). Elevating the Bible-reading layman above prelates, the caricature advocates the sufficiency of the English Bible.

St. Peter's invective against "the grim wolf with privy paw" (line 128) appropriates a memorable anticlerical trope that echoed in Wycliffite sermons, Protestant beast fables, and Spenser's satirical eclogues. In the Sermon on the Mount, Jesus had warned his followers: "Beware of false prophets, which come to you in sheep's clothing, but inwardly they are ravening wolves" (Matt. 7:15). Thomas Warton claims that St. Peter merely targets "what the puritans called unpreaching prelates, and a liturgical clergy, who did not place the whole of religion in lectures and sermons three hours long" (Milton, *Poems*, ed. Warton, p. 22). Nonetheless, the cutting sarcasm makes it far more likely that the "grim wolf" that "Daily devours apace, and nothing said" (line 129) glances both at Jesuit missionary activity under way at the royal court[20] and at Laud and his associates. After all, the predator's "privy paw" hints at the archbishop's role as the king's chief minister, who played a prominent role in both the Privy Council and Privy Chamber.

The wolf's clandestine nature links it to Protestant satire on Roman clerics who disguised themselves as "foxes," despite their "wolfish" nature. Milton's reading of Spenser's May Eclogue accordingly reinforces religious satire in *Lycidas*. In the speech quoted in *Animadversions*, Piers (i.e. Lycidas according to the Cambridge translation of Spenser's *Calender*) inveighs against wolves "That often devoured their own sheep" in the guise of shepherds ("May," line 128). The conversion of the Wolf into "the Fox, master of collusion" (line 219) in Piers's beast fable about the Kid ("the simple sort of faithful and true Christians" according to E.K.'s gloss on line 174) alludes to the Protestant satirical tradition that Catholic clerics conceal themselves as foxes during Protestant regimes, only to reveal themselves openly as wolves under Catholic rulers.[21] Of course, foxes are dangerous in themselves. That attacks of that kind were not antiepiscopal per se may be noted in the September Eclogue, in which "the Wolf in his counterfeit coat" (line 206) is hunted down and slain by Roffy, a thinly veiled figure for Spenser's first patron, John Young, the Puritan Bishop of Rochester. The interplay between covert foxes and overt wolves endured across the seventeenth century. For

---

[20] Leonard, "Trembling Ear," p. 75.
[21] The ecclesiastical-beast fable originates with William Turner's *The Hunting and Finding Out of the Romish Fox* (Bonn, 1543) and John Bale's *Yet a Course at the Romish Fox*, (Antwerp, 1543). See *SPART*, pp. 36–39.

TRIPLE
EPISCOPACIE:
OR,
A THREE-FOLD ORDER
OF BISHOPS:

One of GOD, another of MEN, and another
of the DIVELL; the two later muſt be pluckt up, the
former only muſt continue, and the Reaſons why.

With a declaration of certaine other weighty points concerning
the Diſcipline and Government of the Church:

Matth.15.13. Every plant which mine heavenly Father hath not planted ſhould be rooted up.

Of God,   Of Man,   Of the Divell.

Loe, here are three men, ſtanding in degree,
The leaſt of theſe, the greateſt ought to be.

The other two, of men and of the Devill,
Ought to be rooted out ſoure as evill.

Printed, and are to be ſold by SAMVEL SATTERTHVVAIT

Figure 3   "True" Versus "False" Episcopacy. *Triple Episcopacy: Or, A Threefold Order of Bishops* (1641).

example, William Prynne calls Laud a "Romish Fox" in *Canterbury's Doom* (p. 66). Soon after the Glorious Revolution, *Old Rome's New Church of Knaves and Fools* (1689) portrayed a Jesuit Fox preaching from a pulpit (Figure 4). A verse inscription unfolds the allegory:

> Old Rome's new church of knaves and fools consists,
> Whose auditors are geese, and foxes priests:
> That God the people fear, the priests to mock,
> Who while they seem to feed, devour their flock.[22]

Laudian **wolves** were on Milton's mind during the mid-1630s. Composed only a few years before *Lycidas*, *Comus* associates wolfishness with the hypocritical disguising of Comus and the "vowed priests" of his "foundation." As a "true" pastor, the Attendant Spirit juxtaposes his own "Tending my flocks hard by i' the hilly crofts" with the performance of "abhorred rites" by "stabled wolves," the subhuman followers of Comus (lines 531–34). Bristling with multilingual puns, the striking epithet of **stabled wolves** may imply attack on clerics whose positions in the ecclesiastical establishment or "stable" (from *establir*, the Old French derivation of both "to stable" and "to establish") have enabled them to invade the sheepfold (Lat. *stabulum*). Those connotations may seem far-fetched if one considers *Comus* in isolation, but the connection between that passage and the depredation of a clerical wolf within the sheepfold (i.e. the church) in *Lycidas* reinforces the association.[23] In the Trinity Manuscript, Milton added suggestive revisions to *Comus* close to the time of Edward King's drowning.

Milton employs the wolf trope throughout the antiprelatical tracts to attack voracious clergy who "sought to cover under sheep's clothing . . . threatening inroads and bloody incursions upon the flock of Christ, which they took upon them to feed, but now claim to devour as their prey" (*CPW* I: 856–57). *Of Reformation* derides a pope who "subtly acted the lamb . . . but he threw off his sheep's clothing and started up a wolf," and it concludes with an apocalyptic prayer for salvation of "this thy poor and almost spent, and expiring church" from "these importunate wolves, that wait and think long till they devour thy tender flock" (*CPW* I: 595, 614). According to the *Apology for Smectymnuus*, Laudian prelates "chase away all the faithful shepherds of the flock, and bring in a dearth of spiritual food, robbing thereby the church of her dearest treasure, and

---

[22] Compare a c. 1555 engraving that attacks Bishop Stephen Gardiner, Lord Chancellor under Mary I, as a Romish wolf who slaughters innocent sheep, i.e. Protestant martyrs (*SPART*, fig. 2).

[23] *OED* "stable" v.1 4a. See Wilding, *Dragons Teeth*, pp. 52–54.

Figure 4   The Roman Fox. *Old Rome's New Church of Knaves and Fools* (1689).

sending hoards of souls starving to Hell" (*CPW* 1: 952). The contemporaneity of such barbs may be noted in *A Discovery of the Jesuits' Trumpery*, a revolutionary broadside that defends the Lord's Supper against Laudian "wolves": "Prick your fine Lamb, see if your Lamb will bleed / Ours bled for us: That blood, our soul's purgation" (Figure 5).

It seems likely that Milton reflected upon instances of the wolf trope in *Comus*, *Lycidas*, Spenserian verse, or other texts when, in composing *Paradise Lost*, he incorporated a proleptic stab at ecclesiastical corruption into Satan's predatory invasion of Eden. The conventional language of scriptural pastoral alludes to St. Paul's prophecy that "after my departing shall grievous wolves enter in among you, not sparing the flock" (Acts 20:29):

> As when a prowling wolf,
> Whom hunger drives to seek new haunt for prey,
> Watching where shepherds pen their flocks at eve
> In hurdled cotes amid the field secure,
> Leaps o'er the fence with ease into the fold:
> Or as a thief bent to unhoard the cash
> Of some rich burgher, whose substantial doors,
> Cross-barred and bolted fast, fear no assault,
> In at the window climbs, or o'er the tiles;
> So clomb this first grand thief into God's fold:
> So since into his church lewd hirelings climb. (4.183–93)

That epic simile belittles Satan by comparison to wolfish churchmen unconcerned with pastoral care and in contrast to shepherd-pastors attentive to the spiritual health of "flocks" within the "fold" of the visible church. Intensification of "into the fold" to "into God's fold" assigns an echoing character to clerical corruption over the centuries. Indeed, the word **fold** carries a polemical charge in many of Milton's writings.[24] For example, "On the Late Massacre in Piedmont" (1655) grimly prays for divine vengeance on behalf of Waldensian "saints," members of an Alpine sect recently martyred within "their ancient fold." Their adherence to "truth so pure of old"[25] identifies persecution by the Pope, "the triple tyrant" of Rome, as only the most recent depredation of "the Babylonian woe" associated with the Church of Rome as the Scarlet Whore.

The figure of the **wolf in the fold** exerted a powerful hold on

---

[24] See John Ruskin's *Notes on the Construction of Sheepfolds* (1851), which builds upon Hooker's *Laws of Ecclesiastical Polity* and other early modern sources in applying the **fold** as a figure for the visible church.

[25] Waldensian beliefs included rejection of papal supremacy, the Mass, and religious images.

Figure 5   Pack of Popish Trinkets. *A Discovery of the Jesuits' Trumpery, Newly Packed Out of England* (1641).

Milton's imagination. Indeed, derision of Satan's primal transgression of Edenic boundaries satirizes Restoration ecclesiology as a cyclic return to the infractions of Laudian churchmen and the sacerdotalism of all clergies, including that of Presbyterian churchmen.[26] The epic simile's concluding attack on "lewd hirelings" who "climb" into the seventeenth-century "church" invokes the rhetoric of *The Likeliest Means to Remove Hirelings out of the Church* (1659). Writing that tract during the Learned-Ministry controversy that flared during the waning months of the Commonwealth, Milton adopts a Pauline voice to attack reinstitution of a salaried ministry as a return to the corruption of the early Church, when "hirelings like wolves came in by herds" (*CPW* 7: 280). Such language carried a highly topical charge when Milton's "To the Lord General Cromwell" (1652) expressed scorn for "hireling wolves whose gospel is their maw." Indeed, the poet tempers enthusiasm for Cromwell with a pointed appeal for an end to established ministry salaried by enforced payment of tithes.[27] Milton had long resisted a self-perpetuating, professional clergy on the ground that "New Presbyter is but Old Priest writ large" ("On the New Forcers of Conscience," line 20).

Comparison of Satan to a robber in the second part of the epic simile might seem digressive, but it colorfully likens the exaction of tithes to thievery. After all, equation of the church with a merchant's fortified household, from which people are excluded, may seem highly unflattering. May we discover a hint that the "rich burgher" with his hoard of "cash" is a successor to medieval monastics, who participates in the rapacity of the "prowling wolf?" Such an association might recall Spenser's use of Kirkrapine, a personification of both monastic aggrandizement and Protestant iconoclasm (*FQ* 1.3.16–22), to allegorize misuse of ecclesiastical property. At one and the same time, Kirkrapine is a licentious resident of an unholy convent and a "church robber" (the literal meaning of his name). Satan mirrors him in bringing to mind manifold forms of clerical depredation, stealth, and greed. Nonetheless the simile of the fortified household affords a figure for what requires protection. The barb may attack an ecclesiastical impulse to "lock up" the holy, like an idol, within a richly endowed church establishment, but what lies within is not corrupt per se.

---

[26] See Schwartz, *Remembering and Repeating*, p. 13.

[27] See Blair Worden, "John Milton and Oliver Cromwell," in *Soldiers, Writers and Statesmen of the English Revolution*, ed. Ian Gentles, John Morrill, and Blair Worden (Cambridge University Press, 1998), pp. 243–53.

In *Lycidas*, St. Peter's invective against the "grim wolf with privy paw" concludes with an unambiguous threat to eradicate religious error by means of the "two-handed engine at the door" (lines 128–30). To say that the line has attracted an extravagant range of interpretations is an understatement (see *ME* 5: 55). Warton's comment on the startling clarity of the antiprelatical threat underscores the inefficacy of Laudian censorship:

> It is a matter of surprise, that this violent invective against the Church of England and the hierarchy, couched indeed in terms a little mysterious yet sufficiently intelligible, and covered only by a transparent veil of allegory, should have been published under the sanction and from the press of one of our universities; or that it should afterwards have escaped the severest animadversions, at a period, when the proscriptions of the Star-chamber, and the power of Laud, were at their height. Milton, under pretence of exposing the faults or abuses of the episcopal clergy, attacks their establishment, and strikes at their existence.[28]

Warton lodges the startling claim that the words genuinely prophesied "the execution of archbishop Laud by a two-handed engine" (i.e. the headman's ax). It seems more likely that the "engine" suggests an apocalyptic weapon borne by Archangel Michael, the guardian who presides over the third and final movement of *Lycidas* (lines 161–63). The iconographical attributes of that patron saint of the Church Militant include a coat of mail and a two-handed sword. During the War in Heaven, for example, Michael cuts a swath through squadrons of rebel angels with an avenging "sword" wielded with "huge two-handed sway" (*PL* 6.250–51). In line with the dense biblical texture of St. Peter's diatribe, that image surely undergoes conflation with "the sword of the Spirit, which is the word of God" (Eph. 6:17) and the related figure of "the sharp two-edged sword" that emerges from the mouth of God (Rev. 1:16, 19:15). In sixteenth-century Protestant Bibles, ubiquitous woodcuts of two-edged swords symbolize the divine Word as the bedrock of "true" religion.[29] (Warriors typically used both hands in wielding the straight, double-edged broadsword with a protective pommel.) Indeed, a mid-seventeenth-century engraving brings us full circle to the controversial occasion for the satirical sequence in *Lycidas*. A broadsheet

---

[28] Milton, *Poems*, ed. Warton, p. 23. He bases his observation on an annotation in Milton's *Poetical Works*, 3 vols. (1749–53).

[29] *SPART*, pp. 193–99. The "two-handed engine" recalls the sword with which the Red Cross Knight slays the apocalyptic Dragon (*FQ* 1.11.53) and Satan's acknowledgment of the invincibility of God's "sharp two edged sword" in Fletcher's *The Locusts*, 1.24. See also Leon Howard, "'That Two-Handed Engine' Once More," *HLQ* 15 (1952), pp. 173–84.

published by John Goddard portrays John Bastwick, a victim of Laudian ear-cropping, clad in the Pauline Armor of God, notably the Sword of the Spirit (Eph. 6: 13–17). The scene heroizes his antiformalist opposition to Laudian policies mocked by the engraving, which includesa demon drinking from the chalice of the Roman-rite Mass.[30]

When St. Peter falls silent, the resumption of pastoral elegy makes it clear that the invective on religious corruption constitutes a generic rupture: "Return Alpheus, the dread voice is past,/That shrunk thy streams" (lines 132–33). That jarring shift to the modulated voice of "the uncouth swain" need not constitute a fatal flaw, in line with Samuel Johnson's critique, if we recall that mixing of genres is a distinctive component of satire. Similar ruptures occur at satirical moments in *Paradise Lost* when, for example, jeremiad succeeds heavenly dialogue in the case of the narrator's attack on monasticism at the Paradise of Fools, or when he breaks into a harangue against celibacy in the midst of Edenic epithalamium, or when Roman hymnody intrudes into pastoral idyll.[31] The resurfacing of the river symbolic of "the incorruptibility of truth" (Carey, n. on lines 85–86) initiates a consolatory movement that carries through to the conclusion. Beginning with the catalogue of flowers that "strew the laureate hearse where Lycid lies" (line 151), the closing movement reaffirms the immortality of his soul. Despite the ideological centrality of St. Peter's prophecy of retribution, the conclusion enfolds that outburst within wider apocalyptic expectations of cleansing and renewal.

Echoes of Revelation stud the conclusion, in which death and resurrection supplant all "false surmise" (line 153). A transformative sequence raises Lycidas into the heavenly realm where he joins the company of the "saints" and "hears the unexpressive nuptial song,/In the blest kingdoms meek of joy and love" (lines 176–77). That allusion to the "marriage of the Lamb" (Rev. 19:7) identifies Lycidas with the Spouse, whom theologians interpreted as the antitype of both the human soul and the "true" church. According to the *Apology for Smectymnuus*, "accompanying the Lamb with those celestial songs to others inapprehensible" is the special reward of chaste poets such as Milton and King (*CPW* 1: 892).

The apotheosis of Lycidas into the "genius of the shore" aligns him with St. Peter, "the pilot of the Galilean lake," as one who participates in

---

[30] Arthur M. Hind, *Engraving in England in the Sixteenth and Seventeenth Centuries*, 3 vols. (Cambridge University Press, 1953–1964), 1: 333, pl. 178.

[31] Chapters 5 and 8, below. See Lewalski, *Rhetoric*, pp. 114–24, 178, 238.

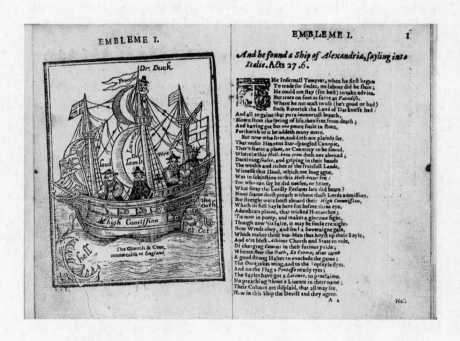

Figure 6   The Ship of the Church and Commonwealth of England. Thomas Stirry, *A Rot Amongst the Bishops, or, a Terrible Tempest in the Sea of Canterbury* (1641), A3ᵛ–A4ʳ.

"the invisible church's mystical body"[32] that is untinged with the corruption of the "fatal and perfidious bark / Built in the eclipse, and
rigged with curses dark" (lines 100–101). The unseaworthiness of the
ship (an ancient symbol for the church) on which Lycidas drowned
suggests yet another stab against corruption in the Church of England.[33]
Transcendence of clerical worldliness anticipates the overt apocalypticism of the prelatical tracts, notably *Of Reformation*, which welcomes the
uprooting of the Laudian bishops with millennial expectations. Indeed,
the ship as a symbol for corrupt Laudianism would occupy a prominent
place in Thomas Stirry's *Rot Amongst the Bishops* (1641), which caricatures
Archbishop Laud as the navigator of a ship symbolic of the High
Commission as a tool for tyrannical authority (Figure 6).

In the manner of Spenser's May Eclogue, St. Peter's harangue
against "Blind mouths" plunged the pre-revolutionary reader into the
world of polemical attack on Roman wolves who feed on unsuspecting
members of the Christian flock. After the destruction of Archbishop
Laud and his associates, revolutionary readers guided by the 1645
addition to the headnote of *Lycidas* were in a position to discover an
ecclesiastical critique far more consistent and explicit than that apparent
in the 1638 edition. The "digression" on clerical corruption in *Lycidas*
anticipates both the polemical rhetoric of Milton's antiprelatical tracts
and, in ways previously unrecognized, encrypted instances of religious
satire throughout *Paradise Lost*.

[32] McLoone, "Hurled Bones," pp. 60–61, 75, 77.
[33] On the ship as a polemical figure for the Church of Rome, see *TRI*, pp. 49, 95–99.

CHAPTER 3

Satan and the demonic conclave

Covert allusions and oblique applications of scriptural typology situate Book 1 of *Paradise Lost* within the contemporary milieu of religious strife. The "hermeneutics of censorship" at work in seventeenth-century England, where press licensers were unable to enforce regulations in the face of indirection and "functional ambiguity,"[1] therefore complicates and enriches our understanding of Milton's poem. Moreover, allusion to idolatrous Pharaoh and proleptic identification of the fallen angels with idolatry contributes to a murmur of antipapal complaint and satire in the opening episodes of Milton's epic. The generic gap between these elements and the conventions of both classical epic (e.g. beginning in medias res, catalogue of heroes, and epic games) and the biblical "epic" of Exodus undercut Satan's claim to heroic stature.[2] Book 1 builds up to a mordant stab that likens the satanic palace of Pandaemonium, in which demons gather in "secret conclave" (1.795), to the Vatican establishment of the Roman pontiff.

Elusive hints concerning antipapal satire coexist with dissident readings discerned at the time of publication, soon after Milton's death, and in modern times. Some early readers aligned Satan with both Charles I and James I, in whose policies militant Protestants perceived the "peril" of Roman Catholic takeover. One critic has discovered common ground between Satan and Charles I, in line with allegations in *Eikonoklastes* concerning the king's infringement upon political liberty and "true" religion.[3] Another interprets Satan in terms of overlapping images of "Stuart, Turkish, and the Roman tyrannies."[4] Others discern

---

[1] Patterson, *Censorship and Interpretation*, pp. 3–31; Keeble, *Culture*, ch. 3.
[2] See Lewalski, *Rhetoric*, pp. 56–62, 76–78.
[3] e.g. Joan S. Bennett, *Reviving Liberty: Radical Christian Humanism in Milton's Great Poems* (Cambridge, MA: Harvard University Press, 1989), ch. 2.
[4] Stevie Davies, *Images of Kingship in "Paradise Lost": Milton's Politics and Christian Liberty* (Columbia, MO: University of Missouri Press, 1983), p. 109 and passim.

Cromwellian arrogance in demonic defeat reminiscent of the failure of the Puritan revolution and Commonwealth.[5] John Toland's "Life of Milton" records that *Paradise Lost* underwent publication despite the licenser's desire "to suppress the whole poem for imaginary treason" because of the comparison of Satan to the eclipsed sun that "with fear of change/Perplexes monarchs" (1.598–99).[6] Suggestive of regicide, that daring innuendo aligns the religio-political establishment with demonic tyranny.

The narrator's sardonic language invites open-ended applications of the gathering of demons to evil in general, the history of the Jews, contemporary ecclesiastical controversy, and crypto-Catholic monarchs. Milton's allusive habit of mind encompasses dazzlingly ambiguous, multiple frames of reference: "Satan then is not a flat allegorical figure, to be equated either with Royalists, Ranters, or major-generals. Milton saw the Satanic in all three."[7] The present chapter investigates traces of religious controversy in Book 1 of *Paradise Lost*, which coexist with allusions to political tyranny and apocalyptic history.

Following Satan's rousing of his stunned cohorts from their fall into hell, an epic simile compares him to hard-hearted Pharaoh, the arch-tyrant of the Pentateuch. The simile fuses the age-old Judaeo-Christian view of Exodus as a figure for providential deliverance of the Chosen People with intimations of the antiformalist view of Restoration England as a land of pharaonic idolatry and oppression.[8] Many Christians identified the wandering Hebrews with the invisible church. The simile recalls allegations in *Eikonoklastes* concerning idolatrous misrule by Charles I. That pamphlet compares the king's defense of the retention of episcopacy to an "excuse" that Pharaoh might have offered for "detaining the Israelites" (*CPW* 3: 516).

When newly roused Satan lurches to the shore of the burning sea to address the fallen angels, biblical typology invites polemical interpretation. He summons his followers, who are strewn like

> scattered sedge
> Afloat, when with fierce winds Orion armed
> Hath vexed the Red Sea coast, whose waves o'erthrew
> Busiris and his Memphian chivalry,

[5] E.g., Worden, "John Milton and Oliver Cromwell," p. 263.
[6] Darbishire, ed., *Early Lives*, p. 180. See also Wilding, *Dragons Teeth*, pp. 237–38.
[7] Hill, *MER*, p. 343.
[8] See Keeble, *Culture*, pp. 254–55, 273–77; Roland M. Frye, *Milton's Imagery and the Visual Arts: Iconographic Tradition in the Epic Poems* (Princeton University Press, 1978), pp. 94–96.

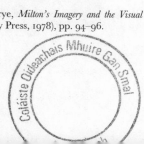

> While with perfidious hatred they pursued
> The sojourners of Goshen, who beheld
> From the safe shore their floating carcasses
> And broken chariot wheels, so thick bestrewn
> Abject and lost lay these, covering the flood,
> Under amazement of their hideous change.
>
> (1.304–13)

In addition to other layers of meaning, the text hints at allusion to the revolutionary defeat and execution of Charles I. After all, *Eikonoklastes* attacks Charles I's sponsorship of Laudian ecclesiastical innovations as subjugation of "true" believers by a latter-day Pharaoh. That pamphlet justifies regicide on the ground that divine providence punishes tyrannical persecutors:

And those kings and potentates who have strove most to rid themselves of this fear, by cutting off or suppressing the true church, have drawn themselves the occasion of their own ruin, while they thought with most policy to prevent it. Thus Pharaoh, when once he began to fear and wax jealous of the Israelites . . . soon found that evil which before slept, came suddenly upon him, by the preposterous way he took to shun it. Passing by examples between, and not shutting willfully our eyes, we may see the like story brought to pass in our own land.

Read in the light of Milton's prose, the epic simile concerning the washing of seawater over the pharaonic host recalls contemporary religious discord. The simile also recollects Milton's *The Ready and Easy Way to Establish a Free Commonwealth* (1660), which asserted on the eve of the Restoration that "choosing . . . a captain back for Egypt" would reverse the course of providential history that concludes with entry into the Promised Land.[9]

A second comparison of Satan to Pharaoh hints that readers may, at least at one level, identify oppression of the Chosen People with "papistry." The proleptic figure compares the fallen angels, springing "upon the wing" (1.332), to innumerable locusts that descend in the eighth of the ten Plagues of Egypt (Exod. 10:1–19):

> As when the potent rod
> Of Amram's son [i.e. Moses] in Egypt's evil day
> Waved round the coast, up called a pitchy cloud
> Of locusts, warping on the eastern wind,
> That o'er the realm of impious Pharaoh hung

[9] *CPW* 3: 509–10; 7: 463. See Marshall Grossman, *"Authors to Themselves": Milton and the Revelation of History* (Cambridge University Press, 1987), p. 20.

>   Like night, and darkened all the land of Nile:
>   So numberless were those bad angels seen
>   Hovering on wing   (1.338–45)

Archangel Michael's prophetic account of a "darksome cloud of locusts swarming down" upon the Nile Valley will expand upon that caustic allusion to Egyptian oppression and idolatry (12.185).

A typological link between the plague of locusts and the insects' emergence from "the bottomless pit" at the blowing of the fifth trumpet (Rev. 9: 1–11) confers a polemical cast upon Satan's mustering of his legions. Militant Protestants had long vilified Roman Catholic clerics, Jesuit priests in particular, as **locusts** swarming in hell. A Geneva Bible gloss on Revelation 9:3 thus identifies demonic **locusts** as "heretics, and worldly subtle prelates, with monks, friars, cardinals, patriarchs, archbishops, doctors, bachelors, and masters which forsake Christ to maintain false doctrine."[10] Sharing many affinities with the Gunpowder Plot satire in Milton's *In Quintum Novembris* (c. 1626), Fletcher's *The Locusts* employs the master conceit of **locusts** swarming in hell to collapse distinctions between Jesuits and Laudian innovators. We may note the topical force of the apocalyptic allusion in Richard Smith's *The Powder Treason Propounded by Satan, Approved by Antichrist, Enterprised by Papists* (c. 1615), engraved in honor of the thwarting of the Gunpowder Plot, which contains a lunette at the base that portrays Guy Fawkes and his co-plotters undergoing metamorphosis into **locusts** in hell (Figure 7).

Locusts continued to swarm in antiprelatical polemics of the revolutionary era.[11] As he composed *Paradise Lost*, Milton may have recalled the apocalyptic prayer that concludes *Of Reformation*. It vilifies Episcopalians, who "stand now at the entrance of the bottomless pit expecting the watch-word to open and let out those dreadful locusts and scorpions, to reinvolve us in that pitchy cloud of infernal darkness, where we shall never more see the sun of thy Truth again"(*CPW* 1: 614). A satirical broadsheet entitled *The Lineage of Locusts or the Pope's Pedigree Beginning with his Prime Ancestor the Devil* (1641?) celebrates the downfall of the bishops even more baldly: "come now and hear from whence the Pope

---

[10] That reading derives from John Bale's *Image of Both Churches* (Antwerp, 1545?), ed. Henry Christmas in *The Select Works of Bishop Bale* (Cambridge: Parker Society, 1849; vol. XXXVI), pp. 349–52. Bale identifies Catholic "bishops, priests and monks, with other disguised locusts" as "instruments of Satan" in *Acts of English Votaries*, 2 vols. (1560), pt. 1, A5v.

[11] Kristen E. Poole notes that conservative pamphleteers appropriated the trope of swarming locusts (or bees or wasps) in "Living with Insects, or Living within Sects: Swarming Wasps, the Liberated Conscience, and Thomas Edwards's *Gangraena*," forthcoming in *Form and Reform in Renaissance England: Essays in Honor of Barbara Kiefer Lewalski*, ed. Amy Boesky and Mary Crane (Newark: University of Delaware Press).

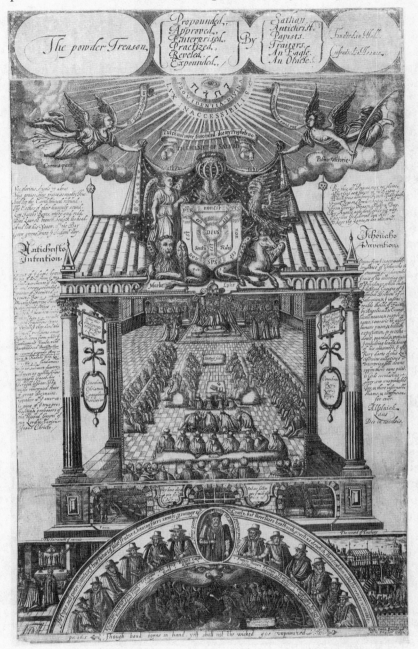

Figure 7   The Gunpowder Plot. Richard Smith, *The Powder Treason Propounded by Satan, Approved by Antichrist, Enterprised by Papists, Practiced by Traitors, Revealed by an Eagle, Expounded by an Oracle, Founded in Hell, Confounded in Heaven* (c. 1615).

descended . . . beginning with his prime ancestor, the Devil" (Figure 8). Likewise the Devil exults that Catholics "swarm, like to the Egyptian locusts, over all the land" in a 1642 broadsheet, *News from Hell, Rome, and the Inns of Court* (A4).

During the Restoration, when *Paradise Lost* found its way to a small but growing audience, the swarming of locusts lived on as a Protestant trope for the proliferation of Roman "error." Thus a banderole emerging from the mouth of a trumpeting demon in *The Devil's Triumph Over Rome's Idol* (1680) prepares the way for the Pope as Antichrist, "that mighty Man of Sin . . . / Whose spawn, like locusts, overspread the world"(Figure 9). The Devil leads his prisoner in chains toward hell. The banner hanging from the trumpet bears the name of Beelzebub, the Philistine Lord of the Flies who serves as Satan's deputy in *Paradise Lost*.[12]

Iconoclastic topoi fill the catalogue of idols that follows Satan's rousing of his cohorts. Those touches are in keeping with a poem that reflects upon an era when intoxicated Roundheads entertained themselves by smashing stained glass windows and altar rails reinstituted in English churches by order of Archbishop Laud (Figure 24). It may be that the narrator's proleptic reference to desecration by backsliding Israelites who permitted erection of Canaanite altars within the sacred precincts of the Temple at Jerusalem suggests iconoclastic attack on sacramental celebrations at high altars:

> often placed
> Within his sanctuary itself their shrines,
> Abominations; and with cursed things
> His holy rites, and solemn feasts profaned.   (1.387–90)

The language recalls Protestant identification of Roman-rite ritual as a latter-day manifestation of Canaanite idolatry. Milton advocated iconoclasm in his antiprelatical pamphlets and *Eikonoklastes* ("The Iconoclast"), the regicide tract in which he defends the dismantling of royal "idolatry."[13]

The narrator's attack on adoration of devils as idols "adorned/With gay religions full of pomp and gold" (1.371–72) corresponds to the contemporary view that vainglorious display falls under the patronage of Satan. For example, the *Catechism* attached to the *Book of Common*

---

[12] For other examples of the locust trope, see Thomas Robinson's *Anatomy of the English Nunnery at Lisbon in Portugal* (1622), pp. 4, 19; Milton's *Tenure of Kings and Magistrates* (*CPW* 3: 258); and Marvell's *First Anniversary of the Government under His Highness the Lord Protector* (lines 311–14).

[13] See Loewenstein, *Drama of History*, pp. 64–66.

Come, come all you that are with ROME offended,
Come now and heare from whence the Pope descended,

THE LINEAGE OF LOCUSTS
OR
THE POPES PEDEGRE

Beginning with his prime ancestor the Divell, plainely set forth to be noted of all good
Christians and true Catholicks, for the avoiding of those subtill snares
continually layd for them by his insinuating Agents.

THE PEDEGREE.

1. THe Divell begat darknesse.
2. And darknesse begat ignorance.
3. And ignorance begat error and his brethren.
4. And error and his brethren begat free-will and selfe-love.
5. Ard selfe-love begat merits.
6. And merits begat forgetfulnes of Gods grace.
7. And forgetfulnes of Gods grace begat mistrust.
8. And mistrust begat satisfaction.
9. And satisfaction begat sacrifice of the Masse.
10. And sacrifice of the Masse begat Popish priest-hood.
11. And Popish priesthood begat prayer for the dead.
12. And prayer for the dead begat sacriledge of soules.
13. And sacriledge of soules begat superstition.
14. And superstition begat hypocrisie the king.

And these are fourtéene Generations.

1. ANd hypocrisie the king begat lucre.
2. And lucre begat purgatory.
3. And purgatory begat foundation of irreligious houses.
4. And foundation of irreligious houses begat patrimonie of the Church.
5. And patrimonie of the Church begat mamon of Iniquity,
6. And mammon of iniquitie begat abundance.
7. And abundance begat crueltie.
8. And cruelty begat domination.
9. And domination begat pompe.
10. And pompe begat ambition.
11. And ambition begat intrusion into the Church right.
12. And intrusion into the Church right begat symonie.
13. And simonie begat universall superintendencie.
14. And universall superintendencie begat the Pope, the Cardinalls and all his brethren.

And these are fourtéene Generations, in the transmigration of abbomination.

1. ANd the Pope begat the mysterie of iniquity.
2. And the mistery of iniquity begat divine sophistrie.

3. And divine sophistrie begat rejection of the Scripture.
4. And rejection of the Scripture begat tyranny.
5. And tyranny begat murder of the Saints.
6. And murder of the Saints begat the despising of God.
7. And the despising of God begat dispensation.
8. And dispensation begat licence to sinne.
9. And licence to sinne begat abomination.
10. And abomination begat confusion.
11. And confusion begat travell in the spirit.
12. And travell in the spirit begat disputation.
13. And disputation begat matter to write of:
By which writing the sonne of perdition Antichrist specified in so many places of Scripture was revealed.

The Protestants Conclusion.

THe Pope, himselfe (the simple to beguile)
Servum servorum Dei doth instile,
The servant of Gods servants, who (we finde)
To seeme his masters better is inclin'd,
Christ humble was, humility requiring,
The Pope is proud to honour still aspiring;
Christ was content to weare a crowne of Thornes,
But the Popes head a crowne of gold adornes,
A triple crowne which hardly him sufficeth
But of his soule ambition what ariseth?
Hunc capit infernum, quem deserit ordo supernus.
Forsaken by the Quire supernall,
Hee's taken by the fiends infernall,
For let false Catholicks say what they can
Hee's neither God nor angell, nor a man,
But a prodigious beast or monster fell
With all his brood hatch'd or begot in hell;

And so I leave him.

Figure 8   Anti-papal Broadsheet. *The Lineage of Locusts* (1641?).

Figure 9   Anti-papal Broadsheet. *The Devil's Triumph over Rome's Idol* (1680).

Prayer urges believers "to forsake the Devil and all his works and pomps, the vanities of the wicked world" (*OED* "pomp" sb.). Furthermore, the language recalls the jargon of antipapal satire. In Spenser's July Eclogue, for example, Thomalin decries the pomp of prelates that "bene yclad in purple and pall" and are "Ygirst with belts of glitterand gold" (lines 173, 177). E.K.'s gloss indicates that the lines refer to "Popes and Cardinalles, which use such tyrannical colours and pompous paynting."

In the first commentary on *Paradise Lost*, Patrick Hume's annotation on "gay religions full of pomp and gold" asserts the presence of an antiprelatical stab. It claims that the idols are "decked and set out with gaudy rites and shows, solemn processions and copes wrought with gold"(n. on 1.371–72). That note on liturgical practices and vestments that Restoration bishops shared with their Roman Catholic and Laudian predecessors insists upon a polemical reading. Hume reads his own concerns into the text, to be sure, but the gloss pinpoints a likely alignment between Milton's language and iconoclastic attacks on formalistic worship of the pre- and post-revolutionary eras. The panoply of demons recalls attacks in his antiprelatical tracts on ritualism, processions, and elaborate clerical robes.[14]

In line with the contemporary belief that ancient societies worshipped the fallen angels as gods, the devils are known proleptically by the names conferred upon them by later civilizations. In a complicated temporal scheme akin to typological exegesis, whereby readers interpret persons and events in the New Testament by reference to shadowy prefigurations in the Old, the "falsities and lies" (1.367) of ancient idolatry anticipate religious practices opposed by Milton's antiprelatical tracts.[15]

In a seeming "travesty of Christ's calling of his disciples,"[16] Satan's calling to his chief lieutenants suggests the assemblage of a demonic church. He summons Moloch, Chemos, Baalim, Ashtaroth, Astoreth, Thammuz, Dagon, Rimmon, Osiris, Isis, Horus, and Belial. Implying no mockery of the New Testament event, such parody would belittle the Church of Rome as a distorted mirror image of the "true" church. This reading cuts against the grain of the traditional assumption that fewer than twelve devils assemble alongside the fiery lake. At issue is whether we are to count Ashtaroth and Astoreth, "whom the Phoenicians called / Astarte" (1.438–39), as separate idols. In Hebrew, Ashtaroth is the

---

[14] See J. B. Broadbent, *Some Graver Subject; An Essay on* Paradise Lost (London: Chatto & Windus, 1960), p. 88; Stephen M. Buhler, "Kingly States: The Politics in *Paradise Lost*," *MiltonS* 28 (1992), p. 61.

[15] On the "double temporal perspective" whereby representation of devils as pagan gods propels them "proleptically . . . out of hell and into human history," see Grossman, *Authors*, p. 38.

[16] Fowler n. on 1.392–490.

singular and Astoreth the plural form for feminine idols. If we follow the narrator in taking them as a pair of deities, Satan's gathering of twelve disciples alongside the fiery lake looks like a distortion of Jesus' summoning of the twelve apostles near the Sea of Galilee (Matt. 4:18–22, 10:1–4).

At the head of the procession of pagan idols, Moloch bears a twisted resemblance to Simon Peter. Foremost among the twelve apostles, Jesus designated him as "this rock [upon which] I will build my Church" (Matt. 16:18). Moloch's precedence may hint at sardonic parody of the Pope's claim to primacy among Christian bishops on the basis of apostolic succession from St. Peter, even though the demons later reject their bellicose colleague's arguments for total war against the Father.[17] Milton's handling of the demonic procession seems characteristic of how he often works with typology. Just as the text fails to make a one-to-one equation between Jesus and Satan, the middle term of the associative chain of Moloch–Peter–Pope escapes contamination. As late as the Glorious Revolution, William Perse would attack the Pope as "the Moloch of Rome; that cruel idol that kills soonest those whom it embraces closest."[18]

The officiation of Canaanite priests at the bloody rites of Moloch suggests a critique of the sacerdotalism and Sacramentarianism of Laudian churchmen and their Restoration successors. The cult of Moloch was notorious for the sacrifice of children burned to death in the uplifted palms of a red-hot brazen idol:

> First Moloch, horrid king besmeared with blood
> Of human sacrifice, and parents' tears,
> Though for the noise of drums and timbrels loud
> Their children's cries unheard, that passed through fire
> To his grim idol.   (1.392–96)

The language hints at Protestant rejection of the Mass as a repeated ritual sacrifice that recreates the shedding of Jesus Christ's blood at a high altar. Both a despot and a seducer of despots, Moloch may remind us of both Charles I and Archbishop Laud. That idol supplanted worship of YHWH at the Temple in Jerusalem, a typological figure for the "true" church,[19] during the reign of King Solomon, whom

---

[17] Lee Erickson, "Satan's Apostles and the Nature of Faith in *Paradise Lost* Book I," *Studies in Philology* 94 (1997): 382–94; see Guibbory, *Ceremony and Community*, pp. 198–99.

[18] Perse, *A Sermon Preached . . . on the Fifth Day of Novemb. 1689* (York, 1689), p. 26.

[19] The preface of the Geneva Bible praises ecclesiastical reform as "the building of the Lord's Temple, the house of God, the Church of Christ, whereof the Son of God is the head and perfection" (***2ʳ).

> he led by fraud to build
> His temple right against the temple of God
> On that opprobrious hill, and made his grove
> The pleasant valley of Hinnom, Tophet thence
> And black Gehenna called, the type of Hell.   (1.401–405)

With epigrammatic brevity, the narrator contrasts Solomon's idolatry with the fidelity of Josiah, an iconoclastic monarch who endorsed smashing of idols and purging pagan cults from the land (2 Kings 22–23): "Till good Josiah drove them thence to hell" (1.418). Coming to the throne of Judah as a child, Josiah occupied a special place in Protestant polemics. His reign afforded a precedent for outbursts of iconoclasm during the reign of Edward VI, known as the New Josiah, and during the 1640s and 1650s. Despite Milton's antimonarchical politics, even *Eikonoklastes* acknowledges Edward as "that godly and royal child" for removing "the images out of churches."[20]

Of all the fallen angels save Satan, the loudest polemical echoes are associated with Belial, who comes at the end of the "apostolic succession" in hell. His cult is not specific to any particular locality:

> Belial came last, than whom a spirit more lewd
> Fell not from heaven, or more gross to love
> Vice for itself: to him no temple stood
> Or altar smoked; yet who more oft than he
> In temples and at altars, when the priest
> Turns atheist, as did Ely's sons, who filled
> With lust and violence the house of God.
> In courts and palaces he also reigns
> And in luxurious cities, where the noise
> Of riot ascends above their loftiest towers,
> And injury and outrage: and when night
> Darkens the streets, then wander forth the sons
> Of Belial, flown with insolence and wine.   (1.490–502)

Denoting both ignorance and unchastity, his "lewd" demeanor anticipates attack on Satan as the forerunner of "lewd hirelings" who would later invade the church (4.193). Patrick Hume identifies him with "excess of luxury and lasciviousness" (n. on 1.499). Belial's sensuality anticipates the blasphemy of Hophni and Phinehas, the riotous sons of Eli, who served as priest when the Ark of the Covenant remained at Shiloh. They devoured sacrificial meat and lay with cult prostitutes at the

---

[20] *CPW* I: 530. See *TRI*, pp. 93–94, 98, 166.

entrance to the sanctuary (1 Samuel 2). Belial's eloquence in demonic debate, where his sophistry makes "the worse appear / The better reason" (2.113–14), bears out Luther's view in *Lectures on the Psalms* that he "can disguise himself as an angel of light . . . and turn God's word into darkness in the hearts of men" (Luther 13: 178).

Belial's universality and polysemous adaptability are well suited to a strategy of indirectness designed to elude censorship. Nonetheless, it is difficult to believe that the press licenser could miss satire on both prelates and courtiers that fills the demon's set-piece portrait. In the most telling stab, use of the present tense intensifies scornful attack on the libertine promiscuity and drunken abandon associated with Charles II and, arguably, foreign monarchs such as Louis XIV: "In courts and palaces he also reigns." Although George Wither's *Vox Pacifica : A Voice Tending to the Pacification of God's Wrath* (1645) aims a nonpartisan stab against political extremists as "sons of Belial" (E4), radical polemicists typically attach that epithet to both churchmen and courtiers during the revolutionary era.[21] One preacher attacks Laudian prelates, for example, as "sons of Belial, who already drunk with the cup of that Scarlet Whore [i.e. the Church of Rome], did forth begin to make a fit daughter [the Church of England], the right spawn of such an abominable and idolatrous mother." [22]

Puritans like Milton employed Belial and his offspring as generic types for adherence to "false" religion. Despite his lack of a particular temple, Belial signifies the worst kind of priest, whose officiation at "temples" and "altars" recalls outrage against the Laudian conversion of communion tables into altars.[23] A contemporary Gunpowder Plot poem thus associates the Laudian ascendancy over "Belial's temple" with Roman Catholicism.[24] Milton himself employs "sons of Belial" and "sons of Eli" as epithets for wicked priests in *Animadversions* and *Means to Remove Hirelings* (*CPW* 1: 893; 7: 296).

---

[21] Davies, *Images*, p. 32. See Christopher Hill, "George Wither and John Milton," in *English Renaissance Studies Presented to Dame Helen Gardner in Honour of her Seventieth Birthday* (Oxford: Clarendon, 1980), p. 215.

[22] Peter Smart, *A Sermon Preached in the Cathedral Church at Durham* (1640), p. 2.

[23] On the Pauline-Protestant belief in the sanctity of the human heart as the only acceptable altar, see Stephen R. Honeygosky, *Milton's House of God: The Invisible and Visible Church* (Columbia, MO: University of Missouri Press, 1993) p. 175; and Christopher Hodgkins, *Authority, Church, and Society in George Herbert: Return to the Middle Way* (Columbia, MO: University of Missouri Press, 1993), p. 172.

[24] Francis Herring, *November 5, 1605. The Quintessence of Cruelty, or Masterpiece of Treachery, the Popish Powder-Plot, Invented by Hellish Malice, Prevented by Heavenly Mercy*, trans. John Vicars (1641), p. 11.

The final set-piece description burlesques Mammon, "the least erected spirit that fell/From heaven" (1.679–80). It makes fun of a benighted
figure who squandered his unfallen state by

> admiring more
> The riches of heaven's pavement, trodden gold,
> Than aught divine or holy else enjoyed
> In vision beatific.   (1.681–84)

Originally an Aramaic term for "riches" or "money," μαμονᾶς or
Mammon denotes wealth that is incompatible with true devotion according to the Sermon on the Mount (Matt. 6:24). Not until the Middle
Ages did Mammon emerge as the devil of avarice, the sense found in
William Tyndale's translation of the New Testament. Tyndale confers
antipapal coloration upon the devil in *The Parable of the Wicked Mammon*
(1528), a full-length exposition of the doctrine of justification by faith
alone on the basis of Jesus' Parable of the Dishonest Steward (Luke
16:1–9). *The Lineage of Locusts* indicates that "Mammon of Iniquity" is an
ancestor of "the Pope,/the Cardinals, and all his brethren" (see Figure
8). Of course, all salaried clerics would remind Milton of Mammon. His
Tenure of Kings and Magistrates accordingly shifts blame to the Presbyterians for supplanting the prelates as "ministers of Mammon" (*CPW* 1:
719; 3: 242), a move reminiscent of the unforgettable line in "On the
New Forcers of Conscience": "New Presbyter is but Old Priest writ
large."

Styling Mammon's gold mining as a proleptic antecedent of Spenser's Den of Mammon, Milton takes that episode in *The Faerie Queene* as
the immediate vernacular model for the nether world of *Paradise Lost*.
Harold Bloom has shown how Milton exploits transumptive allusion to
rewrite literary history by posing as the predecessor of Spenser, his sole
rival as an English Protestant epic poet.[25] Milton had associated the lair
of Spenserian Mammon with religious "error" in *Animadversions*, which
contrasts it with "divine gift of learning" appropriate to "true" ministers
(*CPWI*: 697; 722–3). Only *The Faerie Queene* and *Paradise Lost* represent
Mammon as a pagan god associated with descent into hell, gold mining,
and smelting (*FQ* 2.7.8, 30, 35–36). On the ground that the Spenserian
allusion is complete when Pandaemonium rises "out of the earth . . .
/Built like a temple" (*PL* 1.710–13), however, one critic claims that
Spenserian associations fail to "extend to particularities in the descrip-
tion of the edifice itself."[26] Nevertheless, the temple-like aspect of Pan-

---

[25] Bloom, *Map*, p. 128. The transumptive schemes of both Spenser and Milton bear the imprint of
forebears such as Homer, Virgil, Ovid, and Dante.

daemonium reconfigures the counterfeit splendor of the dwelling of Spenserian Mammon, where "roofe, and floore, and wals were all of gold." The demonic structures share artificial illumination and glittering golden façades (*FQ* 2.7.29; *PL* 1.726–30, 796; 10.452). Satan's palace also recalls Lucifera's Palace of Pride, where an idol-queen clad in "glistring gold" governs within a counterfeit temple whose dazzling façade glitters with "golden foile" (1.4.4, 8).

The anti-Catholic aspect of Spenser's Palace of Pride and Den of Mammon spills over to *Paradise Lost*. Lucifera's palatial splendor and the "throne of royal state" crafted by Mammon for Satan (*PL* 2.1) are both infused with "contemporary associations with Romish pomp."[27] Lucifera thrives on a cult of idolatrous adoration and welcomes Duessa, a variant of the Whore of Babylon who personifies the Church of Rome, into an establishment that houses monk-like Idleness. Located within Mammon's domain, the "glistring glory" of Philotime's court recreates the travesty of glory at Lucifera's Palace of Pride (*FQ* 2.7.46).

Milton renounces Spenserian allegory as an appropriate medium for *Paradise Lost* as a whole, but its imprint remains in the construction of Pandaemonium as a parody of the "true" temple of "the upright heart and pure"(1.18). Even the iconoclastic metamorphosis of Pandaemonium into a darkened place of horror after the Fall of Adam and Eve, when the demons "chewed bitter ashes" in a "grove hard by" their temple (10.548, 566), is proleptic of Spenser's Wood of Error. It also anticipates the deathly Garden of Proserpina, where Mammon's daughter, Philotime, governs near her father's "House of Richesse."[28] Miltonic iconoclasm therefore bears the genetic imprint of a dense pattern of iconoclastic tableaux and anti-Mass satires in *The Faerie Queene* (e.g. Orgoglio's Castle and Geryoneo's Church), in which destruction alternates with construction, and demolition with creation. Spenser characteristically clusters together images of the temple, altar, and idol, apocalyptic figures that recur in Protestant polemics against the Roman-rite Mass and Book 1 of *Paradise Lost*.[29]

The erection of Pandaemonium as "high capital/Of Satan and his peers" (1.756–57) by Mammon's band of goldsmiths hints at satire on the

[26] Guillory, *Poetic Authority*, pp. 138–39.
[27] Radzinowicz, "Politics," pp. 209, 212. See *SPART*, pp. 52–54, 62–63 n. 41, 87–89, 101–103, 118–20, 130–31.
[28] *FQ* 2.7.51–56. Phineas Fletcher provides a bridge between Spenser and Milton, once again, because the "world of Mammon" is related to Philotimus (Ambition), a descendant of Spenser's Philotime, in *The Purple Island* (gloss on 8.4; 8.38).
[29] *SPART*, pp. 79-109, 119; Kenneth Borris, *Spenser's Poetics of Prophecy in "The Faerie Queene" V*, English Literary Studies Monograph Series, vol. LII (Victoria, British Columbia: University of Victoria Press, 1991), pp. 53–54.

Church of Rome. The site's Babylonian aspect (1.717–20) recalls Protestant attacks upon papal Rome as the Whore of Babylon.[30] Explaining the meaning of Pandaemonium as "All-Devil-Hall, or Satan's Court," Patrick Hume likens it to Rome (n. on 1.756). The organ-like "sound/Of dulcet symphonies and voices sweet" that accompanies its construction recalls polyphonic church music associated with ritualistic worship (1.711–12). (The importance of hymnody in heaven suggests that Milton opposes "abuse" of church music rather than its "right use.")[31] The baroque architecture of Pandaemonium refers in some sense to the reconstruction of St. Peter's Basilica, which incorporated "pilasters," "pillars," "architrave," and "frieze" (1.713–16) even in the incomplete state witnessed by Milton when he visited Rome.[32] By associating the aggressive program of Caroline church-building and Archbishop Laud's "beauty of holiness" with both Mammon and Antichrist, *Of Reformation* had offered a polemical prefiguration of the counterfeit splendor of Pandaemonium:

an excessive waste of treasury . . . in the idolatrous erection of temples beautified exquisitely to outvie the papists, the costly and dear-bought scandals, and snares of images, pictures, rich copes, gorgeous altar-cloths. . . . What other materials than these have built up the spiritual Babel to the height of her abominations? Believe it Sir right truly it may be said, that Antichrist is Mammon's son.[33]

Antipapal connections adhere to Babel, the Hebrew name for Babylon.

Satirical associations infuse the demonic council that meets "with awful ceremony" (1.753) at the end of Book 1: "The great seraphic lords and cherubim/In close recess and secret conclave sat" (1.794–95). Milton did not invent the satanic council, a modification of assemblies of gods and warriors in classical epic that we encounter in Christian epics from Vida's *Christiad* to Tasso's *Gerusalemme liberata*.[34] Irony pervades

---

[30] John Vicars, *Babylon's Beauty: Or, the Romish Catholics' Sweetheart* (1644).

[31] See *ERL*, pp. 222–23.

[32] Marjorie Hope Nicolson, *John Milton: A Reader's Guide to His Poetry* (New York: Noonday Press, 1963), pp. 196–98. See also William A. McClung, "The Architecture of Pandaemonium," *MiltonQ* 15 (1981): pp. 109–12. For a counterclaim, see Frye, *Imagery*, pp. 134–35.

[33] Leighton's *An Appeal to the Parliament; Or, Sion's Appeal Against the Prelacy* (Amsterdam, 1629) and Prynne's *A Looking-Glass* (1636) lodged related attacks (*CPW* 1: 589–90, nn. 61, 63). Milton's *Tenure of Kings and Magistrates* attacks the prelates furthermore as "ministers of Mammon" (*CPW* 3: 242). *The True Emblem of Antichrist: Or Schism Displayed* (1651), an anonymous broadsheet, allegorizes Mammon as the offspring of "patrimony of the Church," itself a descendant of the Devil, and an ancestor of "the Pope, the Cardinals and all his brethren."

[34] John M. Steadman, *Milton and the Renaissance Hero* (Oxford: Clarendon Press, 1967), p. 87. See Gertrude C. Drake, "Satan's Councils in 'The Christiad,' 'Paradise Lost,' and 'Paradise Regained'," in *Acta Conventus Neo-Latini Turonensis*, ed. Jean-Claude Margolin (Paris: Vrin, 1980), p. 979; and Sister Mary Christopher Pecheux, "The Council Scenes in *Paradise Lost*," in *Milton*

Milton's reconfiguration of a device in Tasso's great Counter-Reformation epic in order to mock, at some level, corruption in the Roman and English churches. The "deepe Conclave" in Phineas Fletcher's *Apollyonists* (1.17) furnishes an English vernacular model for associating Catholic clerics with an underworld assembly presided over by Satan. The oration to Jesuitical demons (or Apollyonists) delivered by Fletcher's Lucifer (Cantos 1–2), enthroned in monarchical splendor in the manner of Miltonic Satan, consolidates into one speech alternative rhetorical strategies for revenge that Milton distributes among Moloch, Belial, Mammon, Beelzebub, and Satan. Lucifer's worldly guise as Equivocus anticipates the mastery of equivocation demonstrated by Miltonic Satan and Belial.[35]

A recognizable conceit in sixteenth- and seventeenth-century religious satire, the conclave in hell recalls ridicule of "councils and conclaves that demolish one another" according to *Of Reformation* (*CPW* 1: 569). We may locate a prominent instance of that device in Bernardino Ochino's *A Tragedy or Dialogue of the Unjust Usurped Primacy of the Bishop of Rome* (1549), in which Pope Boniface III joins his overlord when Lucifer orates to a conclave of "faithful brethren" in hell (A3). Other examples of the conceit are Donne's *Ignatius His Conclave* (1611), in which the Pope attends a satanic consistory, and Fletcher's *Apollyonists*. Among many contemporary satires that identify demonic conclaves with the Church of Rome and/or England is George Walley's *I Marry Sir, Here is News Indeed. Being a Copy of a Letter which the Devil Sent to the Pope of Rome, and Kept at the Conclave of Cardinals Ever Since the Year 1623* (1642).

Although hellish councils recur in political propaganda, it is difficult, if not impossible, to differentiate between religious and political controversy. Partisans of opposing sides followed the highly malleable strategy of plunging enemies into hell. During the revolutionary era, for example, royalist pamphleteers generated the sub-genre of "the Parliament of hell" to mock opponents. Although royalists identified Satan with the parliamentary opposition rather than monarchy or episcopacy, their rhetorical schemes anticipate certain elements in Milton's poem.[36]

and Scriptural Tradition: The Bible into Poetry, ed. James H. Sims and Leland Ryken (Columbia, MO: University of Missouri Press, 1984), pp. 82–103.

[35] David Quint, "Milton, Fletcher, and the Gunpowder Plot," *Journal of the Warburg and Courtauld Institutes*, 54 (1991): 264. For a more complete development of that argument, see Quint's *Epic and Empire: Politics and Generic Form from Virgil to Milton*, Literature in History (Princeton University Press, 1993).

[36] Achinstein, *Revolutionary Reader*, pp. 177–210. See also Diana T. Benet, "Hell, Satan, and the New Politician," in *Literary Milton: Text, Pretext, Context*, ed. Diana T. Benet and Michael Lieb, Duquesne Studies: Language and Literature Series, vol. XVI (Pittsburgh: Duquesne University Press, 1994), 91–113, 235–37.

Polemical associations cling to the "secret conclave" that meets at the end of Book 1. Patrick Hume points out that the phrasing alludes to "the place where the election of the Pope is made at Rome" (n. on 1.795). Indeed, debate within the conclave culminates in the election of Satan to take revenge on newly created Adam and Eve (2.388–89). Protestant pamphleteers employed **conclave**, a word that denotes a private ec-clesiastical assembly, especially of the cardinals who gather at the deaths of popes, as a cant term for attacking alleged Catholic conspiracies. Jesuitical locusts swarm, for example, in the "conclave" portrayed at the base of Richard Smith's *Powder Treason* (see Figure 7). Pictured as a vassal of the Devil, the Pope presides over conclaves of cardinals and Jesuits in Gunpowder Plot and Popish Plot broadsheets such as *To God, In Memory of His Double Deliverance* (Figure 10) and *Happy Instruments of England's Preservation* (Figure 11). A 1680 pamphlet features a consistory analogous to the one that convenes at Pandaemonium: *News from Rome, or a Dialogue Between his Holiness and a Cabal of Cardinals at a Late Conclave* (Figure 12). The anonymous author satirizes Charles II as an ally of the Pope and cardinals, who debate the "most effectual remedies to recover the lost credit of Holy Church in England" (A1).

Anti-Roman associations pervade the frontispiece for Book 1 in the fourth edition of *Paradise Lost* (1688). Published during the year of the Glorious Revolution by Jacob Tonson and the bookseller, Richard Bentley, the first folio edition is also the first illustrated version of the poem. In the foreground of the engraving, Satan adopts a classicized stance and manipulates a pike as he rouses his suffering cohorts from the fiery lake (Figure 13). Iconographical analysis has determined that his visage bears the features of James II. Portrayal of a royal court at Pandaemonium in the background is a key feature of that engraving.[37]

The frontispiece gives visual form to the highly politicized views of the text's anti-Jacobite editors, one of whom, Henry Aldrich, designed the engravings for Books 1 and 12, and in all likelihood Book 2.[38] He projected a layer of virulent anti-Roman Catholic satire onto the de-monic world of Satan and the fallen angels. Indeed, the engraving per se

---

[37] Estella Schoenberg, "Seventeenth-Century Propaganda in English Book Illustration," *Mosaic* 25 ii (Spring 1992): 1–6.

[38] The engravings include an illustration for Book 4 by Bernard Lens and Peter Paul Bouche and plates by Michael Burghers (or Burgesse) for each of the remaining eleven books. The Aldrich designs were previously attributed to John Baptista de Molina. See Suzanne Boorsch, "The 1688 *Paradise Lost* and Dr. Aldrich," *Metropolitan Museum Journal* 6 (1972), pp. 133–50; *ME* 2:136–37, 4:58, 7:113; John T. Shawcross, *Milton: A Bibliography for the Years 1624-1700* (Binghamton, NY: MRTS, 1984), nos. 345–46.

Figure 10   The Eye of Providence. Samuel Ward, *To God, In Memory of his Double Deliverance from the Invincible Navy and the Unmatchable Powder Treason* (Amsterdam, 1621).

Figure 11   Heaven Shall Turn Thy Weapons Against Thee. *The Happy Instruments of England's Preservation* (1681).

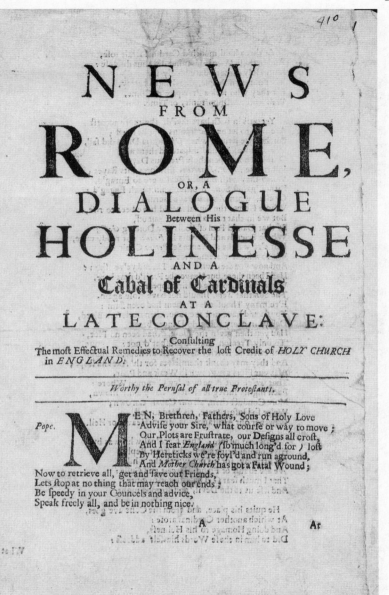

NEWS
FROM
ROME,
OR, A
DIALOGUE
Between His
HOLINESSE
AND A
Cabal of Cardinals
AT A
LATE CONCLAVE:

Consulting
The most Effectual Remedies to Recover the loft Credit of *HOLY CHURCH* in *ENGLAND*.

Worthy the Perufal of all true Proteftants.

Pope.

MEN, Brethren, Fathers, Sons of Holy Love
Advife your Sire, what courfe or way to move;
Our Plots are Fruftrate, our Defigns all croft,
And I fear *England* (fo much long'd for) loft
By Hereticks we're foyl'd and run aground,
And *Mother Church* has got a Fatal Wound;
Now to retrieve all, get and fave our Friends,
Lets ftop at no thing that may reach our ends;
Be fpeedy in your Councels and advice,
Speak freely all, and be in nothing nice.

A   At

Figure 12   A Cabal of Cardinals at a Late Conclave. *News from Rome* (1680), A1ʳ.

Figure 13   Satan With the Face of James II. Illustration for Book 1 of Milton, *Paradise Lost*, 4th ed. (1688).

is not antimonarchical, because it supports the claim to the throne of Mary, daughter of James II, and William of Orange, her spouse.[39] The portrayal of Pandaemonium at the left rear focuses on figures absent from the text itself: an enthroned king and queen, miter-wearing courtiers, and a woman bearing an infant at the viewer's right (Figure 14). Given the date of publication of the Tonson-Bentley edition, the queen is Mary of Modena, consort to James II. The female attendant carries the heir to the throne whose birth precipitated the Revolution of 1688. The wearing of miters contributes to the Whig attack on a Roman Catholic royal establishment. It seems likely that Aldrich's caricature glances not only at courtiers, but also at Jesuit priests who enjoyed entrée at the Jacobite court.[40]

In both inception and design, the first folio edition presents *Paradise Lost* as a text deeply embedded in religio-political topicality. The addition to that expensive volume of a frontispiece for each of the twelve books represents a profound shift from the poem's prior publication, in affordable quarto and octavo format, as an unillustrated text by a defeated republican who had difficulty engaging a publisher and whose work sold poorly.[41]

An anti-Jacobite group associated with Christ Church, Oxford, initiated the first folio edition. It included Francis Atterbury and Henry Aldrich. Later Dean of Christ Church, Aldrich designed the parodic frontispiece in collaboration with Jacob Tonson, who commissioned the engraving by Michael Burghers. In a 15 November 1687 letter to Tonson, Atterbury discusses his role in procuring the plates. Appending the names of thirty-one subscribers, he volunteers to pay the engraver's fee out of payments collected at Oxford University: "You talkd a good while ago of pay in subscription money for Burghers: if your mind be the same still, I'll pay him 6 pound upon a word's notice." Accounting for a delay in publication, Atterbury's reference to "ye expectations people are in of greater affairs" may allude to the pregnancy of Mary of Modena, which resulted in the birth of the Old Pretender.[42]

The prime mover behind the edition appears to be John, Lord Somers. After playing a key role in the parliamentary declaration that

[39] Their accession brought to the throne first cousins who shared Charles I as their grandfather.

[40] A heroine to seventeenth-century Protestant militants, Elizabeth I would have turned over in her grave had she known of *A Sermon Preached Before Their Majesties in Their Chapel at St. James's* (1687), delivered by James Dormer, SJ, in celebration of **her** Accession Day.

[41] See Peter Lindenbaum, "John Milton and the Republican Mode of Literary Production," *Yearbook of English Studies* 21 (1991): pp. 121–136.

[42] Folger Shakespeare Library MS C.c.1 (3).

Figure 14   The Royal Family in Hell. Detail from Figure 13.

James II had abdicated the throne during the Revolution of 1688, Somers was the architect of the Declaration of Rights, the prototype for the British Bill of Rights. It set forth the conditions governing the 1689 accession of William and Mary as constitutional monarchs, under whom Somers served as Lord Chancellor. After their death, he became an influential member of the Whig party.[43]

It may be that many politically and socially prominent subscribers to the first folio were attracted by Milton's repudiation of royal absolutism, which James II had attempted to consolidate by securing the repeal of the Test Acts of 1673 and 1678 and by suspending statutory law concerning habeas corpus. The birth of a male heir on 10 June 1688 provided the last straw for anti-Jacobites unwilling to countenance a Roman Catholic succession. The king's consort, Mary of Modena, was far more influential than Henrietta Maria and Catherine of Braganza, the king's mother and sister-in-law, had been; she furthered her husband's introduction of Roman Catholicism at court; and she would serve as regent for her son in the event of the king's death.[44] Her potential influence as a power behind the throne of a Catholic successor instilled fear among Protestants of the reinstitution of "idolatry" that Milton and Marvell had railed against in *Of True Religion* and *An Account of the Growth of Popery* (1677). It is an irony of history that *Paradise Lost* returned to favor as a republican classic in the year that witnessed the flight from England of James II and his heir (James, the Old Pretender). They were the son and grandson of the king whose deposition and death Milton had celebrated in the *Tenure of Kings and Magistrates* and *Eikonoklastes*.

The polemical slant of the 1688 engraving for Book 1 of *Paradise Lost* accords with a gloss that Francis Atterbury inscribed in the margin of a copy of the third edition (1678). That notation concerning the demeanor of Moloch in debate at Pandaemonium affords a tantalizingly rare glimpse of the interpretive habits of a contemporary reader. Atterbury instinctively senses a veiled allusion in the Moloch description: "He ended frowning, and his look denounced/Desperate revenge, and battle dangerous/To less than gods" (2.106–108). The scholar states that "this [is] probably ye picture of some great man in Milton's time." Even though he is uncertain about specifics, he assumes that the text affords a topical commentary on contemporary affairs.[45] From such a vantage

[43] Shawcross, *Bibliography*, nos. 345–47; *ME* 7: 113.
[44] J. R. Jones, *Country and Court: England, 1658–1714*, The New History of England, vol. V (London: Edward Arnold, 1978), pp. 13, 234–35.
[45] Osborn Collection, pb 9, Beinecke Library, Yale University; as cited in Zwicker, *Lines*, pp. 4–5.

point, Milton's polemical outlook differs only in degree of obliquity from Dante's habit of plunging hated enemies such as Pope Boniface VIII into the depths of hell.

Entering into the English language as a term for wild uproar, Milton's coinage of Pandaemonium out of παν + δαίμων (Greek for "assembly of all demons") has retained hyperbolic, satirical connotations to the present day. The broad parody of the Homeric council of war contributes to the debasement of Satan's claim to heroic stature. The demonic gathering "In close recess and secret conclave" hints at sly innuendoes against "papistry" without sacrificing either the universality of biblical epic or the obliquity necessitated by Restoration censorship. The swarming of apocalyptic locusts and Satan's gathering of his disciples in what looks like a mordant travesty of Jesus' commission of the twelve apostles prepare the way for that climactic assembly. The tendentious frontispiece for Book 1 in the 1688 folio edition of *Paradise Lost* foregrounds anti-Catholic innuendoes akin to those pointed out in Patrick Hume's 1695 annotations. It would be facetious to claim that Milton's poem foretells the Revolution of 1688, and I lodge no such claim here. Nonetheless, such a view would perhaps be no more outlandish than the addition to the 1645 headnote that declares that *Lycidas* "by occasion foretells the ruin of our corrupted clergy then in their height." The engraved portrait of James II both as Satan and as head of the royal family in hell brings Milton's radical religio-political agenda posthumously into the mainstream of English culture under William and Mary.

CHAPTER 4

Milton's Den of Error

Satan's encounter with Sin and Death has troubled modern readers as a problematic intrusion of Spenserian allegory into *Paradise Lost*. By contrast, Milton's contemporaries tolerated the incident. For example, Andrew Marvell's "Last Instructions to a Painter" incorporates an appreciative parody of Sin and Death in its allegory of Monster Excise and its incestuous spawn.[1] Marvell may have worked with a prepublication manuscript of Milton's poem in his satire on religious and social abuses detested by both poets. Patrick Hume's 1695 annotations upon Virgilian and Spenserian antecedents reflect no distaste for Sin and Death. Joseph Addison set the stage for later disapproval of Milton's inclusion of that monstrous pair: "such allegories rather savour of the spirit of Spenser and Ariosto, than of Homer and Virgil" (*The Spectator*, no. 297). Addison recognizes the burlesque aspect of Sin and Death, but he condemns it. On neoclassical grounds favored by Addison, eighteenth-century criticism rejected the Spenserian allegory as a lapse in taste.

Unmindful of the satirical dimension that Addison recognized, Dr. Johnson's sharp attack establishes a foundation for later criticism:

Milton's allegory of Sin and Death is undoubtedly faulty. Sin is indeed the mother of Death, and may be allowed to be the portress of hell; but when they stop the journey of Satan, a journey described as real, and when Death offers him battle, the allegory is broken . . . This unskillful allegory appears to me one of the greatest faults of the poem, and to this there was no temptation but the author's opinion of its beauty.[2]

Nineteenth- and twentieth-century readers have continued to deny the legitimacy of the Spenserian allegory, but they follow Johnson rather than Addison in forgetting its ludicrously parodic aspect. William

---

[1] Frank Kermode and Keith Walker, eds., *Andrew Marvell* (Oxford University Press, 1990), lines 131–46.   [2] Johnson, "Life of Milton," in *Lives of the Poets*, p. 108.

Empson simply rejects what he terms "bad allegory."[3] Parodying Dryden's preface to *The Fables*, another scholar asks: "In what sense, then, was Spenser Milton's original?" In an essay that startlingly ignores Sin and Death, he answers that a sharp conflict between allegory and mimesis leads Milton to reject Spenserian allegory.[4] Nevertheless, the presence of Archangel Raphael's quasi-allegorical mode of narration, which likens "spiritual to corporal forms, / As may express them best" (5.573–74), undermines that claim that Milton renounces allegory.[5] The unfolding of the prophetic history of humanity born in original sin accordingly mingles allegory and mimesis in Archangel Michael's vision of the universality of death: "but many shapes/Of death, and many are the ways that lead/To his grim cave, all dismal" (11.467–69).

The objections of Addison, Johnson, and Empson notwithstanding, the present study argues that the allegory of Sin and Death plays an important role in Milton's allusive critique of failures in the Christian church. Recovering parody of Spenser's Den of Error (*FQ* 1.1.13–27) as a foundation for ecclesiastical complaint and satire in *Paradise Lost*, it explores anticlerical rhetoric grounded upon Spenserian allegory of monstrous incest and **rape**. Milton shares Spenser's profound multigenericity, and we may locate parodic analogues to a variety of epic romances in Satan's "mini-*Odyssey*" from hell to Eden. On the model of Book 1 of *The Faerie Queene*, Satan accordingly functions as a "parodic Red Cross who pursues evil rather than holiness" in his encounter with Sin, a composite type who participates in the iconography of Spenserian Error and Duessa.[6]

Religious controversy has gone unnoticed as a component of Miltonic Sin, despite her status as an allegorization of the theological doctrine of original sin or innate depravity, "which our first parents, and in them all their posterity committed when they abandoned their obedience and tasted the fruit of the forbidden tree" (*CD* 1.11; *CPW* 6: 382). It appears that Sin reflects the standing of her Spenserian prototypes, Error and Duessa, as a polemical figure for the Roman Church as an unholy mother.[7] Catholic belief in Holy Mother Church reflects

---

[3] Empson, *Milton's God*, rev. ed. (London: Chatto & Windus, 1965), p. 59.

[4] Gordon Teskey, "From Allegory to Dialectic: Imagining Error in Spenser and Milton," *PMLA* 101 (1986): pp. 9–23, quoting from p. 9. For a counterargument, see Victoria Kahn, "Allegory, the Sublime, and the Rhetoric of Things Indifferent in *Paradise Lost*," in *Creative Imitation: New Essays on Renaissance Literature in Honor of Thomas M. Greene*, ed. David Quint, et al. (Binghamton: MRTS, 1992), 127–52. For Dryden's recollection, see chapter 1, n. 54 above.

[5] Kenneth Borris, "Allegory in *Paradise Lost*: Satan's Cosmic Journey," *MiltonS* 26 (1990): pp. 101–33; Mindele Treip, *Allegorical Poetics and the Epic: The Renaissance Tradition to* Paradise Lost (Lexington, KY: University of Kentucky Press, 1991), pp. 126–27.

[6] Lewalski, *Rhetoric*, pp. 67–69. See *SPART*, pp. 56.   [7] See Bloom, *Map*, pp. 125–43.

veneration of the Virgin Mary as a maternal intercessor between communicants and Jesus Christ, but patriarchal Protestantism rejects all mediators. At the level of historical allegory, Error joins Duessa as variant of the Whore of Babylon and personification of the Church of Rome and its central rite, the Mass. Milton's Sin recalls their polymorphous sexuality and grotesque physique. Those monstrous females recall the long-standing Protestant slur on the Mass as "spiritual fornication," which builds on Old Testament denunciations of Canaanite and Philistine idolatry as "whoring after false gods."[8] Milton's *Apology for Smectymnuus* supplies an analogous attack on a Romanized Church of England for giving "up her body to a mercenary whoredom under those fornicated arches which she calls God's house" (*CPW* 1: 849). Wordplay on *fornix*, a Latin word for "brothel" that originally meant "arch," mocks the Laudian revival of neo-Gothic ecclesiastical architecture. John Bale's commentary on Revelation, *The Image of Both Churches*, had popularized interpretation of the chaste Woman Clothed with the Sun and Whore of Babylon (Rev. 12, 17) as prophetic figures for conflict between the "true" church and the "false" church governed by the papal Antichrist. It became a commonplace feature of seventeenth-century Protestant thought.[9]

A contemporary broadsheet entitled *Arminius Between Truth and Heresy* (1641) documents the currency of apocalyptic associations of that kind. It stigmatizes Jacobus Arminius as a crypto-Catholic adherent of the Whore of Babylon or Heresia (Heresy). Originally published during the 1620s, this broadsheet underwent republication in celebration of the downfall of Archbishop Laud (Figure 15). Its verses appeal in vain to Charles I to "protect us with thy gracious hand,/Or else Arminius will o'erspread this land." As a variant of the Woman Clothed with the Sun, Veritas (Truth) tramples symbolic objects associated with Roman ritual. They include a monstrance, crucifix, scourge, rosary, tiaras, and cardinal's hat. Heresia clasps the hand of the theologian, whose head supports a windmill symbolic of his homeland, Holland. Her tiara identifies her with papal Rome. Arminius' rejection of the Bible proffered by sun-bright Veritas symbolizes his alleged departure from the Protestant

---

[8] *SPART*, pp. 82–97. See also Gilman, *Iconoclasm*, p. 153; D. Douglas Waters, "Milton and the 'Mistress-Missa' Tradition," *MiltonQ* 6 (1972), pp. 6–9; and his *Duessa as Theological Satire* (Columbia, MO: University of Missouri Press, 1970), pp. 6-8.

[9] On the seminal impact of Bale's *Image*, see *ERL*, pp. 61–64; Paul Christianson, *Reformers and Babylon: English Apocalyptic Visions from the Reformation to the Eve of the Civil War* (University of Toronto Press, 1978), passim.

England's Petition, to her gratious King,
That he Arminius, would to ruine bring,
Who, by his Doctrine, priuie plotts, and hate
To verity, doth ruine Church and State.
&c:

Figure 15   The Woman Clothed with the Sun Versus the Whore of Babylon. *Arminius Between Truth and Heresy* (Amsterdam, 1641).

doctrine of *sola scriptura* ("scripture alone"). As a Jesuit stoops to whisper into one ear, Pelagius uses an ear trumpet to whisper heretical denial of original sin and concomitant advocacy of the sufficiency of free will into the other ear of Arminius.[10]

The mythological antecedents of both Error and Sin include Scylla, a beautiful nymph, and Echidna, the mother of Cerberus, the canine guardian of Hades. Scylla's loins became "barking dogs" when Circe transformed her into a biform monster: "Instead of them she found / The mouths of Cerberus, environed round/With ravening Curs."[11] Scylla came to symbolize uncontrollable appetite of sin according to Dante and the *Ovide Moralisé*.[12] Milton's figuration of Scylla as "less abhorred" than Sin and her offspring (*PL* 2.659) attaches a pun on **whore** to personification of Pauline-Protestant understanding of innate depravity and original sin. The Circe association affords a link to Milton's *Mask at Ludlow*, which contrasts the unchastity of Comus, son of Circe and Bacchus, with the invulnerable continence of the Lady as a symbol for the victory of "truth" over "falsity."

Indelicate figural associations appear to link religious satire to the grotesque body of Sin, who describes the feeding of her monstrous offspring, sired by Death, upon her own body, into and out of the womb of which they creep. Addressing their grandfather, Satan, whose coupling with his self-born daughter conceived Death, she states:

> of that rape begot
> These yelling monsters that with ceaseless cry
> Surround me, as thou sawest, hourly conceived
> And hourly born, with sorrow infinite
> To me, for when they list into the womb
> That bred them they return, and howl and gnaw
> My bowels, their repast. (2.794–800)

Sin mirrors the sinister maternity of Spenserian Error, whose suckling remains incapable of sating the hunger of her famished brood of a "thousand yong ones" (1.1.15). When that Spenserian monster under-

---

[10] The first four lines of text in the 1641 version here reproduced (Wing E3011) represent an addition to a unique copy of the 1628 broadsheet preserved at the Bodleian Library (*STC* 5028).

[11] Ovid, *Metamorphosis*, 14.50–74; quoted from *Ovid's Metamorphoses Englished, Mythologized, and Represented in Figures*, trans. George Sandys (Oxford, 1632), pp. 456–57. On Echidna, see Hesiod, *Theogony*, 295–305. On the pagan gods as figures for evil in Spenser and Milton, see Joan L. Klein, "From Errour to Acrasia," *HLQ* 41 (1977), pp. 173–99; and "The Demonic Bacchus in Spenser and Milton," *MiltonS* 21 (1985) pp. 93–118. See also Judith E. Browning, "Sin, Eve, and Circe: *Paradise Lost* and the Ovidian Circe Tradition," *MiltonS* 26 (1991), pp. 135–57.

[12] *Inferno* 6.13–33; Fowler n. on *PL* 2.659–61.

goes dismemberment, its brood devours her **body** and **blood** in a lurid travesty of transubstantiation and the Mass offered by yet another **mother**, the Roman church:

> They flocked all about her bleeding wound,
> And sucked up their dying mothers blood,
> Making her death their life, and eke her hurt their good.
>
> $(FQ\ 1.1.25.7\text{--}9)^{13}$

Rabelaisian inversions relate the "bowels" upon which Sin's younglings "gnaw" to incessant birth, death, digestion, and defecation. As in both *The Faerie Queene* and *Gargantua and Pantagruel*, hyperbolic birth suggests a broad theological parody of faith.[14] The scene also evokes, ironically, Milton's image of Time's devouring womb ("On Time") and the notion of sin as self-consuming (as in *Comus*).

Censorship restrictions imposed under the harshly punitive Licensing Act (19 May 1662) may have led Milton to veil the polemical aspect of the **genealogy of evil**. By contrast, Spenser and preceding Protestant publicists had employed that allegorical figure openly to explore the ontology of vice. Anti-Mass satires published under Edward VI partici-pate in a widespread Protestant cultural practice that we encounter in the Sin and Death episode. For example, Luke Shepherd's *Pathos, Or an Inward Passion of the Pope for the Loss of His Daughter the Mass* (1548?) incorporates a funeral elegy for Mistress Missa,[15] a scurrilous personifi-cation of the Roman rite who looks like an ancestress of Spenserian Error and Duessa, **and** Miltonic Sin. The demonic descent of Mistress Missa as granddaughter of Pluto, illegitimate daughter of the Pope, and niece of Mohammed allegorizes the Protestant accusation that transub-stantiation and the Mass are demonic inventions. Like Miltonic Sin, she commits incest with her papal father. Duessa's related status as the "sole daughter" of the Pope anchors Book 1 of *The Faerie Queene* in Reforma-tion controversy (1.2.22). The revolutionary broadsheet *The Lineage of Locusts* reverses the polemical line of descent with its claim that "sacrifice of the Mass" is an ancestor of the Pope (Figure 8).

Genealogies of papal evil were a conventional feature of Spenserian allegories comparable to Milton's Sin and Death episode. For example,

---

[13] In *Of True Religion*, Milton attacks "the Romish Church [as] Mother of Error" (*CPW* 8: 419–21).

[14] Bakhtin, *Rabelais and His World*, pp. 163, 227.

[15] The name derives from the sacerdotal Mass salutation: "ite, missa est" ("go, you are released"). See *ERL*, pp. 265–66, 289; Lana Cable, *Carnal Rhetoric: Milton's Iconoclasm and the Poetics of Desire* (Durham, NC: Duke University Press, 1995), pp. 43–44. Edited by Janice Devereux, Shepherd's complete works are forthcoming from the Renaissance English Text Society.

Francis Herring's *Pietas pontificia* (1606–1609) contains a close analogue to the family romance of Satan, Sin, and Death. That text features a parodic Trinity made up of Lucifer, the Great Whore, and the serpentine monster that they beget in hell. Even more closely attuned to the Miltonic episode is Herring's *The Quintessence of Cruelty, or Masterpiece of Treachery, the Popish PowderPlot* (1641). According to its allegorical reconfiguration of the Gunpowder Plot, the "infernal copulation" of Satan and the Babylonian Whore produces Treason, a Vice character identified with the Pope (pp. 1–2).[16]

Spenserian allegories by Phineas Fletcher provide a bridge between Spenser's Error and Miltonic Sin and Death. Appropriation of the Gunpowder Plot as a focus for anti-Catholic satire is a critical component in Fletcher's *Purple Island* and *The Locusts*. (Milton composed his own Gunpowder Plot poem, *In Quintum Novembris*, at virtually the same time as the latter poem.) *The Locusts* features a personification of Sin who originates her namesake's role as portress of the gate of hell in *Paradise Lost*. The daughter of Eve ("that first woman") and Satan ("th'old serpent"), Fletcher's Sin shares the femininity and biform aspect of both Spenserian Error and Miltonic Sin:

> Her former parts her mother seemes resemble,
> Yet onely seemes to flesh and weaker sight;
> For she with art and paint could fine dissemble
> Her loathsome face: her back parts (blacke as night)
> Like to her horride Sire would force to tremble
> The boldest heart; to th'eye that meetes her right
>   She seemes a lovely sweet, of beauty rare;
>   But at the parting, he that shall compare,
> Hell will more lovely deeme, the divel's selfe more faire.
>
> *(Locusts*, 1.11–12)[17]

Milton's Death shares the "shapeless shape" of Fletcher's Sin (1.10). His leering response to the Satanic commission to feed upon mortal life (*PL* 2.846–48) "recalls none other than Fletcher's Guy Fawkes himself, contemplating the ruin of the House of Parliament" in *The Locusts* (5.10).[18]

---

[16] The latter text is a loose translation of *Pietas pontificia* by John Vicars. Filled with nostalgia for the *Pax Anglicana* of Elizabeth I's reign, William Bedell's *A Protestant Memorial: or, the Shepherd's Tale of the Powder Plot* (comp. c. 1630–40; publ. 1713) constructs the Gunpowder Plot as an attack generated by Rome as a new Babylon, a Circean whore who transforms men into beasts.

[17] Compare Error's appearance as an "ugly monster plaine,/Halfe like a serpent horribly displaide,/But th'other halfe did womans shape retaine,/Most lothsome, filthie, foule and full of vile disdaine" (*FQ* 1.1.14).   [18] Quint, *Epic and Empire*, pp. 271–74.

Milton personifies the unfolding multiplicity of error in Sin, mother of Death, and the hideous hell-dogs that they incestuously spawn. Hypocritical dissembling of corruption with superficial beauty is the common attribute of Error, Duessa, and both Fletcherian and Miltonic Sin. Milton's Sin also reflects the biform femininity of Hamartia (from ἁμαρτία, "error, sin"), the hideous daughter of Eve and "the firie Dragon." At the apocalyptic conclusion of _The Purple Island_, that draconic father mimics the emetic response of Spenserian Error when he vomits his daughter and her serpentine siblings:

> The first that crept from his detested maw,
> Was Hamartia, foul deformed wight;
> More foul, deform'd, the Sunne yet never saw;
> Therefore she hates the all-betraying light:
>   A woman seem'd she in her upper part;
>   To which she could such lying glosse impart,
> That thousands she had slain with her deceiving art. (12.27)[19]

On the model of its Spenserian antecedents, Milton's profound emphasis upon coarse bodily activity, notably alimentary and sexual aggression, hints at anti-Catholic innuendo. Polemical undertones pervade Satan's encounter, at the gate of hell, with the daughter whom he fails to recognize because of her metamorphosis into one who

> seemed woman to the waist, and fair,
> But ended foul in many a scaly fold
> Voluminous and vast, a serpent armed
> With mortal sting; about her middle round
> A cry of hell hounds never ceasing barked
> With wide Cerberian mouths full loud, and rung
> A hideous peal: yet, when they list, would creep,
> If aught disturbed their noise, into her **womb**,
> And **kennel** there, yet there still barked and howled,
> Within unseen. (2.650–59)

The alliterative sibilants and fricatives recall gross bodily sounds. Although the overt allusion is Shakespearean,[20] Spenser's Den of Error

---

[19] Compare Error's spewing of Roman Catholic propaganda on the model of Rev. 16:13: "Her vomit full of bookes and papers was,/With loathly frogs and toades, which eyes did lacke" (_FQ_ 1.1.20). The Geneva Bible gloss explains the frog-like spirits as "this great devil the Pope's ambassadors, which . . . come out of Antichrist's mouth, because they should speak nothing but lies . . . to maintain their rich Euphrates [i.e. Babylonian Rome] against the true Christians."

[20] Queen Margaret thus baits the Duchess of York for mothering Richard III: "From forth the kennel of thy womb hath crept/A hell-hound that doth hunt us all to death" (Shakespeare, _Richard III_ 4.4.47–48). Assuming an antimonarchical tinge in the seventeenth century, that birth

affords a subtext for Sin's construction as a grotesque mother who invokes Protestant hostility toward the Mother Church of Rome.

Emphasis upon Sin's hideous fecundity recalls not only Spenserian Error, but also Milton's prose attack on Rome as the "**womb** and center of apostasy," a figure diametrically opposed to the "mystical body" of the "true" church. *Of Reformation* anticipates the kenneling of monstrous hell-dogs in its denunciation of English bishops, whose failures mean "we shall see Antichrist shortly wallow here, though his chief **kennel** be at Rome" (*CPW* 1: 547, 590). Milton's complete œuvre contains only those two instances of the indecorous word **kennel**. An attack on an "apostate" Catholic as "the stinking and filthy **kennel** of Satan" suggests that that term functioned as a term of abuse in the Protestant polemical lexicon.[21] The usage may also allude to St. Paul's warning to "Beware of dogs" in Philippians 3:2, which the Geneva editors interpret with reference to "false apostles" who engage in "tearing asunder of the Church." *The Lineage of Loust* lodges an analogous attack on the Pope as "a prodigious beast or monster fell/With all his brood hatched or begot in hell" (see Figure 8).

The central trope of false feeding focuses not upon mother's milk, but the **body and blood** upon which the hell-dogs feast. The grotesque tableau would appear to invoke Protestant attack on transubstantiation and the Mass as cannibalism. Sin's fate recalls attack on "Masse-Priests, Priests-Cannibal,/Who make their Maker, chew, grinde, feede, grow fat/With flesh divine" in Fletcher's *The Locusts* (1.1). The spawning of the "hell hounds" through Sin's incestuous rape by Death constitutes an expansion upon James 1:15: "Then when lust hath conceived, it bringeth forth sin, and sin when it is finished, bringeth forth death." At the same time, their retreat within her womb to "gnaw" upon their mother's "bowels" (2.798–800) alludes to the feeding of Error's younglings upon their "dying mother's blood" (*FQ* 1.1.25).[22] We should recall Error's status as a personification of the Roman sacrament.

Anti-Mass parody that equates transubstantiation with cannibalistic gorging upon flesh and blood appears to play a previously unrecognized

---

allusion may glance at Charles I. In *Eikonoklastes*, Milton accuses the king of dissembling and hypocritical piety on the model of Shakespeare's Richard III (*CPW* 3: 361–62).

[21] Lady Jane Grey, *An Epistle of the Lady Jane to a Learned Man of Late Fallen from the Truth of God's Word* (London? 1554?), A2; reprinted in Foxe's *Book of Martyrs*. On "dumb dogs" as a polemical figure for ignorant clergy, see Barbara Brumbaugh, "'Under the Pretty Tale of Wolves and Sheep': Sidney's Ambassadorial Table Talk and Protestant Hunting Dialogues," forthcoming in *Spenser Studies* 13.

[22] Compare the putative kenneling of "many Dragonets" within the womb [i.e. stomach] of the apocalyptic Dragon slain by the Red Cross Knight (1.12.10). See *SPART*, p. 87.

role in Milton's representation of Sin. Travesty of that kind accords with Bakhtin's observation that gorging is a conventional attribute of medieval and early modern anticlerical satire. The fecundity of Sin illustrates his recognition that grotesque bodily feeding is tightly linked to "procreation (fertility, growth, birth)." Bakhtin perceives that in "the comic banquet there are nearly always elements parodying and travestying the Last Supper."[23] His insights accord with Miltonic definition of the Mass as "a cannibal feast" in *Christian Doctrine* (*CPW* 6: 554). Glutting also characterizes Death as the archetypal predator delegated by Satan, his unholy grandfather, to gorge upon living beings in the created world: "there ye shall be fed and filled / Immeasurably, all things shall be your prey" (*PL* 2.843–44). After the Fall, we learn that the hell-dogs' repulsive eating habits represent an inherited trait, because the "scent of living carcasses designed/For death" whets their father's fulsome appetite (10.277–78).

The polemical discourse of false feeding associates the ravening appetites of the hell-dogs with the devouring wolves of *Lycidas* and attacks on "Blind mouths" in that poem and *Of Reformation*. That tract castigates the "belly" worship of idolatrous clerics associated with "new-vomited paganism of sensual idolatry" and "belching the sour crudities of yesterday's popery." Readers may identify in Milton's "dialectic of digestion and regurgitation" a radical strain of rhetorical zeal. In accordance with commentaries on the Book of Revelation by John Bale, Thomas Brightman, and others, it affords an antidote to the lukewarmness of the established church.[24] The underlying trope is scriptural: "As a dog turneth again to his own vomit, so a fool turneth to his foolishness" (Prov. 26:11). The demise of monstrous Error in the opening episode of Spenser's *Faerie Queene* provides the paramount instance of allegorical emesis. Among many polemical analogues, John Vicars's *Behold Rome's Monster on his Monstrous Beast* incorporates a lurid confluence of false feeding and anal aggression (Figure 16). That broadsheet caricatures the Church of Rome as the Whore of Babylon, a poisonous feeder in both senses of that term.

Milton's allegory of Sin and Death intermingles crude gibes from the "low" world of antipapal broadsheets and street processions with scriptural texts, "high" cultural monuments of classical Greece and Rome,

---

[23] Bakhtin, *Rabelais and His World*, pp. 279, 293–94, 296, 300.
[24] *CPW* 1: 520, 540, 577. Thomas Kranidas, "Milton and the Rhetoric of Zeal," *Texas Studies in Language and Literature* 6 (1965), pp. 425, 432.

Figure 16   The Pope Seated Atop the Seven-headed Beast. Wenceslaus Hollar, engraving for John Vicars, *Behold Rome's Monster on his Monstrous Beast!* (1643).

and allusions to Spenser and Shakespeare. Bakhtin has taught us how transgressive uses of coarse bodily language are firmly grounded in popular cultural practices of early modern Europe. Carnivalesque laughter degrades by reducing objects of attack to "the reproductive lower stratum." Such humor associates hell with the functioning of the womb, gut, penis, and testicles: "the underworld is always linked with the lower bodily stratum."[25] Asserting that Milton broadens the register of discourse to discuss theological matters via sexual and excretory language, one scholar lodges a well-taken defense against charges of obscenity on the ground that vulgarity was permissible "in a serious discourse in defense of 'virtue.'" Nevertheless, his claim that Milton fashions a "new decorum of abuse" requires qualification.[26] After all, sexual and scatological innuendo was a notable feature of anticlerical satire long before Milton's time. It played an important role in the discourse of theologians as various as Martin Luther and Sir Thomas More.[27]

Satan's encounter with Sin and Death further dramatizes a ludicrous travesty of the Trinity.[28] It is important to note that it ridicules not the Father, the Son, or the Spirit, but rather the ontology of sin whereby Satan generates his hideous offspring out of his own mind. The status of Sin and Death as unreal abstractions accords, furthermore, with Augustinian ontology, whereby evil lacks essential being because it constitutes privation or absence of good. For St. Augustine, the emptiness of evil functions as a negative argument for the good. The simultaneity of Satan's fall, on the one hand, and his parthenogenetic birth of Sin on the other, indicates that she constitutes "the allegorical embodiment of Satan's turning from God."[29] In a parody of divine creation, Satan's conception of Sin *ex nihilo* exculpates God from blame for the origination of evil. At the same time, Sin's generation contradicts the doctrine of Pelagianism associated with Arminianism in the popular mind (see Figure 15).

Multilayered Trinitarian and Incarnational parodies are in keeping with Sin's aspect as an apparent precursor of the "false" church.[30] The

---

25 Bakhtin, *Rabelais and His World*, pp. 21, 311. See also pp. 314–21, passim.

26 Thomas N. Corns, "Obscenity, Slang and Indecorum in Milton's English Prose," *Prose Studies* 3 (1980), pp. 5–14, quoting pp. 6, 13.   27 *ERL*, pp. 93–94. See Chapter 7, below.

28 Hill, *MER*, p. 366.

29 Stephen M. Fallon, *Milton Among the Philosophers: Poetry and Materialism in Seventeenth-Century England* (Ithaca, NY: Cornell University Press, 1991), p. 185. See Augustine, *City of God*, 12.7. A vanishing motif in *FQ* also demonstrates that embodiments of evil such as Orgoglio and Busirane constitute absence rather than presence (*SPART*, pp. 79–80, 104–05).

30 See Sister Mary Christopher Pecheux, "The Second Adam and the Church in *Paradise Lost*," *English Literary History* 34 (1967), pp. 173–87.

association of Trinitarian parody, a conventional feature of Gunpowder Plot satires, with anti-Catholic polemics and illicit sexuality veils the anti-Trinitarian heresy that Milton records unambiguously in *Christian Doctrine*. According to one construction, the infernal Trinity of Satan, Sin, and Death is a distorted mirror image of the Father, Son, and Holy Spirit. Of course, we know that Milton affirms neither that the Son is coeternal with the Father nor that the Holy Spirit participates as a member of the Trinity. According to another construction, Satan's conception of Sin and her rape by Death travesty both the Immaculate Conception of the Blessed Virgin Mary and the Virgin Birth of Christ Jesus.[31]

Even Sin's recollection of her incestuous rape, in a sinister reversal of the initial encounter of Eve and Adam, suggests a laughable theological charge when she describes assault by her son, Death: "Me overtook his mother all dismayed" (2.792). The knotty wording punningly echoes the theological-erotic allegory of the fall of the Redcross Knight when Orgoglio discovers him in flagrante delicto with that giant's own paramour, Duessa. "Disarmd, disgrast, and inwardly dismayde" (*FQ* 1.7.11), the knight's inward awareness of his sinful condition puns on the past tense of **dismaiden**, because the exhausted hero has just lost his virginity. Low comic decorum similarly pervades the absurdity of Sin's flight from her lustful son, Death.[32]

The monstrous femininity of Sin and her poetic ancestresses may reflect a gynophobic aspect of Protestantism.[33] Nonetheless, it could also parody Mariological devotion. Does Sin function as a perverse Mary, who receives praise in Roman Catholic tradition both as Christ's virgin mother and his queenly wife in heaven? In a variation of that typological scheme, Sin's (im)maculate conception through the parthenogenetic agency of a male and Minerva-like birth from the left side of Satan's head parodies the advent of Eve through the Father's withdrawal of a rib from Adam's "left side" (8.465), with its **sinister** (Latin for "left") connotations. Parodic twists of such kind are disrespectful to neither the Father, Son, Eve, nor Mary per se. Indeed, Protestant belief that Christ's mother deserves honor not as a miracle-working mediator, but because of the role that she plays in Christian history, pervades her presentation in *Paradise Regained*.

---

[31] Hill, *MER*, pp. 285–96.   [32] See Grossman, *Authors*, pp. 45–46.

[33] On the psychodynamics of Sin's wombless birth and that of Eve, see William Kerrigan, *The Sacred Complex: On the Psychogenesis of "Paradise Lost"* (Cambridge, MA: Harvard University Press, 1983), pp. 184–87.

Puns and iconographical details associated with both Sin and Death suggest parodies of the papal assertion of ecclesiastical primacy. Sin's bearing of her "fatal key" as "portress of hell gate" (2.725, 746) hints at the papal claim to apostolic succession from St. Peter as the first Bishop of Rome.[34] Sin's key is proleptic of the "key of the bottomless pit" conferred upon a fallen angel, most likely Satan, in Revelation 9:1. The Geneva gloss refers to papal heraldry: "This authority chiefly is committed to the Pope in sign whereof he beareth the keys in his arms." The scene recalls the antipapal overtones of Orgoglio's castle, where Ignaro bears rusted keys as a personification of spiritual ignorance and, in the historical allegory, papal suzerainty (*FQ* 1.8.30). The **rocky** nature of Sin's "adamantine gates" hints further at a parodic inversion of Jesus' commission: "Thou art Peter, and upon this rock I will build my church: and the gates of hell shall not overcome it" (Matt. 16:18). Protestants construe those words as a parabolic pun on the name of Peter in Koine Greek: Πέτρος ("rock"). The Geneva gloss interprets the "true" rock as faith. Miltonic parody directs blame not against Peter per se, whose positive role in Christian tradition is apparent in the "Massy keys" that he bears in *Lycidas* (line 110), but against the alleged episcopal perversion of the apostle's role in the primitive church.[35]

Antipapal humor suffuses innuendoes attached to Death's employment of his "mace petrific" to petrify inchoate matter of Chaos for the bridge from hell to earth "by wondrous art/Pontifical" (10.294, 312–13). Derived from πέτρος, the Greek word for stone, "petrific" suggests a pun on Peter.[36] The scene punningly inverts the Spenserian identification of petrification with faith.[37] The "rock" upon which Jesus ordered Peter to establish the church undergoes parody in both the "Massy iron or solid rock" of hell gate (2.878) and the "ridge of pendent rock" out of which Sin and Death build their bridge (10.313). Denominating Satan's offspring as a demonic "pontiff," reference to Death's "pontifical" (from Lat. *pontificalis*) art and "new wondrous pontifice" (i.e. bridge; 10.348), travesties the papal epithet of *Pontifex Maximus* ("supreme bridge-maker"), a title once held by the chief priests of pagan Rome. An annotation by Patrick Hume demonstrates the accessibility of that

---

[34] Composed during Milton's Cambridge years, *In Quintum Novembris* mocks the Pope's style as an imperial overlord who wears a triple crown and carries a pair of golden keys.

[35] See Chapter 2; *SPART*, pp. 97–100.

[36] See Flannagan n. on *PL* 10.294; Thomas M. Corns, *Milton's Language* (London: Basil Blackwell, 1990), pp. 90–91.

[37] *FQ* 1.7.35. See Darryl J. Gless, *Interpretation and Theology in Spenser* (Cambridge University Press, 1994), p. 132.

antipapal joke to Milton's contemporaries: "Their successors the Roman bishops, though they found this infernal bridge built to their hand, have made bold to erect a baiting-place of purgatory by the way, more poetical and fictitious than it" (n. on 10.313). From Hume's vantage point, the doctrine of purgatory is more far-fetched than Milton's fanciful allegory.

Punning representation of Death as a parodic pontiff ramifies into a quibble upon his phallic dart.[38] Sin's account of the birth of a well-armed son who immediately rapes his mother outrageously fuses allusion to 1 Corinthians 15:55 with quibbling on "death" as orgasm:

> but he my inbred enemy
> Forth issued, brandishing his fatal dart
> Made to destroy: I fled, and cried out Death.　　(2.785–87)

A phallic nuance attached to the bridging of Chaos with a "mole [i.e. causeway] immense wrought on/Over the foaming deep high arched, a bridge/Of length prodigious" (10.300–302) supplies a risqué overlay upon the punning attack on the claim of Roman pontiffs to **Petrine** supremacy.[39] The womb-like construction of Chaos further suggests that demonic insemination parodies inspiration by the Holy Spirit that bridges it, as it were,

> with mighty wings outspread
> Dove-like sat'st brooding on the vast abyss
> And madest it pregnant.　　(1.20–22)

(The Spirit's androgyny sustains the double sense of "brooding" and "breeding.")

Given the polymorphous sexuality of the Satanic family, Patrick Hume's annotation on the "**secret** conclave" that sits at Pandaemonium suggests the possibility of an even more outrageous pun. He defines that site as "a private place into which no person can come without a key" (n. on 1.795). Sin is associated with the key to hell, the papacy, and **the** primal scene: "such joy thou [Satan] took'st/With me

---

[38] Milton's *Defensio Secunda* also employs ribald wordplay upon *pontifex*. It attacks Alexander More, a Huguenot clergyman, for seducing Pontia, a servant of the wife of Claude Salmasius, a severe critic of Milton's defense of regicide: ". . . for if *carnifex* (an executioner) be supposed to be derived from *conficienda carne* (from dispatching flesh) why should you think it less likely, that from a priest you should be made *pontifex* (a high-priest) *conficiendo Pontiam* (from dispatching Pontia)". Quoted from Columbia, 8: 89.

[39] On Miltonic bawdry, see John Rumrich, "'Milton's God and the Matter of Chaos," *PMLA* 110 (1995): 1039; and John T. Shawcross, "Assumptions and Reading Spenser," *Explorations in Renaissance Culture* 21 (1995), pp. 1–20.

in **secret**, that my womb conceived/A growing burden" (2.765–67). The prefix in *con-clave* (Latin "with a key") provides a false cognate for the common vernacular term for the female genitalia in both English and French, hence a suggestive connection between bawdy humor and antipapal satire.[40] It is worthy of note that William Prynne uses "secret conclave" as an epithet for sexual irregularity in attacking a theater tinged with Catholicism as a hotbed of sodomy.[41] Phallic puns on "key" are at least as old as Anglo-Saxon riddles.

Sexual quibbles were commonplace in pre-1700 religious polemics, but an unforgettable instance bears an association to yet another secret conclave: *I Marry Sir, Here is News Indeed. Being a Copy of a Letter which the Devil Sent to the Pope of Rome, and Kept at the Conclave of Cardinals* (1642). Far more coarse than Miltonic parody, that burlesque records a lurid message from Lucifer to his "dear son," the Pope. References to the residence at the Vatican of "whores . . . punks . . . and strumpets" and to the enshrinement of a papal lieutenant's "stones" as a holy relic (A3–4) recall Chaucer's *Pardoner's Tale* and scabrous allegations about the Borgias and other early modern popes.[42]

Defining puns as "false wit," Joseph Addison and his neoclassical successors condemned recourse to figures of speech that "agree in the sound, but differ in the sense" (*The Spectator*, no. 61). Dr. Johnson thus rejects Milton's "equivocations" and habitual "play on words."[43] Nonetheless, Milton conforms to pre-Enlightenment canons of taste. Recollection of Hamlet's bawdy quibbles or squibs by Milton's contemporary, the Earl of Rochester, demonstrates that puns were a mark of satirical wit in early modern discourse. In *Paradise Lost*, puns often represent a form of *grammatica jocosa* that transgresses conventional orthodoxy.[44] They often embody a carnivalesque aspect that may lend

---

[40] For a feminist response to the genital allegory, see Gregerson, *The Reformation of the Subject: Spenser, Milton, and the English Protestant Epic* (Cambridge University Press, 1995), pp. 208–209. After Sin opens the gates of hell, Satan enters oceanic Chaos, which contains "secrets of the hoary deep" (2.891). An arguable pun on whore-y affords Jonathan Swift a bawdy quibble in "The Lady's Dressing Room": "O ne'er may such a vile machine/Be once in Celia's chamber seen!/O may she better learn to keep/Those secrets of the hoary deep!" As quoted in Le Comte, *Dictionary of Puns*, p. 160.   [41] Prynne, *Histrio-Mastix* (1633), pp. 211–12.

[42] The slur recalls John Bale's allegations concerning papal lechery and the inducement to polymorphous sexuality afforded by the clerical vow of celibacy. Profuse instances may be located in his *Acts of English Votaries* (1548), which recounts a tale about Pope Sylvester, who "gelded himself" in order to dedicate "his stones in a foul sacrifice to Satan" (pt. 2, p. x). On the homophobic aspect of Bale's anti-Catholic propaganda, see Donald N. Mager, "John Bale and Early Tudor Sodomy Discourse," in *Queering the Renaissance*, ed. Jonathan Goldberg (Durham, NC: Duke University Press, 1994), 141–61.

[43] Johnson, *Lives of the Poets*, ed. Hardy, pp. 61, 66–67, 109.

[44] Stallybrass and White, *Politics and Poetics of Transgression*, p. 11.

itself to mockery of the ecclesiastical (and monarchical) establishment by analogy to the antiprelatical tracts.

According to Archangel Michael's prophetic account of future history, the proliferation of Sin's offspring, human inheritors of the original sin of Adam and Eve, will be stamped with the disorderly sexuality of their ancestors. Indeed, the first consequence of the Fall is the discovery of crude recreational sex by Adam and Eve, inflamed with "carnal desire" (9.1013). Their first fallen coupling mirrors the lust for Sin shared by both Satan and his grandson Death. Discord, the "first/Daughter of Sin" (10.707–708), personifies the conflicted nature of the postlapsarian relationship of Eve and Adam, the latter of whom initially believes that sexuality is infected with the consequences of original sin and with death:

> All that I eat or drink, or shall beget,
> Is propagated curse. O voice once heard
> Delightfully, *Increase and multiply*,
> Now death to hear! (10.728–31)

Of course, his faulty reasoning does not imply that sexuality bears the stamp of original sin and death.

The satirical point seems palpable. At the level of topical parody, Sin and Death look like progenitors of generations of Roman pontiffs and English prelates, whose sinister construction of the "false" church has committed a metaphorical rape upon humanity that results in death, not birth, as reprobate souls hasten toward hell during history past, present, and future.[45] The rape conceit is conventional in tracts that attack the Laudian church for ravishing England, but we may note its long-standing place in Protestant polemical discourse in John Bale's scabrous attack on papal "buggery" of England.[46] In *Canterbury's Pilgrimage* (1641), for example, Laud is "the Ork of Canterbury, that great monster, [who kept away] the Church of England, from Christ her spouse, and . . . polluted her with popery" (A3^v, 4^v). According to *The Times Dissected* (1641), Laud introduced "innovations into the Church, making her of a pure virgin a very strumpet" (A4^v).[47]

Disorderly sexuality is a key feature in the portrayal of the Spenserian allegory of Sin and Death in the first folio edition of *Paradise Lost*. The frontispiece for Book 2 situates Satan's encounter with his hideous

---

[45] *News from Hell: Or the Relation of a Vision* (1660) reverses the satirical point in an ironic account of Satan's outrage against the Restoration as an act of treason against the demonic takeover he had perpetrated during the Puritan Commonwealth.

[46] Bale, *Acts of English Votaries*, p. xxiii. [47] I am grateful to Deborah Burks for these examples.

Figure 17   Satan With the Face of Charles II. Illustration for Book 2 of *Paradise Lost*, 4th ed. (1688).

offspring within the milieu of contemporary religio-political strife. Following a design attributed to Henry Aldrich, the anti-Jacobite editor at Christ Church, Michael Burghers's engraving caricatures Charles II by conferring his features on Satan in the company of Sin and Death at the gates of hell (Figure 17). It may be that Jacob Tonson commissioned that plate prior to the king's death in 1685, at an early stage in the planning of an edition published during the period leading up to the Revolution of 1688. The picture may reflect the circumstances of Charles's successful defense of the status of his brother, James, Duke of York, as heir to the throne.[48] Referring to that picture, Daniel Defoe interprets Sin as "the very emblem of a Jacobite high-flyer."[49] The barrenness of the king's legitimate sexuality had led to the Exclusion Crisis (1679–81), the Whig effort to exclude James from the royal succession because of his Roman Catholicism. The debauchery of Charles II's court imparted a polemical tinge to other details in *Paradise Lost*, notably the celebration of the chaste married love of Adam and Eve in Book 4.[50]

The frontispiece for Book 2 indicates that early modern editors discerned, or imposed, allusion to religio-political strife in the presentation of Sin and Death. Accurately incorporating iconographical details embedded in the text, that portrayal of Satan's meeting with his daughter and grandson infuses topical religious and political concerns into Milton's allegorization of James 1:15. The frontispiece associates the Restoration with a "pontifical" bridge that enabled the importation of Roman "corruption" into England. The engraving mocks Charles II's notorious promiscuity, which contributed both to the festering crisis concerning the royal succession and to the witty obscenity of the royal court. Like Satan, Sin, and Death, that crypto-Catholic monarch gained notoriety as a prolific father of bastards. For the anti-Jacobite editors, the threat of a Roman Catholic royal succession functions as a new Gunpowder Plot aimed not **against** a Stuart monarch, but **by** a Stuart monarch who collaborated with High Church prelates against the Protestant cause in England.[51] Incest and rape within the Satanic

---

[48] Schoenberg, "Seventeenth-Century Propaganda," pp. 4–6. Alterations in Satan's face and hands in the frontispiece for Book 1 raise the possibility that it once portrayed Charles II.

[49] *The Review* (Tuesday June 14 1708). As quoted in *ME* 2: 137.

[50] Zwicker, *Lines*, pp. 92–95, 120–26, passim.

[51] On the linkage of Sin and Death to "monarchy and popery," see Quint, *Epic and Empire*, pp. 271, 278. Reversals of the topos of diabolical incest and birth are featured in royalist broadsheets that recount the monstrous delivery of the Devil's grandson by Mistress Rump, a personification of the Rump Parliament, the remnant of the Long Parliament dissolved before the Restoration: *Mistress Rump brought to Bed of a Monster* (1660) and *The Life and Death of Mistress Rump* (1660). She was born of the Devil's Arse. That scatological conceit bears some relationship to the anti-

family thus participate in contentious allusion to alleged failures in the Church of England.

Catholic satirical associations of a summit in the Peak District. They are apparent in "A Pass for the Romish Babble, To the Pope of Rome through the Devil's Arse of Peak" (c. 1620), an engraving attributed to the atelier of Claes Jansz Visscher (Piscator). It portrays the Devil devouring and excreting Jesuits. See F. W. H. Hollstein, *Dutch and Flemish Etchings, Engravings, and Woodcuts c. 1450–1700*, 43 vols. (Amsterdam: Hertzberger, 1949–), vol. 28, no. 22; 29 pl. 22. *To the Praise of Mistress Cellier the Popish Midwife: On Her Incomparable Book* (1680), a mock-epideictic broadside published during the Exclusion Crisis, continues in a related vein: "You're skilled, what Nature's fabric is below,/ And all the secret arts of groping know,/Sexes defect with D——do can supply."

CHAPTER 5

The Paradise of Fools

The attack on the four chief orders of mendicant friars during Satan's sojourn at the futuristic Paradise of Fools (or Limbo of Vanity) is the most explicitly sustained outburst of ecclesiastical controversy in *Paradise Lost*. It constitutes a discordant generic intrusion en route from the exalted dialogue between the Father and Son and the "sacred song" of heaven, on the one hand, to the pastoral idyll of unfallen Eden, on the other. Limbo is located within the sphere of the fixed stars, the next stop on Satan's itinerary after he exits from Chaos. Echoing the linguistic practices of satirical broadsheets of the revolutionary era and Milton's own antiprelatical pamphlets, the narrator's misrepresentation of Catholic devotion invokes the demotic discourse of contemporary Protestant propaganda. In addition to explicit attack on the Church of Rome, the Paradise of Fools affords a screen for mockery of formalistic practices in the Church of England in particular and sacerdotalism in general. Recovery of antiformalistic polemicism as a discursive field in which *Paradise Lost* is deeply embedded illuminates our understanding of the poem's participation in the bitter ecclesiastical controversies of seventeenth-century England.[1]

Milton models the Paradise of Fools on Astolfo's journey to the terrestrial paradise in Ariosto's *Orlando furioso* (34.70–91), the poem that triggered the European vogue for romantic epic. The opening invocation of *Paradise Lost* pays ironic homage to that Italian masterpiece in its claim to pursue "Things unattempted yet in prose or rhyme" (*PL* 1.16). Milton polemicizes the lighter comedy of the flight to the Moon undertaken by Astolfo to recover Orlando's lost wits. Indeed, Milton develops Ariosto's parody of Dante's *Purgatorio* into a frontal assault on the

---

[1] Among the few serious considerations of the Paradise of Fools are Merritt Y. Hughes, "Milton's Limbo of Vanity," in *Th'Upright Heart and Pure*, ed. Fiore, pp. 7–24; and Kantra, *All Things Vain*, pp. 75–83, passim.

sacramental and purgatorial system at the heart of the *Commedia*.[2]
Religious satire is such an intangible presence in Ariosto's Limbo of
Vanity that it goes without comment in Sir John Harington's annotated
translation. By contrast, Milton's own translation of the following Arios-
tan verses in *Of Reformation* reframes the episode within an attack on
Archbishop Laud's policies as the most recent manifestation of age-old
corruption in the Christian church:

> Then past he to a flowery mountain green,
> Which once smelled sweet, now stinks as odiously,
> This was that gift (if you the truth will have)
> That Constantine to good Silvestro gave.   (st. 79)

Pope Sylvester I allegedly received temporal authority as a gift from
Emperor Constantine I, but Lorenzo Valla, the Italian humanistic
scholar, exploded the Donation of Constantine as a forgery.[3]

Although John Dryden and Alexander Pope imitate Milton's burlesque in their own mock-heroic satires, *Mac Flecknoe* and *The Rape of the
Lock*,[4] critics since the time of Joseph Addison have expressed profound
dismay over the episode. Addison protests that "Milton has interwoven
in the texture of his fable some particulars which do not seem to have
probability enough for an epic poem, particularly in the actions which
he draws of the Limbo of Vanity" (*The Spectator*, no. 297). Although Dr.
Johnson acknowledges the success of the episode per se, he claims that
laughter at ludicrous happenings ruptures epic decorum. Thus Milton's
"desire of imitating Ariosto's levity has disgraced his work with the
'Paradise of Fools'—a fiction not in itself ill-imagined, but too ludicrous
for its place."[5]

Even though Satan experiences absolute solitude at a location where
"other creature in this place/Living or lifeless to be found was none,"
the narrator's proleptic account fills the void with "all things transitory
and vain" (3.442–43, 446). Roman Catholic belief in Limbo as the
residence of souls temporarily or permanently denied entry into heaven
(e.g. the patriarchs under the Old Law, unbaptized infants, suicides, and
virtuous pagans) falls under the general Protestant rejection of purgatory. Furthermore, the attack develops into an affirmation of justification by faith alone versus justification by good works, the Roman
Catholic belief that human beings could take an active part in atone-

---

[2] John Wooten, "From Purgatory to the Paradise of Fools: Dante, Ariosto, and Milton," *English Literary History* 49 (1982), pp. 741–50.

[3] *CPW* 1:553–60; quoting p. 560.

[4] Pope models the apotheosis of Belinda's lock (*Rape* 5. 123–28) on *PL* 3.459, 481–83. See below concerning *Mac Flecknoe*.   [5] Johnson, "Life of Milton," in *Lives of the Poets*, p. 109.

ment. Indeed, the latter doctrine takes on a "demonic" aspect because superstitious works find their source in Sin, the daughter of Satan, who

> With **vanity** had filled the **works** of men:
> Both all things **vain**, and all who in **vain** things
> Built their fond hopes of glory or lasting fame,
> Or happiness in this or the other life;
> All who have their reward on earth, the **fruits**
> Of painful **superstition** and blind zeal,
> Naught seeking but the praise of men, here find
> Fit retribution, **empty** as their deeds.   (3.447–54)[6]

An oxymoronic pun informs the idea of filling **works** with **vanity** because the literal meaning of the Latin root of **vanity** (*vanus*) is "empty" or "void." Chiasmic mockery of "things **vain**" and "**vain** things" makes light of both empty **works** and those who believe in them. Empty **works** are **fruits** not of spiritual faith, but worldly superstition.[7]

The narrator's use of **vanity** invokes a highly charged term that Protestant polemicists used to stigmatize Roman "error."[8] A satirical broadsheet thus mocks the Pope, a surrogate for Laudian prelates, as "This load of **vanity**, this peddlar's pack" (Fig. 18). The Paradise of Fools parodies the Catholic doctrine of good works by defining "the works of men" and "fruits/Of painful superstition and blind zeal" as weightless errors that would fly "Up hither like aerial vapours" (3.445, 447, 451–52). Patrick Hume discerns a stab at Catholic devotional practices of "worship of saints" and "fastings, scourgings, processions, pilgrimages" (n. on 3.452). In *Christian Doctrine*, by contrast, Milton advances the standard Protestant view that good works play an essential role as **posterior** signs of a living faith: "So we are justified by faith without the works of the law, but not without the works of faith; for a true and living faith cannot exist without works, though these may be different from the works of the written law" (*CPW* 6: 490).

In employing figures of lightness versus weight to present vanity as the

---

[6] Capitalization of Sin as a personification follows *PL* 3.446, ed. Flannagan.

[7] The absurd debate of theologian-devils "Of providence, foreknowledge, will and fate,/Fixed fate, free will, foreknowledge absolute,/And found no end, in wandering mazes lost" (2.559–61) anticipates Limbo. Fidelia's tutelage "Of God, of grace, of justice, of free will" at Spenser's House of Holiness affords a non-ironic model (*FQ* 1.10.19). See *SPART*, pp. 61–63. On the proleptic aspect of Limbo, see John Wooten, "The Metaphysics of Milton's Epic Burlesque Humor," *MiltonS* 13 (1979), p. 256; Grossman, *Authors*, p. 66.

[8] Thus John Bunyan describes Vanity Fair where "as in other fairs, some one commodity is as the chief of all the fair, so the ware of Rome and her merchandise is greatly promoted in this Fair: only our English nation, with some others, have taken a dislike thereat." See *The Pilgrim's Progress*, ed. Roger Sharrock (Harmondsworth: Penguin, 1965), p. 125.

opposite of "truth," the text jokingly incorporates a variation of the iconography of the Last Judgment. A woodcut in Foxe's *Book of Martyrs* affords a good analogy. It portrays the "heaviness" of the Bible out-weighing a heap of decrees, decretals, rosaries, images, and wealth of the crowned Pope and Catholic clerics. The attendant demon cannot tip the Scales of Justice in their favor. A conventional feature in Last Judgment scenes, the upward movement of the demon resembles the trajectory of Satan's flight to Limbo, a false paradise whose close proximity to heaven belies its ontological status as a different kind of hell, where all is "Abortive, monstrous, or unkindly mixed" (3.456).[9] The iconography of the Weighing of Souls becomes explicit when the Father employs "his golden scales" (4.997) to weigh the respective claims of Satan and Gabriel concerning fighting versus peace:

> The fiend looked up and knew
> His mounted scale aloft: nor more; but fled
> Murmuring, and with him fled the shades of night.   (4.1013–15)

The Paradise of Fools is the future residence of giants and suicides, "Embryos and idiots" (3.474), but Roman Catholics receive most atten-tion. The long list of anti-Catholic allegations constitutes the most extensive and topically explicit satirical sequence in *Paradise Lost*:

> eremites and friars
> White, black and gray, with all their trumpery.
> Here pilgrims roam, that strayed so far to seek
> In Golgotha him dead, who lives in heaven;
> And they who to be sure of Paradise
> Dying put on the weeds of Dominic,
> Or in Franciscan think to pass disguised;
> They pass the planets seven, and pass the fixed,
> And that crystalline sphere whose balance weighs
> The trepidation talked, and that first moved;
> And now Saint Peter at heaven's wicket seems
> To wait them with his keys, and now at foot
> Of heaven's ascent they lift their feet, when lo
> A violent cross wind from either coast
> Blows them transverse ten thousand leagues awry
> Into the devious air; then might ye see
> Cowls, hoods and habits with their wearers tossed
> And fluttered into rags, then relics, beads,
> Indulgences, dispenses, pardons, bulls,
> The sport of winds: all these upwhirled aloft

---

[9] See *TRI*, fig. 56, pp. 171–72; and Eugene R. Cunnar, "Milton's 'Two-Handed Engine': The Visionary Iconography of *Christus in Statera*," *MiltonQ* 17 (1983), pp. 29–38.

Fly o'er the backside of the world far off
Into a limbo large and broad, since called
The Paradise of Fools, to few unknown
Long after, now unpeopled and untrod.   (3.474–97)

Catalogues of that kind are a conventional feature in satires by Skelton, Rabelais, Swift, and others. The passage echoes Tyndale's attack on purgatory: "Priests, monks, canons, friars, with all other swarms of hypocrities, do but empty purgatory, and fill hell."[10]

Recalling the blind "'folly" of friars in Milton's *In Quintum Novembris*, the episode participates in the poet's lifelong hostility to "papistry." On the ground that Jesus Christ "lives in heaven" following the Ascension, the narrator mocks the alleged worldliness of Catholicism by scoffing at credulous pilgrims who seek salvation at Golgotha, the site of the Crucifixion. The attack includes lay people who superstitiously believe they may gain entry into heaven by donning a friar's habit at the point of death. Nevertheless, satirical attack focuses on the four chief orders of begging friars, including Carmelites, Dominicans, and Franciscans, who wear white, black, and gray habits, in addition to Augustinians or Austin friars and hermits, whom the narrator terms "eremites."

The Limbo of Vanity recalls a tradition of anticlerical satire that stretches back to the Goliardic poets of the twelfth and thirteenth centuries. In this approach Milton returns to the familiar terrain of the antiprelatical tracts in which he cites Chaucer's *Friar's Tale* and the pseudo-Chaucerian *Plowman's Tale* as prototypes for satirizing Laudian prelates.[11] In *Areopagitica*, stigmatization of prior censorship takes an antifraternal turn in mockery of "two or three glutton friars" who function as Italianate censors: "Sometimes five Imprimaturs are seen together, dialoguewise, in the piazza of one title page, complimenting and ducking each other with their shaven reverences" (*CPW* 2: 503–4). The friars could supply a screen for attacking formalistic abuses of both Episcopalianism and Presbyterianism. Even though it is comparatively easy to identify "false" clerics, we should remember that Milton's belief in the priesthood of all believers attaches "little significance to the distinction between clergy and laity."[12]

The epic narrator's contempt for Catholic **trumpery** invokes the

[10] Tyndale, *Doctrinal Treatises*, ed. Henry Walter, Parker Society vol. XLII (Cambridge University Press, 1848), p. 303.
[11] See Chapter 2, above; and Michael Lieb, "Milton among the Monks," in *Milton and the Middle Ages*, ed. John Mulryan (Lewisburg, PA: Bucknell University Press, 1982), pp. 103–14. By contrast, Samuel Pordage constructs a "Fantastic Region" akin to Milton's Limbo as a place occupied by Presbyterians, Independents, Dippers, Quakers, Monarchists, Enthusiasts, and Fanatics. See his *Mundum Explicatio* (1661), G8[r-v].   [12] Hill, *MER*, p. 421.

discourse of coarse Protestant polemics against allegedly superstitious devotional modes, rites, and images.[13] Hume glosses the word by reference to the friars' "beads, baubles, tricks, and cheats" (n. on 3.475). The French root, *tromperie*, refers to deception or cheating. Although conservative critics had mocked Puritan linguistic habits ever since the 1580s, Milton emulates them at a mock-heroic moment. Objecting specifically to the scurrility of **trumpery**, the editor, Richard Bentley, proposes that the Paradise of Fools is a spurious addition in his 1732 edition of *Paradise Lost*:

... all this long description of the outside of the world, the Limbo of Vanity, was not Milton's own, but an insertion by his editor ... in its several parts it abounds in impertinencies ... 'tis a silly interruption of the story in the very middle. (n. on 3.444–98)

Like Bentley's other efforts to "purify" *Paradise Lost* of supposed textual errors, the proposed emendation exemplifies newly fashionable neoclassical decorum. As such, it accords with Addison's attack on the episode. Concerning the particular term, Bentley states: "Tis a doubt, whether the word *Trumpery* here in epic style is not as great a fault in a poet, as the thing itself in the friars" (n. on 3.475).

Nevertheless, we should remember that Milton embraces jarring generic mixtures and satirical breaks in decorum. Bentley's objection affords a counterintuitive proof that the vernacular term of abuse is appropriate to a passage that undercuts Satan's claim to heroic grandeur. Indeed, Thomas Newton defends the authenticity of **trumpery** and the integrity of the episode as a whole: "Bentley is for rejecting this verse and fifty more which follow as an insertion of the editor; but I think there can be no doubt of their genuineness." Newton continues:

Our author here, as elsewhere, shows his dislike and abhorrence of the Church of Rome, by placing the religious orders with all their trumpery, cowls, hoods, relics, beads, etc., in the Paradise of Fools, and not only placing them there, but making them the principal figures.[14]

The harangue against **trumpery** invokes a vulgar epithet linked to the iconographical figure of the **peddler's pack** in contemporary

---

[13] Association of **trumpery** with Protestant contempt for allegedly superstitious religious practices emerged c. 1540 (*OED* "trumpery" 2c). E. K.'s gloss on Spenser's May Eclogue defines the "trusse of tryfles" carried by the Fox "as a poore pedler" (lines 237–40) with "the reliques and ragges of popish superstition, which put no smal religion in Belles: and Babes .s. Idoles: and glasses .s. Paxes, and such lyke **trumperies**." Prominent attacks on Catholic **trumpery** are in the third part of the sermon "Of Good Works" in the 1548 *Book of Homilies* and the preface to vol. 1 of Thomas Becon's *Works* (1560), C6ᵛ-C7.

[14] *PL*, ed. Newton, 2nd ed. (1750), nn. on 3.444, 475.

visual satire. The pack typically contains "trinkets" cited in the narrator's list of "relics, beads,/Indulgences, dispenses, pardons, bulls."[15]
These associations inform polemical broadsheets such as *A Discovery of the
Jesuits' Trumpery, Newly Packed Out of England*, with its caricature of "a
popish pack,/A truss of trinkets, holy crosses, beads,/Religious relics,
Ave-Marias, creeds; / Our Lady's images, images of saints" (see Figure
5); Wenceslaus Hollar's *Time Carrying the Pope from England to Rome* (Figure
18), with its burlesque of the Pope and Roman impedimenta as "this
peddler's pack/This trunk of trash and Romish trumperies"; and *The
Solemn Mock Procession of the Pope, Cardinals, Jesuits, Friars*, with its attack
against "Catholic trumpery" (Figure 19). The title-page woodcut of
Lambeth Fair, Wherein You Have All the Bishops' Trinkets Set to Sale (1641)
portrays the revelation of religious "corruption" through the ministration of Time, the father of Truth, who presides over the moment when
the Romish "pack's laid open, all's revealed" (Figure 20).

Bentley also rejects the joking allusion to St. Peter and his keys "'at
heaven's wicket" as a "low and doggerel" usage that violates epic
decorum (n. on 3.484). That observation ignores the biblical resonances
of a palpable allusion to the Sermon on the Mount: "Enter in at the
strait [i.e. narrow] gate: for it is the wide gate, and broad way that
leadeth to destruction . . . and the way narrow that leadeth unto life, and
few there be that find it" (Matt. 7:13–14). By contrast to Bentley, Patrick
Hume discerns the text's polemical edge:

How the Romanists have conferred this office of door-keeper on St. Peter, and
for what reason I know not, unless they interpret the power of the keys our
Savior gave him, (which is generally by them understood, the absolute power
and authority of the governing Christ's Church on earth delegated to him) to be
exercised literally by him now in heaven, the popes (his pretended successors)
managing the other magisterially enough on earth. (n. on 3.484)

By contrast, antiformalists used the **wicket** or **gate** as a figure for the
progress of the elect soul through the vanity of the world and toward
heavenly salvation. The best-known example may be the Wicket Gate
through which Christian passes en route to the Celestial City in *Pilgrim's
Progress*, a text roughly contemporary to *Paradise Lost*. The usage recurs
in militantly Protestant tracts and devotional treatises of the sixteenth
and seventeenth centuries.[16]

The topos of false feeding, found throughout Milton's antiprelatical
pamphlets and *Paradise Lost*, governs the metaphorical flatulence ("A

---

[15] See *OED* "trinket" sb.1 3.
[16] *Wyclif's Wicket* (Nuremberg, i.e. London, 1546); Keeble, *Culture*, pp. 268–72.

This Burden backe to *Rome*, Ile beare againe:
From thence it came, there let it still remaine.

When Times Great Maker (the most high Eternall)   He to his daughter Truth gaue straight Command   This trunke of trash & Romish Trumperies
In mercy loked from his Throne supernall: That shee those dang'rous Errors should withstand   Deluding showes infernall forgeries
And saw the Euils which began to grow   Then vp I tooke vpon my aged backe,   And therefore am I hence in post this riding
In his deare Vine here Militant below,   This load of vaniti, this Pedlers packe   To Rome againe, for here is no abiding

Figure 18   This Burden Back to Rome I'll Bear Again. Wenceslaus Hollar, *Time Carrying the Pope from England to Rome* (c. 1641).

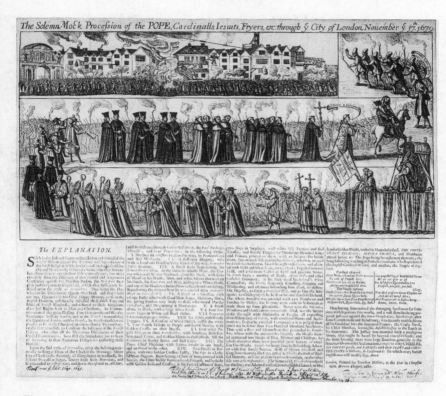

Figure 19   Pope Burning Procession. *The Solemn Mock Procession of the Pope, Cardinals, Jesuits, Friars, Etc. Through the City of London* (1680).

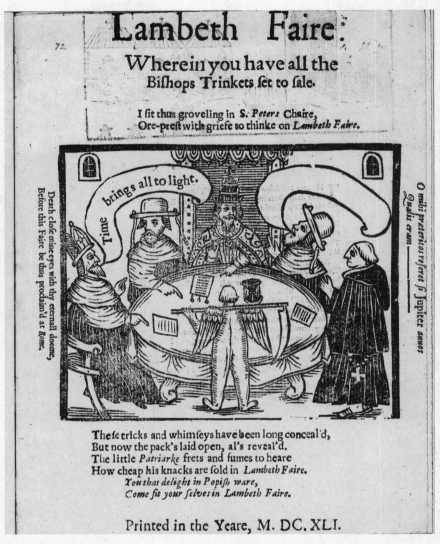

Figure 20 Bishops' Trinkets Set to Sale. *Lambeth Fair: Wherein You Have All the Bishops Trinkets Set to Sale* (1641).

violent cross wind") that blows the mendicant friars with their "Cowls, hoods and habits" over "the backside of the world" and into the Paradise of Fools. Having exited from what one critic terms "the hole of Chaos,"[17] Satan encounters Limbo at the "bare outside of this world" (3.74). This cosmic instance of breaking wind recalls Bakhtin's observation that early modern popular culture commonly likened entrances into purgatory or hell to the rump. He notes that grotesque bodily humor of that kind "degrades and materializes" by linking alleged ecclesiastical abuses to the "bodily lower stratum."[18] The satirical moment is akin to Canto 18 of the *Inferno*, where Dante witnesses souls of the damned immersed in excrement. Breaking wind epitomizes the offensiveness of moral corruption that infects the universe following the Fall of the rebel angels.

The scatological joke recalls bodily humor in Milton's antiprelatical tracts, such as the conceit of the stinking "bishop's foot," whose toes signify clerical pluralism (the holding of multiple benefices), "besides the metropolitan toe, and sends a foul stench to heaven." The foul odor of the world's posterior recalls Milton's claim that Jesus compared "unsavory traditions" to "'the dunghill and the jakes" (*CPW* 1: 894–95). His final divorce tract, *Colasterion*, furthermore defames the anonymous confuter as "the backside of posterity, not a golden, but a brazen ass" (*CPW* 2: 757). Puns on "sphincter" and "posterior" in Milton's undergraduate *Prolusions* show that flatulence had been on his mind for a long time (*CPW* 1: 278).

In an addition to the windiness of classical Limbo, a broad parody of the Epistle for Whitsunday (Pentecost) in the *Book of Common Prayer* (or the Roman-rite liturgy that underlies it) furthers Milton's scatological satire on the friars as "false" apostles. That conceit inverts the birth of the Christian church at the descent of the Holy Spirit upon the apostles:

And suddenly there came a sound from heaven, as it had been the coming of a mighty wind, and it filled all the house where they sat. . . . And they were all filled with the Holy Ghost, and began to speak with other tongues, even as the Spirit gave them utterance. (Acts 2:2–4; *BCP*, p. 169)

The parody is rooted in what Bakhtin has defined as the long-standing tradition of scriptural parody: "Not a single saying of the Old and New Testaments was left unchallenged as long as it could provide some hint

---

[17] Lieb, *Dialectics*, p. 30. On the "oral-anal-sexual imagery" of Chaos and Limbo, see pp. 28–33.
[18] Bakhtin, *Rabelais and His World*, pp. 19–20, 41, 377.

of equivocal suggestion that could be travestied and transposed into the language of the material bodily lower stratum."[19]

A learned pun upon prophetic "inspiration" (from Lat. *inspirare*, "to blow upon, inspire") informs the "violent cross wind" at the Paradise of Fools. False inspiration parodies the Genesis account of the creation of Adam by the "breath of life," the life-giving spirit of the Father (Gen. 2:7; compare *PL* 7.525–26).[20] Allusion to apostolic speaking "with other tongues" (Acts 2:4) affords a witty contrast to the linguistic confusion of the "builders next of Babel on the plain/Of Sennaar," (3.466–68), who precede the friars in the catalogue of future inhabitants of the Paradise of Fools. According to Archangel Michael, the Pentecostal inspiration of the apostles to "speak all tongues" would undo the Babylonians' loss of "their native language" (12.54, 501). A thick cluster of polemical associations adheres to Babel, the Hebrew name for Babylon. Luther points out that the formation of the "true" church at Pentecost reverses the semantic confusion of the Tower of Babel. *Of Reformation* attacks a Church of England tinged with Romanism as a "spiritual Babel" (*CPW* 1: 589–90). The city functions as a ubiquitous type for papal Rome in Protestant propaganda such as *Behold Rome's Monster on His Monstrous Beast*, with its attack on "Babel's Bishops" (see Figure 16).

Symbolic flatulence affords a sequel to the alimentary aggression of Sin, Death, and the hell-dogs that they spawn and a counterpoint to the absence of flatulence in prelapsarian Eden, where the "pure digestion" of Adam soundlessly generates

> temperate vapours bland, which the only sound
> Of leaves and fuming rills, Aurora's fan,
> Lightly dispersed   (5.5–7)

The reader later learns that after the Fall "envious winds/Blown vaga-

[19] Ibid., p. 86. See *OED* "wind" sb.[1] 10; and *PL* 11.14–16 and Fowler n. Wycliffite tradition associates friars with the backside of the Devil or Antichrist. The angelic command in Chaucer's *Summoner's Tale* may, therefore, have a Lollard tinge: " 'Hold up thy tayl, thou Sathanas!' quod he;/Shew forth thyn ers, and lat the frere se/Where is the nest of freres in this place' " (lines 1689–91). The ensuing division of the argument burlesques scholastic disputation. It results in the ludicrous decision that each of twelve friars in a mendicant house "sholde have yliche his part/As of the soun or savour of a fart". (lines 2225–26). See Alan Levitan, "The Parody of Pentecost in Chaucer's *Summoner's Tale*," *University of Toronto Quarterly* 40 (1970–71): pp. 236–46; Penn Szittya, *The Antifraternal Tradition in Medieval Literature* (Princeton University Press, 1986), p. 233. Centuries later John Bale's *Acts of English Votaries* claimed that "these pilled [i.e. tonsured] friars are the tail which covereth his [i.e. Antichrist's] most filthy part" (D8ᵛ). Vulgar antifraternal humor thus represents a point of continuity between late medieval and early modern religious satire.

[20] For a catalogue of winds as false inspiration, see Janet Adelman, "Creation and the Place of the Poet in *Paradise Lost*," in *The Author in His Work: Essays on a Problem in Criticism*, ed. Louis L. Martz, Patricia Meyer Spacks, and Aubrey Williams (New Haven: Yale University Press, 1978), pp. 66–67 and n. 9.

bond or frustrate," which emanate from Limbo, fail to interrupt the heavenward course of Adam and Eve's prayers. Michael's concluding prophecy reverses the model of Limbo with its précis of the scriptural account of the apostolic church, which would endure for a brief moment following Pentecost:

> for the Spirit
> Poured first on his apostles, whom he sends
> To evangelize the nations, then on all
> Baptized, shall them with wondrous gifts endue
> To speak all tongues, and do all miracles,
> As did their Lord before them.   (12.497–502)

The "teachers, grievous wolves" (12.508) who would soon subvert the church necessarily include the proleptic friars of the Paradise of Fools.

The Limbo of Vanity expands upon the trope of false feeding that readers encounter in *Lycidas*, where St. Peter denounces false shepherds who fatten themselves while their "hungry sheep look up, and are not fed,/But swoll'n with wind" (lines 125–26).[21] Roman Catholic doctrine, the Mass, and clerical aggrandizement allegedly substitute coarsely material feeding and digestion for clerical "feeding" of the Christian flock with scriptural truth. The mode of religious pastoral familiar from *Lycidas* further suffuses the epic narrator's ridicule of Satan by likening him to "a vulture on Imaus bred," which gorges on the "flesh of lambs or yeanling kids/On hills where flocks are fed" (3.431–35). His orgiastic predation affords a prototype both for the Pope as a "false" St. Peter and for false "shepherds" who deny pastoral care to their congregations.

Where Addison would discern "false wit," Dryden, who appreciated Miltonic satire, imitates the burlesque of the wind-whipped friars, who undergo a precipitous drop following a fraudulent "flight." He secularizes a conceit grounded in anticlerical satire when the "yet declaiming bard," Flecknoe, descends through the trapdoor of the Barbican stage at the conclusion of *Mac Flecknoe* (1682):

> Sinking he left his drugget robe behind,
> Borne upwards by a subterranean wind.
> The mantle fell to the young prophet's part,
> With double portion of his father's art.   (lines 214–17)

Over and beyond the stench of raw sewage that envelopes Thomas Shadwell's mock-heroic progress on the River Thames, alliterative

---

[21] The wording may allude further to 2 Peter 2:1, 18, which attacks "false prophets" who "speak swelling words of vanity" according to John C. Ulreich, Jr., " 'And by Occasion Foretells': The Prophetic Voice in *Lycidas*," *MiltonS* 18 (1983), p. 7.

plosives contribute to the **fart** that concludes the implied triplet at the end of the poem. Dryden transfers the burden of Miltonic satire against the friars, and the English bishops who perpetuate their ways, to burlesque of bad poets as "false prophets" who emulate Satan's proleptic disguise.[22]

The cultural practices of Reformation polemics remain in play when Satan assumes the "habit" of a "stripling cherub" (3.636, 643) upon departure from the Paradise of Fools. He does so in preparation for his encounter with Uriel, one of seven archangels who execute divine commands. That "theatrical" disguise supplies a proleptic link to the religious dress of the friars who would inhabit Limbo in the future: "Cowls, hoods and habits." Underlying the scheme of demonic disguising is the conviction that the Roman-rite Mass constitutes a theatrical performance akin to magic, trickery, or juggling.[23] By the late 1620s, militant Protestants had transferred the trope of prelatical "disguising" from Roman clergy to Arminian churchmen who de-emphasized preaching in favor of a return to highly "theatrical" vestments, ceremonialism, and sacramentalism. For example, *Of Reformation* yokes "the unmasking of hypocrites" with attack upon "the Pope and papists." Of course, Milton does not limit hypocrisy to an ecclesiastical context. Attacking *Eikon Basilike* as a piece of hypocritical "stage work," *Eikonoklastes* undermines the image of Charles I for incorporating "the common grounds of tyranny and popery, dressed up, the better to deceive, in a new Protestant guise, and trimly garnished over."[24] According to *The Lineage of Locusts*, Hypocrisy is the ancestor of "the Pope, the Cardinals and all his brethren" (see Figure 8).

The narrator's retrospective judgment indicates that Satan, the "false dissembler," functions as a personification of Hypocrisy (3.681), a recurrent object of attack in antiformalistic polemics. Because of their emphasis upon spiritual inwardness, antiformalists believed that "hypocrisy

---

[22] Dryden's scene also travesties Elisha's assumption of Elijah's mantle (2 Kings 2: 9–13); see Broadbent, *Some Graver Subject*, p. 263 n. In the *Dunciad*, Pope imitates *Mac Flecknoe* in the description of the court of Dullness: "And now had Fames posterior trumpet blown,/And all the nations summoned to the throne" (4.71–72).

[23] John Bale, *The Vocacyon of Johan Bale*, ed. Peter Happé and John N. King, Renaissance English Text Society, vol. 14 (Binghamton, NY: MRTS, 1990), lines 1238–43 and n; hereafter cited as *Vocation*. See Jonas A. Barish, *The Anti-Theatrical Prejudice* (Berkeley and Los Angeles: University of California Press, 1981), pp. 160–65; Greenblatt, *Self-Fashioning*, p. 158.

[24] *CPW* 1: 527; 3: 339, 530. See also the attack in *Apology* against "mitered hypocrisy" (1: 924). Instances in other tracts are at 1: 590, 679, 894; 3: 195, 545. On acting as a trope for prelatical "disguising," see Barish, *Prejudice*, p. 162.

and formalism were above all the vices to guard against."[25] Patrick Hume's 1695 commentary parts company with Milton's republican politics in glossing "zeal" with reference to "those zealous hypocrites our author's contemporaries, an age so impiously godly, and so zealously wicked, that prayer was the prologue to the murder of a monarch" (n. on 2.486), but his annotation on Satan's status as a personification of Hypocrisy accords with the narrator's view that Satan "was the first/ That practiced falsehood under saintly show" (4.121–22). According to Hume, **hypocrisy** is "a counterfeiting virtue, religion and piety, the better to gain an opinion of sanctity, and under that disguise covertly to commit all manner of villainy and impiety" (n. on 3.683).

Hypocritical costuming marks the furtiveness of Satan's character throughout *Paradise Lost* as he undergoes transformation, at the level of simile or outright metamorphosis, into the form of a toad, cormorant, and serpent. Nevertheless, Satan's "likeness of an angel bright" fails to conceal his family resemblance from Sin and Death, in a telling reversal of his deception of Archangel Uriel:

> Disguised he came, but those his children dear
> Their parent soon discerned, though in disguise.   (10.330–31)

Although the primary allusion is to his disguising as an "angel of light" (2 Cor. 11:14), his deception participates in a widespread cultural practice whereby Protestant polemicists attacked Catholic clerics as manifestations of demonic hypocrisy. The Gospels supply the scriptural source in Jesus' frequent applications of ὑποκριτής ("a stage actor, dissembler") in its figurative sense of "hypocrite" to Jewish priests, Pharisees, and Sadducees (e.g. Matt. 23: 27–28).

Satan therefore takes part in an allegorical performance akin to a late medieval morality play. His soliloquies bear a faint generic resemblance to clerical self-confession in interludes such as John Bale's *Three Laws*, in which Hypocrisy wears the costume of a Franciscan friar and Sodomy

---

[25] Keeble, *Culture*, p. 219; see also Davis, "Against Formality," pp. 268–69. Pre-1642 drama mimics polemics against "malignant hypocrites" according to Maus, *Inwardness and Theater in the English Renaissance* (University of Chicago Press, 1995), pp. 35–47, et seq. Milton's *Civil Power* attacks reestablishment of a state church because it would breed hypocrisy (*CPW* 7: 269). On Milton's general disdain for hypocrisy, see Honeygosky, *House*, pp. 8, 45, 49, 52, 63. Quakers transferred such concerns from the state church to nonconformist congregations. Bunyan's Pilgrim struggles against formalistic hypocrisy in *Pilgrim's Progress*, which satirizes formalism when personifications of Hypocrisy and Formalist attempt to take a short cut to the Celestial City. See Hill, *A Tinker and a Poor Man: John Bunyan and his Church, 1628–1688* (New York and London: W. W. Norton, 1988), pp. 304–09; *The Collected Essays of Christopher Hill*, 3 vols. (Brighton: Harvester, 1985), vol. I, p. 147; and Ann Hughes, "The Frustrations of the Godly," in *Revolution and Restoration: England in the 1650s*, ed. John Morrill (London: Collins & Brown, 1992), p. 83.

appears as a monk.[26] Satan's disguising recalls Comus' costume as a false hermit. Their mastery of illusory appearances associated with both "idolatrous" religion and "'false' poetry" labels them as descendants of Spenser's Archimago.[27] Among the most compelling instances of demonic disguise are those assumed by Satan Tentator (Medieval Latin, "assailant") in John Bale's *John Baptist's Preaching* (c. 1547) and Satan during the first temptation in *Paradise Regained*, whom the narrator describes as

> an aged man in rural weeds,
> Following, as seemed, the quest of some stray ewe,
> Or withered sticks to gather.   (1.314–16)

Gunpowder Plot associations invade kindred seventeenth-century texts, moreover, when the reader recalls Satan's worldly disguise as a Franciscan friar in Milton's *In Quintum Novembris* (lines 81–85). That early poem invokes the long-standing Protestant gibe that the Fiend may walk the earth in disguise as a member of the mendicant orders or a Jesuit priest. Clad as a Jesuit Vicar General, the Devil in Fletcher's *The Locusts* shares Archimago's Protean ability to change shape at will (2.5–9).

Despite Uriel's status as the "sharpest sighted spirit of all in heaven" (3.691), his inability to see through Satanic disguise penetrable only by divine providence inspires the narrator to comment on a fundamental epistemological problem:

> So spake the false dissembler unperceived;
> For neither man nor angel can discern
> **Hypocrisy**, the only evil that walks
> Invisible, except to God alone,
> By his permissive will, through heaven and earth:
> And oft though wisdom wake, suspicion sleeps
> At wisdom's gate, and to simplicity
> Resigns her charge, while goodness thinks no ill
> Where no ill seems   (3.681–89)

The "Uriel defense" raises the broad issue of the "unavoidability and moral neutrality of intellectual/perceptual error."[28] Even an archangel must wrestle with the task of discriminating between "true" and "false" images, an important paradigm of early modern consciousness.[29] We

---

[26] See Barish, *Prejudice*, pp. 91, 117, 125, 155; White, *Theatre*, p. 76. On monastic disguise, see Lieb, "Monks," p. 110; and *SPART*, pp. 50–54, 57. Fletcher's *Purple Island* groups Hypocrisy with Idolatry, Pharmacus (i.e. Witchcraft), and Hæreticus (7.28–39).   [27] *SPART*, pp. 47, 67–70.

[28] Stephen Fallon, *Milton's "Peculiar Grace": Self-representation, Intention, and Authority*, forthcoming.

[29] See Bale's *Image of Both Churches*; *ERL*, pp. 63, 153–60. Borris discovers "epistemological

may locate an apposite comment on the issue of religious hypocrisy in *The Racovian Catechism* (Amsterdam, 1652), a text controversial because of its Socinian ideas (followers of Socinus denied the divinity of Christ):

> But it can hardly be known by the outward actions where true faith is; for outward actions, proceeding from a corrupt heart, may carry the same appearance with those that flow from a heart which is sincere. In short, he that is evil-minded, may put on the outward garb of a good man: but it is otherwise in a good man, who never laboreth to put on the garb of an evil man. (M6^{r-v})

As a Commonwealth censor, Milton approved it for publication.

That *Paradise Lost* associates both hypocrisy and disguising with religious "falsity" may be noted in the jarring intrusion of satirical attack on those who believe that human sexuality is corrupt into epithalamic celebration of wedlock when Adam and Eve retire to their bower for the night. Recalling the moment when "Eve decked first her nuptial bed,/ And heavenly choirs the hymenean sung," the narrator's witty wordplay stresses their lack of hypocrisy before the Fall, when innocent nakedness "eased the putting off/These troublesome **disguises** which we wear" (4.710–11, 739–40). Implicitly contrasting their spontaneous prayer with liturgical prayer, the narrator articulates a positive response to the vexed theological issue of whether Adam and Eve partake in sexual relations in their unfallen state. Patrick Hume cites the contrary opinion of patristic and Scholastic authorities who claim that "if Adam had not sinned, mankind had been multiplied in some more angelical manner, and not by carnal corruption" (n. on 4.744).

Affirming that Adam and Eve participate in worshipful "rites/Mysterious of connubial love" (4.742–43), the narrator lodges an invective attack on

> Whatever **hypocrites** austerely talk
> Of purity and place and innocence,
> Defaming as impure what God declares
> Pure, and commands to some, leaves free to all.
> Our maker bids increase, who bids abstain
> But our destroyer, foe to God and man?
> Hail wedded love, mysterious law, true source
> Of human offspring. (4.744–51)

Interpreting that passage as an elaboration of 1 Timothy 4:1–3, which attributes prohibition of marriage to demonic "hypocrisy," Hume rules

perversity" at work in Satan's "posing as a cherub" ("Allegory," pp. 117–18). Fallon discerns "fallen epistemology, the perverse refusal of Satan and his devils to acknowledge the unity of a monist universe" in "Milton's Sin," p. 341.

out the Roman Catholic vow of clerical celibacy as a higher state than matrimony. He thus insists on the validity of the divine blessing, "Bring forth fruit and multiply" (Gen. 1:27–28), "which the Catholic encouragers of the celibate will by no means understand as a command, but as a benediction" (n. on 4.748).

Protestant eradication of external, worldly authorities turned the search for "truth" into an inward process capable of resolution only by the individual believer. The narrator's scorn for the latter-day **trumpery** of hermits and friars accordingly echoes Tyndale's attack against the "hypocrisy of outward works."[30] The projection of this conflict onto the struggle of Adam and Eve to fulfill the divine commandment of obedience indicates how their dilemma encapsulates the problem of discriminating between "true" and "false" faith. *The Faerie Queene* allegorizes that issue when Archimago, a figure for Antichrist as the source of false images, confounds the Red Cross Knight, who cannot distinguish between Una and Duessa. By contrast, Milton's *Of True Religion* draws an absolute distinction between "true worship and service of God, learnt and believed from the Word of God only" and "false religion or . . . the Romish Church, Mother of Error, School of Heresy" (*CPW* 8: 419–21).

Satan's personification of Hypocrisy marks him, in line with Harold Bloom's theory,[31] as the proleptic forefather of Archimago. That master disguiser is the only figure in Spenser's *Faerie Queene* whose status is clarified by a headnote, which identifies him as Hypocrisy (1.1. Argument). Archimago's ability to change shape at will links him to Proteus, who "To dreadfull shapes he did himselfe transforme" (*FQ* 3.8.41). Like Archimago, Milton's Satan is a metamorphic master of disguise whose unstable form replicates "In various shapes old Proteus from the sea" (*PL* 3.604). In Fletcher's *The Locusts*, the skill at equivocation and shape-changing aspect of Lucifer's personification of Jesuitical casuistry functions as yet another bridge between Spenser and Milton:

> Once Proteus, now Equivocus he hight,
>   Father of cheaters, spring of cunning lies,
>   Of slie deceite, and refin'd perjuries,
> That hardly hell it selfe can trust his forgeries.
>
> To every shape his changing shape is drest,
> Oft seemes a Lambe and bleates, a Wolfe and houles.   (2.5–6)

Henry Peacham's *Minerva Britannia: Or a Garden of Heroical Devices* (1612)

---

[30] *Whole Works of William Tyndale, John Frith, and Doctor Barnes,* ed. John Foxe (1573), G4ᵛ.
[31] See Bloom, *Map,* pp. 125–43.

affords a further iconographical link in its portrayal of the Hypocrite's "feigned zeal of sanctity" as a Satanic pilgrim whose habit affords "false disguise" (p. 198).[32]

Dissembling by those figures, along with the Protean disguising that constitutes Satan's proleptic bequest to Archimago, involves a self-reflexive consideration of the nature of poetry (i.e. fiction) because both Satan and Archimago function as sinister mirror images of Milton and Spenser as makers of images.[33] Protestant suspicion of the mimetic function of the "fancy" (i.e. fantasy or imagination), a deceptive faculty capable of undermining human understanding by transmitting false and misleading ideas, contributes to the epic narrator's declaration concerning the incompatibility between "heroic song" and allegorical romantic epic (9.25), the vestigial presence of which undergoes travesty in the Spenserian allegory of Sin and Death. After all, "fantasies" are akin to "dreames" and "lies" (*FQ* 2.9.51), and rhetoricians have defined allegory as the "figure of false semblant" (i.e. resemblance or image).[34] The imagination may deceive not only by recreating an inaccurate image of the external world, but also by creating false concepts.

Because the "fancy" is most vulnerable during sleep, when the reason is at rest, both Archimago and Satan initiate temptations in the form of dreams. Satan accordingly assumes a ridiculous posture to launch revenge:

> Squat like a toad, close at the ear of Eve;
> Assaying by his devilish art to reach
> The organs of her fancy, and with them forge
> Illusions as he list, phantasms and dreams.   (4.800–803)

(Toads symbolize both lust and death.) His deception constitutes an anticipation of Archimago's tricking of the Red Cross Knight into abandoning Una by employing the "false shewes" of an erotic dream (*FQ* 1.1.46).

The aurality of Satanic temptation, here and in Book 9 of *Paradise Lost*, anxiously interrogates Protestant insistence upon the priority of hearing the Word over seeing images. Satan's goal of infiltrating Eve's mind with "discontented thoughts,/**Vain** hopes, **vain** aims, inordinate desires/Blown up with high conceits" (4.807–809) returns the reader full circle to the satire on the windy vanity of the Paradise of Fools, with all

[32] See also the use of deceptive "habit" to disguise the "coal-black conscience of an Hypocrite" in George Wither, *A Collection of Emblems, Ancient and Modern* (1635), book IV, illustration 21.

[33] See Guillory, *Authority*, pp. ix–x, 1, 4, 18, 36, 58, 108, 123.

[34] George Puttenham, *The Art of English Poesy*, in *Elizabethan Critical Essays*, ed. G. Gregory Smith (London: Oxford University Press, 1904), vol II, p. 169. See also *SPART*, pp. 69–70.

of its antimonastic associations. Indeed, Satan's whispering into her ear
may hint at parody of the Annunciation, an important image in Catholic iconography, when the Holy Spirit delivered news of the Incarnation into the ear of Mary, the antitype of Eve.[35] Demonic temptation
thus represents a distorted mirror image of divine inspiration. The
tableau involves a subtle recreation of the baldly polemical moment
when Satan whispers into the Pope's ear in Milton's *In Quintum Novembris*. Variations of that conventional scene recur in contemporary visual
satires (see Figures 11 and 19).

During the morning after Eve's disturbed sleep, she experiences
anxiety over Satan's aural penetration of her dream world. He visited in
disguise as "One shaped and winged like one of those from heaven,"
who made the Tree of Knowledge appear "Much fairer to my fancy
than by day" (5.53, 55). As an antidote, Adam instructs her concerning
the image-making function of the wakeful "fancy" as a faculty subordi-
nate to the reason versus the subversion of rationality when "mimic
fancy" governs during sleep, "most in dreams" (5.110, 112). In response
to the epistemological problem posed by the invasion of Eve's mind by a
Satanic nightmare, a reprise of his employment of cherubic disguise to
deceive Uriel, Adam declares:

> Evil into the mind of god [i.e. angel] or man
> May come and go, so unapproved, and leave
> No spot or blame behind.   (5.117–19)

Satan's laughable posture at the ear of Eve undermines the prevalent
view that he is "never ridiculous."[36] The degradation of his toad-like
disguise recalls clerical "disguising" at the Limbo of Vanity. A moment
of sardonic humor at Satan's initial temptation of Eve is jarringly
appropriate to the presence of ecclesiastical complaint and satire in
Paradise Lost. Satan's effort to inspire in Eve "Vain hopes, vain aims"
recalls the vain windiness of the Paradise of Fools in a discordant sequel
to epithalamic celebration of the "wedded love" of Adam and Eve. The
deceptively insubstantial dream images that Satan projects into his
intended victim's mind anticipate futuristic instances of what the narrator has already attacked as demonic **trumpery**. The dark comedy at
the conclusion of Book 4 is generically appropriate to Satan's disruption
of the pastoral idyll of prelapsarian Eden. Eve's initial encounter with
Satan constitutes a sour introduction to the dwindling remainder of
Edenic bliss.

---

[35] Frye, *Imagery*, p. 100.   [36] Guilhamet, *Satire and the Transformation of Genre*, p. 9.

CHAPTER 6

Laughter in heaven

In the course of exalted dialogue between the Father and Son at the court of heaven, divine mirth frames Satan's sojourn at the Limbo of Vanity. Heavenly merriment affords divine sanction for the narrator's satirical perspective. The reader is privy to the Father's irony as he scrutinizes Satan winging his way toward the Paradise of Fools: "High throned above all highth, bent down his eye,/His own works and their works at once to view" (3.58–59). The Son shares the Father's scorn in his own boast about the prospect of victory against the "powers of darkness" at the time of the Last Judgment:

> Thou at the sight
> Pleased, out of heaven shalt look down and smile,
> While by thee raised I ruin all my foes,
> Death last, and with his carcass glut the grave.   (3.256–59)

That paradoxical gibe alludes to St. Paul's assurance concerning resurrection, "O death, where is thy sting! O grave where is thy victory!" (1 Cor. 15:55). Irony imbues the Son's prophecy of victory over his demonic double, Death, the son not of the Father, but of Satan. Archangel Michael's prophecy concerning the builders of the Tower of Babel indicates, furthermore, that divisive linguistic confusion will evoke divine mirth in a replay of cosmic mockery of Satan and the rebel angels:

> great laughter was in heaven
> And looking down, to see the hubbub strange
> And hear the din; thus was the building left
> Ridiculous, and the work Confusion named.   (12.59–62)

Pleasure at the damnation of the fallen angels underpins the Father's sarcastic response to the moment when Satan "Drew after him the third part of heaven's host." Intense dramatic irony envelops the actions of rebels unaware of the Father's constant surveillance, when his "eternal eye" perceived "Rebellion rising, saw in whom, how spread." Peering through darkness, he saw "what multitudes/Were banded to oppose his high decree" (5.710–11, 715–17). Satirical detachment underlies the Father's pretence to vulnerability when, speaking in a deadpan manner, he feigns uneasiness to the Son: "Nearly it now concerns us to be sure/Of our omnipotence" (5.721–22). His "smiling" charade (5.718) disingenuously admits the possibility of Satanic victory:

> Let us advise, and to this hazard draw
> With speed what force is left, and all employ
> In our defense, lest unawares we lose
> This our high place, our sanctuary, our hill.   (5.729–32)

Apprehending the Father's derisory mood, the Son is amused by a scornful joke intended to glorify his own quelling of Satanic pride:

> Mighty Father, thou thy foes
> Justly hast in derision, and secure
> Laugh'st at their vain designs and tumults vain,
> Matter to me of glory, whom their hate
> Illustrates, when they see all regal power
> Given me to quell their pride, and in event
> Know whether I be dextrous to subdue
> Thy rebels, or be found the worst in heaven.   (5.735–42)

Reference to "**vain** designs and tumults **vain**" anticipates the "**vain** things" that will fill the Limbo of Vanity (3.448).

Although the Son insists upon the justness of divine disdain, readers have resisted the contemptuous mockery of the Father and the Son. The reaction of most twentieth-century readers is comparable to Adam's initial puzzlement at punishment of his disobedience: "Inexplicable/Thy justice seems" (10.754–55). William Empson's memorable critique therefore focuses on the poem's crux, which is addressed not only by Adam and the Father, but also the narrator in the opening invocation:

> That to the highth of this great argument
> I may assert eternal providence,
> And justify the ways of God to men.   (1.24–26)

Focusing on contradictions and discontinuities in *Paradise Lost*, Empson decries the presence of divine comedy, which leads him to conclude that the Father is a tyrannical dictator with sadistic tendencies who feigns vulnerability and provokes the War in Heaven. To Empson, the collaboration of the Father and Son as divine ironists is problematic in the extreme.[1] His view expands upon the Romantic heroization of

Satan typified by William Blake's epigrammatic remark that the "rea-son Milton wrote in fetters when he wrote of angels and God, and at liberty when of devils and hell, is because he was a true poet and of the Devil's party without knowing it" (*The Marriage of Heaven and Hell*, plate 5). Like Blake, Empson engages in satirical reversal of standard pieties of Christian orthodoxy. His argument builds explicitly upon the Satanist inversions of Percy Bysshe Shelley's *A Defence of Poetry*, which declares:

Milton's Devil as a moral being is as far superior to his God, as one who perseveres in some purpose which he has conceived to be excellent in spite of adversity and torture, is to one who in the cold security of undoubted triumph inflicts the most horrible revenge upon his enemy, not from any mistaken notion of inducing him to repent of a perseverance in enmity, but with the alleged design of exasperating him to deserve new torments.[2]

Like Shelley, Empson praises Satan for sheer tenacity and condemns the Father for ethical perversity.

The trenchancy of *Milton's God* has influenced more than one gener-ation of critics who have taken spirited stands for or against Empson, who has a subtle eye for the impossibility of eradicating ambiguity in *Paradise Lost*. Directing the anti-Miltonic views of T. S. Eliot and F. R. Leavis into an unexpected swerve, he attacks "neo-Christian" critics who defend religious orthodoxy.[3] As such, *Milton's God* is the product of a moment in mid-twentieth-century criticism when figures such as C. S. Lewis,[4] with his Anglican confessional biases, and E. M. W. Tillyard[5] were among the dominant voices in Milton studies. By contrast, Empson's acknowledgment of Milton's heterodoxy is compatible with Christopher Hill's thesis concerning Milton's heretical radicalism.[6]

Having endured censure by conservative Miltonists when *Milton's God* first appeared, Empson continues to influence contemporary criticism. For example, Frederic Jameson has retheorized his thesis

less as testimony about Milton's theological beliefs, than as a demonstration of the way in which the requirement to give anthropomorphic figuration to the ideology of Providence ends up denouncing itself, and undermining the very

---

[1] Empson, *Milton's God*, ch. 3. For precedents in *FQ* 1 and other sixteenth-century texts, see *SPART*, pp. 221–26.

[2] Shelley, *Complete Works*, 10 vols. (London: Ernest Benn, 1926–30), vol. 7: p. 129. See Empson, *Milton's God*, pp. 19–21.

[3] Empson, *Milton's God*, p. 229. Other "pro-Satanist" critics include A. J. A. Waldock and Edgar Stoll. On Empson's "anti-Satanist" opponents, see John Carey, "Milton's Satan," in *The Cambridge Companion to Milton*, ed. Dennis Danielson (Cambridge University Press, 1989), p. 132, et seq.

[4] Lewis, *A Preface to "Paradise Lost"* (London: Oxford University Press, 1942).

[5] Tillyard, *Milton* (London: Chatto & Windus, 1930); *Studies in Milton* (London: Chatto & Windus, 1951).   [6] Empson, *Milton's God*, p. 11; Hill, *MER*, p. 3, et seq. See Rumrich, *Milton Unbound*, p. 1.

ideology it set out to embody.[7]

Recent studies continue to take Empson's attack on Miltonic theodicy (defense of divine justice) quite seriously.[8] His insistence upon indeterminacy of meaning is compatible with postmodernist theory. Critics who antagonized Empson, such as Tillyard and Lewis, have come under attack for positing a critical model grounded upon reflectionistic and essentialistic assumptions.[9]

Addressing the consternation of the "Christian reader" at the Father's confession of vulnerability at the outset of the War in Heaven, Empson interprets the Son's above-quoted reply as reassurance "that this is merely one of God's jokes." He takes the Father's tortuous sense of humor as proof of divine authorship of evil, yet another perennial theological issue: "The joke becomes appallingly malignant if you realize that God has a second purpose in remaining passive; to give the rebels a false evidence that he is a usurper, and thus drive them into real evil." With reference to Adam and Eve, Empson concludes that the Father's indifference "to the mass of suffering he causes by his sustained trickery" negates any theodicy based upon the Fortunate Fall (felix culpa), the belief that the Fall was a fortunate event because it supplies the precondition for Christian redemption. He claims that Milton insists, "with harsh and startling logic, that God was working for the Fall all along."[10] By contrast, one critic proposes an alternative "hypothesis of the Unfortunate Fall" in order to save Milton's theodicy from Empson's countercharge that it constitutes "little more than a useless façade over the nightmare abyss of 'divine' intentions."[11]

The present chapter offers a previously unrecorded, historicized explanation of laughter in heaven. Unlike Empson, who reads *Paradise Lost* as a text isolated from history, I frame the poem within its contemporary historical moment and in dialogue with seventeenth-century

[7] Jameson, "Religion and Ideology," pp. 47–48.
[8] See John Rumrich, *Matter of Glory: A New Preface to Paradise Lost* (University of Pittsburgh Press, 1987), pp. 132–34.
[9] Among many examples, see Jonathan Dollimore, *Radical Tragedy: Religion, Ideology, and Power in the Drama of Shakespeare and His Contemporaries*, 2nd ed. (Durham, NC: Duke University Press, 1993), pp. 89–90; and Shuger, *Habits*, pp. 2–3, et passim. Tillyard's critics focus on *The Elizabethan World Picture* (London: Chatto & Windus, 1943), his little handbook of commonplaces concerning organic models for human society and the cosmos.
[10] Empson, *Milton's God*, pp. 96–97, 189–92, 272–73. For a counterargument, see Arthur O. Lovejoy, "Milton and the Paradox of the Fortunate Fall," *English Literary History* 4 (1937): pp. 161–79.
[11] Dennis Danielson, *Milton's Good God: A Study in Literary Theodicy* (Cambridge University Press, 1982), pp. 202–203, et seq.

religious polemics. Granting that Empson interprets the text in ways that resonate with twentieth-century readers, I try to show that such responses are ahistorical. The present argument aims to recover from oblivion an entire discursive field within which the anthropomorphic trope of divine mirth functions as a gratingly harsh element of contemporary religious controversy. Grounding the present argument in the discursive field of seventeenth-century ecclesiastical controversy, the present investigation offers an alternative interpretation of evidence selected by Empson. Built upon a broad range of scriptural texts, heavenly mirth is not a capricious Miltonic invention. Instead, it is a nearly predictable element in a general strategy of bad-tempered religious satire. Indeed, the poet joins contemporary polemicists in modeling scoffing insults and wordplay upon the lexicon of YHWH and his prophets in the prophetic books of the Old Testament.[12]

Contemporary sermons and commentaries contextualize divine merriment as an expansion upon God's scorn for his enemies according to Psalms 2:4: "But he that dwelleth in the heaven shall laugh: the Lord shall have them in derision." To seventeenth-century readers immersed in the Bible, that text and Proverbs 1:26 ("I will also laugh at your destruction, and mock, when your fear cometh") would help to explain the grotesque irony of the Father's belligerent denial of responsibility for the invasion of the defenseless Garden of Eden by Sin and Death:

> had not the folly of man
> Let in these wasteful furies, who impute
> Folly to me, so doth the prince of hell
> And his adherents, that with so much ease
> I suffer them to enter and possess
> A place so heavenly, and conniving seem
> To gratify my scornful enemies,
> That laugh, as if transported in some fit
> Of passion. (10.619–27)

Hume paraphrases the Father's joke thus: "Winking at their wickedness seem[s] to oblige my proud enemies" (n. on 10.624).

In an invective mode, the Father rails against the **folly** of Satan, Adam, and Eve. Even Sin, in yet another expansion of Psalms 2:4, shares the Son's insight that the Last Judgment will constitute the ultimate cosmic joke. When Satan and Death threaten to slay each other as unwitting instruments of divine providence, Sin declares:

[12] Jemielity, "Divine Derision and Scorn," pp. 47–68.

> and know'st for whom;
> For him who sits above and laughs the while
> At thee ordained his drudge, to execute
> What e'er his wrath, which he calls justice, bids,
> His wrath which one day will destroy ye both.　　　(2.730–34)

Milton's own theory of satire derives from scriptural rebukes uttered by God and Jesus.[13] Heavenly mirth alludes to a messianic formulation in Psalms 2:1–7. Composed in 1653 at the outset of the Protectorate, Milton's own translation of Psalm 2 predates intense work on *Paradise Lost* by only a few years. The contemporary context of revolution and counterrevolution confers topical immediacy upon words concerning divine victory over "kings of the earth":

> he who in heaven doth dwell
> Shall laugh, the Lord shall scoff them, then severe
> Speak to them in his wrath, and in his fell
> And fierce ire trouble them.

Milton translated that text during his tenure as Secretary for the Foreign Tongues in service to a government that claimed legitimacy on the ground that God aided its battlefield victory over Charles I and the royalist cause. In *Paradise Lost*, application of the Psalmist's declaration enables the reader to infer that the Father is a wry ironist.[14]

Ironic commentary by the narrator or Father or Son affords a means for deflating the feigned heroism of the fallen angels. It corresponds to the Geneva Bible gloss on Proverbs 1:26, which explains laughter in heaven as an anthropomorphic accommodation "spoken according to our capacity, signifying that the wicked, which mock and jest at God's word, shall have the just reward of their mocking." As such, divine mirth accords with Milton's application of the theory of accommodation, ultimately derived from Augustine's *City of God* (15.25), to representation of the Father, angelic life, and the War in Heaven. In *Christian Doctrine*, Milton explains accommodation with reference both to description of God "not as he really is but in such a way as will make him conceivable to us" and to formation of "just such a mental image of him as he, in bringing himself within the limits of our understanding, wishes us to

[13] *CPW* 1: 875. See Chapter 1, above.
[14] Hume annotates the important allusion to Ps. 2:4 (n. on 5.736). On that text's centrality in *PL*, see Stella Revard, *The War in Heaven: "Paradise Lost" and the Tradition of Satan's Rebellion* (Ithaca, NY; Cornell University Press, 1980), pp. 99–101; Lieb, *Poetics*, pp. 277–78. See also Paul Rovang, "Milton's War in Heaven as Apocalyptic Drama: 'The Foes Justly Hast in Derision,'" *MiltonQ* 28 (1994): p. 33.

form."[15] Empson's intentionalistic argument ignores contextual evidence of that kind, which affords a contemporary model for derisory laughter as a response to fallen error.

From the moment when the Father "bent down his eye" (3.58) to scrutinize Satan en route from hell toward earth, divine irony undergoes iconographical representation in the Eye of Providence, a scriptural symbol that comes into use in the sixteenth century. Analogous to the use of an eye as a hieroglyph for Osiris in early printed editions of Horapollo's *Hieroglyphica*, that emblematic figure skirts overtly anthropomorphic representation of the inaccessible deity in an iconographical response to the problem of accommodation. It appears within sunlit clouds symbolic of the veiling of divine glory on the well-known title page of Sir Walter Ralegh's *History of the World* (1614).[16] Milton is known to have owned or read that text.[17]

The Eye of Providence came into play as a conventional figure for divine intervention against religio-political peril in engravings of the Gunpowder Plot and other "providential" occasions in the nationalistic calendar filled with sequels to the Spanish Armada and Guy Fawkes Day. The Eye of Providence is comparable to the sun-bright Tetragrammaton (the Hebrew consonants for YHWH, the divine name too sacred to pronounce) within a radiant field sometimes encircled by clouds pierced by a beam or beams of shining light. Even committed Protestants who disapproved of religious images condoned nonanthropomorphic representations of the deity.[18]

The recurrence of the divine eye in Fifth of November broadsheets enables us to recover a long-forgotten polemical nuance in the presentation of God as a divine ironist. The figuration is biblical, but numerous instances in Protestant publications take on a highly polemical cast. We may note a further association between the Eye of Providence in *Paradise Lost* and the Gunpowder Plot in the earliest instance of laughter in heaven in Milton's writings, the overtly antipapal attack in *In Quintum Novembris*: "Meanwhile the Lord who sends the lightning from his skyey

[15] *CPW* 6: 133. See William G. Madsen, *From Shadowy Types to Truth: Studies in Milton's Symbolism* (New Haven: Yale University Press, 1968), pp. 74–80, and passim; and *ME* 1:13–14.

[16] Margery Corbett and Ronald Lightbown, *The Comely Frontispiece: The Emblematic Title-page in England 1550–1660* (London: Routledge and Kegan Paul, 1979), pp. 41–42, 135, fig. 10. See also Hind 2: 342, 394; and Edgar Wind, *Pagan Mysteries in the Renaissance*, rev. ed. (New York: Norton, 1968), ch. 14 ("The Concealed God"), esp. pp. 222–24, 232–34, figs. 84, 86.

[17] Boswell, *Milton's Library*, no. 1209.

[18] *ERL*, pp. 96–97, figs. 2, 11. See also Karl Josef Höltgen, "The Reformation of Images and Some Jacobean Writers on Art," in *Functions of Literature: Essays Presented to Erwin Wolff on His Sixtieth Birthday*, ed. Ulrich Broich, et al. (Tübingen: Max Niemeyer Verlag, 1984), pp. 123–27, passim.

citadel and bends the heavens in their wide arc looks down and laughs at the vain attempts of the evil mob, intending to defend His people's cause Himself" (lines 166–69).[19]

Many instances of the Eye of Providence in contemporary broadsheets demonstrate how Milton's poem, at a highly topical level of historical reference, participates in the satirical practices of contemporary Protestant propaganda. Although William Empson blames Milton alone, divine mockery of Satan is not unique to *Paradise Lost*. For example, a remarkable visual analogue to the tropes of laughter in heaven and the dispensation of "light from far" by the Father's "lordly eye" (*PL* 3.578–79) dominates an inflammatory broadsheet, *To God, in Memory of His Double Deliverance* (1621). Juxtaposing the Spanish Armada and Gunpowder Plot as instances of providential deliverance, it portrays the Pope and attendant clerics in conference with Satan (see Figure 10). The sunbeam that emanates from the Tetragrammaton and the divine Eye illuminates Guy Fawkes's "deed of darkness" beneath the House of Lords. The Latin-English-Dutch epigram alludes to texts such as Psalms 2:4 and Proverbs 1:26: "Video Rideo. I see and smile. Ick sie en lach." Samuel Ward's verses declare:

> But he whose never slumbering EYE did view
> The dire intendments of this damned crew
> Did soon prevent what they did think most sure
> Thy mercies LORD for evermore endure.

In maturity, Milton rejected the politics of Richard Smith's *The Powder Treason* (see Figure 7), which incorporates Michael Droeshout's engraving of James I in parliament at the time of the Gunpowder Plot. It presents the king as a worldly extension of the Eye of Providence and Tetragrammaton. Based on common biblical sources, however, the overlapping accommodations of the godhead in terms of the Tetragrammaton, Divine Providence (*Providentia Divina*), and Inaccessible Light (*Lux Inaccessibilis*) share iconographical ground with the language of emanation in the second invocation in *Paradise Lost*:

> Hail, holy Light, offspring of heaven first-born,
> Or of the eternal co-eternal beam
> May I express thee unblamed? since God is light,
> And never but in unapproached light

---

[19] "Interea longo flectens curvamine coelos/Despicit aetherea dominus qui fulgurat arce,/ Vanaque perversae ridet conamina turbae,/Atque sui causam populi volet ipse tueri." See Revard, *War*, p. 99.

Dwelt from eternity, dwelt then in thee,
Bright effluence of bright essence increate.   (3.1–6)

That passage combines generalized allusions to nonanthropomorphic representation of the deity in the Old and New Testaments (e.g. John 1:4–9) with Neoplatonic theory of emanation. The epic narrator consistently associates vision and light with the eternal providence of "God beholding from his prospect high,/Wherein past, present, future he beholds" (3.77–78).

The iconography of providential vision played a vital role in Gunpowder Plot pamphlets such as Francis Herring's *The Quintessence of Cruelty* (1641), which praises King James as a vehicle for divine providence in interpreting enigmatic clues concerning Guy Fawkes's plot. The frontispiece portrays the confounding of Fawkes "and his Father-Satan" by a beam of light emanating from "Heaven's All-Seeing-Eye" (Figure 21). That conventional formulation of the discovery of the lantern-bearing figure of Guy Fawkes focuses on the kegs of gunpowder beneath parliament, which undergo more stylized representation in Droeshout's engraving for Smith's *Powder Treason* (see Figure 7).

The Eye of Providence was in use throughout Milton's lifetime and beyond. Propagandists therefore interpreted the Popish Plot in terms of providential intervention akin to that credited with exposure of the Gunpowder Plot. Published during the Exclusion Crisis, *Happy Instruments of England's Preservation* (Figure 11) thus portrays the Pope, serving as the Devil's minion, as the butt of a cosmic joke because Titus Oates and his companions, as divine agents, see through the clouded obscurity of the Popish Plot. The beam of light emanating from heaven proclaims "prophetic" words: "Heaven Shall Turn Thy Weapons Against Thee." The sun-bright manifestation of YHWH confounds the Spanish Armada and Gunpowder Plot in insets of the engraved title page of George Carleton's *A Thankful Remembrance of God's Mercy* (Figure 22).

The polemical character of laughter in heaven is clearly evident in the homiletic discourse of Fifth of November sermons.[20] Generally devoid of Miltonic motifs, pre-1640 Gunpowder Day sermons delivered at the Chapel Royal universally celebrate the achievements of the Stuart

---

[20] The present chapter distills findings based on a reading of all Gunpowder Day sermons in the collections of the Folger Shakespeare Library and the Huntington Library for the years 1606–1702 (and sermons preached before Queen Anne, 1702–14). For the recurrence in Gunpowder Day sermons of tropes other than laughter in heaven and the Eye of Providence, see Revard, *War*, pp. 89–103, passim. The Gunpowder Plot is an important model for Satan's impulse "to bring about a reversion of God's works back to the volatile state of Chaos" (Quint, "Plot," p. 264).

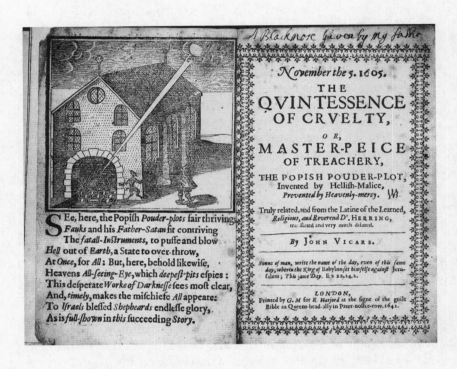

Figure 21   Guy Fawkes and the Devil. Francis Herring, *November the 5, 1605. The Quintessence of Cruelty, or Master-Piece of Treachery, the Popish Powder-Plot,* translated by John Vicars (1641).

Figure 22   The Triumph of the True Church. George Carleton, *A Thankful Remembrance of God's Mercy*, 3rd ed. (1627).

dynasty. A rare pre-revolutionary instance of laughter in heaven does occur, however, in Robert Willan's juristic sermon, *Conspiracy Against the Kings, Heaven's Scorn* (1622), which acknowledges the problem of accommodation in glossing the seminal text of Psalm 2:4 as an example of "Prosopopeia [i.e. personification], attributing improperly, but significantly, a spleen and laughter unto God. So the catastrophe and conclusion of all conspiracy, is the sarcasmos, and bitter scorn of God" (p. 5).

The prominence of laughter in heaven in sermons of the 1640s and 1650s affords further evidence concerning the involvement of *Paradise Lost*, at a typological level, with the politics of the revolutionary era. In one instance, Matthew Newcomen preached for upwards of three hours at the parliamentary church of St. Margaret's, Westminster. His apocalyptic sermon, *The Craft and Cruelty of the Church's Adversarie* (1643), urges members of the House of Commons to emulate divine sarcasm in attacking the royalist opposition: "Let the Kings of the Earth, and the people rage as much as they will; he that sits in Heaven shall laugh them to scorn" (p. 40). Following parliamentary victory, a sermon preached by Henry Haggar subverts royal iconography by likening Charles I not to Christ, but to the tyrants Nebuchadnezzar and Ahab, antiregal types who recur in Milton's tracts.[21] The preacher treats the theatrical spectacle of the late king's execution as divine comedy: "Therefore now the Lord that sitteth in heaven, is laughing them to scorn, and hath them in derision, and is vexing of them in his sore displeasure" (p. 16).

Laughter in heaven retained currency as a homiletic trope after publication of *Paradise Lost*. A familiar generic shift in Henry Dove's *Sermon Preached before the Honorable House of Commons, at St. Margaret's Westminster, November 5. 1680* marks the preacher's treatment of the Popish Plot by reference to the *theatrum mundi* ("theater of the world") conceit: "That the actors should be apprehended on the stage, when they were just ready to begin the tragedy, and all the danger blown over in a moment." Although the performance is tragic from a human perspective, from the vantage point of heaven the unknowing actors are butts of a cosmic joke: "But he that sits in heaven laughed them to scorn; the Lord had them in derision" (pp. 12, 15).

At the level of religio-political topicality, *Paradise Lost* exemplifies a

---

[21] Haggar's *No King but Jesus: Or, the Walls of Tyranny Razed* (1652) affords a grisly variation upon a renowned royalist slogan with the claim "that when that Lord [Archbishop Laud] that anointed him [Charles I] lost his head, he that was anointed by him could not keep his long: And so their old proverb was verified, *No Bishop, No King*" (p. 17).

shift away from the original thrust of Gunpowder Plot satires and sermons as pro-Stuart propaganda. During the Commonwealth and at the time of the Exclusion Crisis, militant Protestants enunciated the antithetical view that Charles I, Charles II, and his heir, James, Duke of York, were co-conspirators in a new Gunpowder Plot to reimpose "popery" upon England. Belial's association with courtly profligacy thus infuses a sly suggestion concerning monarchical irreligion into his cowardly fear of the Eye of Providence:

> for what can force or guile
> With him, or who deceive his mind, whose eye
> Views all things at one view? He from heaven's highth
> All these our motions vain, sees and derides.
>
> (2.188–91)

Despite the demon's lack of spiritual insight, he possesses dim awareness of divine irony.

Repetition of the figure of the Eye of Providence in the narrator's judgment following the Fall of Adam and Eve styles their disobedience as a proleptic archetype for future acts of rebellion, which presumably include the Gunpowder Plot:

> for what can scape the eye
> Of God all-seeing, or deceive his heart
> Omniscient, who in all things wise and just,
> Hindered not Satan to attempt the mind
> Of man, with strength entire, and free will armed,
> Complete to have discovered and repulsed
> Whatever wiles of foe or seeming friend.
>
> (10.5–11)

Despite its eloquence, Miltonic language recalls Gunpowder Plot satires such as Herring's *Quintessence of Cruelty*, which boasts that divine providence perceives "This desperate work of darkness" and "timely, makes the mischief all appear" (see Figure 21).

Gunpowder Plot tropes infiltrate Raphael's account of the War in Heaven. Although scholars debate whether the battle in its entirety is mock-epic, agreement exists that hyperbolic satire on warfare and the heroic code come into play by the time that the demons invent cannon.[22] The discovery of gunpowder and invention of artillery by the fallen angels are modeled upon *Orlando furioso*, *The Faerie Queene*, and

---

[22] Arnold Stein, *Answerable Style* (Minneapolis: University of Minnesota Press, 1953), pp. 20–23; Lewalski, *Rhetoric*, p. 147.

battles in heaven in Christian epics such as Valvasone's *Angeleide*,[23] but they coexist with more humble native Protestant precedents for their mining operation:

> in a moment up they turned
> Wide the celestial soil, and saw beneath
> The originals of nature in their crude
> Conception; sulphurous and nitrous foam
> They found, they mingled, and with subtle art,
> Concocted and adjusted they reduced
> To blackest grain, and into store conveyed.   (6.509–515)

The establishment of a demonic powder magazine is akin to Guy Fawkes's concealment of ammunition kegs beneath parliament. Smith's *The Powder Treason* (see Figure 7) portrays that event with the flanking inscription, "They have digged a pit for me, and are fallen into the midst of it" (Ps. 7:15). Ward's *To God, In Memory of his Double Deliverance* and the title page of Herring's *Quintessence of Cruelty* portray variations of that scene (see Figures 10, 21). According to Milton's *In Quintum Novembris*, laughter in heaven rings out in response to the emplacement of gunpowder beneath parliament at the instigation of the Pope and the Devil.

Although the loyal angels in *Paradise Lost* share the Father's "controversial merriment" at the prospect of rebellion, according to Archangel Raphael's eye-witness report concerning the War in Heaven, their mood takes a seriocomic turn because they are excluded from the Father's ironic perspective. In a passage that alludes to the Gunpowder Plot, the loyal angels become the butts of a joke when they innocently face cannon fire from what Raphael and the loyalists perceived as "new and strange" devices borne by "triple mounted row of pillars laid / On wheels" (6.571–74):

> while we suspense,
> Collected stood within our thoughts amused,
> Not long.   (6.580–82)

Artillery fire bowls over the loyalists in a ludicrous pratfall:

> with such impetuous fury smote,
> That whom they hit, none on their feet might stand,
> Though standing else as rocks, but down they fell
> By thousands, angel on archangel rolled.   (6.591–94)

Divine mirth has a demonic counterpart when the rebels greet the

---

[23] See Fowler n. on 6.484–90; Revard, *War*, pp. 188 ff.

apparent defeat of the loyalists with amusement. Satan affords a sinister mirror image of the Father when he "beheld their plight,/and to his mates thus in derision called" (6.607–608). In contrast to the derisory humor of the Father and Son, which excludes puns, Satanic wit is grounded upon wordplay. Although puns occur in some of the most elevated segments of *Paradise Lost*, Satan's quibbling call to battle affords an index of degradation because its wordplay is appallingly bad. Walter Savage Landor wittily observes: "It appears then on record that the first overt crime of the refractory angels was punning: they fell rapidly after that."[24] In itself, the contemptuousness of demonic wordplay invokes a satiric perspective.[25]

Described by Raphael as "scoffing in ambiguous words" (6.568), Satan employs anatomical quibbles on "overture" (or hole), "back perverse," and bodily emission: "Heaven witness thou anon, while we discharge/Freely our part" (6.562; 564–65). He shares sportive puns and quips with Belial, who continues "in like gamesome mood" concerning the loyalists' derisory rejection of their negotiating position: "the terms we sent were terms of weight,/Of hard contents, and full of force urged home,/Such as we might perceive amused them all" (6.620–23). Satan leads his cohorts in attempting to make the Father the butt of a cosmic joke:

> So they among themselves in pleasant vein
> Stood scoffing, highthened in their thoughts beyond
> All doubt of victory, eternal might
> To match with their inventions they presumed
> So easy, and of his thunder made a scorn,
> And all his host derided. (6.628–33)

The language used by Raphael (and Satan) to describe the War in Heaven problematizes the traditional reputation of *Paradise Lost* as the outstanding English instance of poetic sublimity by indicating how Miltonic gravity coexists with a vulgar satirical strain. By rupturing epic decorum, the nonstop punning at the outset of the War in Heaven should remind the reader that the jarring mixture of styles, genres, and modes is a hallmark of satire. Although Patrick Hume appreciates the abundance of puns, Joseph Addison's neoclassical principles lead to condemnation: "This passage I look upon to be the most exceptionable in the whole poem, as being nothing else but a string of puns, and those

---

[24] Landor, *Imaginary Conversations*, in *The Complete Works of Walter Savage Landor*, ed. T. Earle Welby, 16 vols. (London: Chapman and Hall, 1927–36), vol. V: p. 258.

[25] Christopher Ricks, *Milton's Grand Style* (Oxford: Clarendon Press, 1963), p. 67.

too very indifferent." Despite his view that "laughter can very seldom be admitted with any decency into an heroic poem," Addison does recognize the comic tenor of the episode: "The only piece of pleasantry in *Paradise Lost*, is where the evil spirits are described as rallying the angels upon the success of their new invented artillery." By contrast, Dr. Johnson, whose distaste for puns is famous, enumerated among the faults of Milton's poem his "play on words, in which he delights too often."[26]

In accordance with Bakhtin's identification of excrement as "gay matter" that simultaneously "degrades and relieves," the anal and oral aggression of the fallen angels represents a return to grotesque alimentary imagery. Puns on defecation and flatulence that fill Satan's boast concerning the "discharge" of ammunition (6.564) and Raphael's eyewitness account of the demons' newly invented cannon are in keeping with the black comic aspect of the War in Heaven. Bakhtin reminds us further that the visceral force of the lower body associates the demons with Rabelaisian appetites for feeding, sex, and evacuation. Laughter at demonic transgressiveness constitutes a paradoxical affirmation of "true" faith, however, because the "negative derisive element" affirms the positive significance of "bodily regeneration and renewal."[27] The fallen angels' unbridled appetites for "food, sex, and violence" may remind us of the Protestant effort to supplant the indulgences of carnival with a year-long practice of "Lenten" abstention.[28]

Carnivalesque language suggests that the devilish invention of cannonry during the War in Heaven involves travesty upon both sacramentality and sexuality. After all, Milton's antiprelatical tracts associate the trope of **false feeding** with the perception that Laudian sacramentalism involves reimposition of the Roman-rite Mass. A topsy-turvy mingling of anatomical quibbles in Satan's description of the invention of artillery may therefore add an antic undertone of ecclesiastical controversy to Milton's imitation of *Orlando furioso* and *The Faerie Queene*:

> These in their dark nativity the deep
> Shall yield us pregnant with infernal flame,
> Which into hollow engines long and round
> Thick rammed, at the other bore with touch of fire

---

[26] Addison, *The Spectator*, no. 279; Johnson, "Life of Johnson," in *Lives of the Poets*, p. 109.

[27] Bakhtin, *Rabelais and His World*, pp. 75, 317–19, 335. See Revard, *War*, pp. 188–91; Wilding, *Dragons Teeth*, p. 179.

[28] Peter Burke, *Popular Culture in Early Modern Europe* (New York University Press, 1978), pp. 18, 186–90, 234, ch. 7, passim.

Dilated and infuriate shall send forth
From far with thundering noise among our foes. . . . (6.482–87)

Bombastic diction filled with anatomical puns distinguishes Raphael's account of the discovery of gunpowder, in continuing emulation of Ariosto and Spenser:

> sulphurous and nitrous foam
> They found, they mingled, and with subtle art
> Concocted and adusted they reduced
> To blackest grain, and into store conveyed:
> Part hidden veins digged up (nor hath this earth
> Entrails unlike) of mineral and stone,
> Whereof to found their engines and their balls
> Of missive ruin.   (6.512–19)

Over and beyond the references to "hollow engines," "entrails," and "balls," the "sulphurous and nitrous" smell of gunpowder reminds us of the latrine. The soil of heaven becomes "pregnant with infernal flame." The ramming of fire at "the other bore" (i.e. the hind end) causes the "dilated" hole to emit "thundering noise."

Raphael's eye-witness description of demonic artillery also involves hyperbolic wordplay upon digestion and excretion, insemination and birth:

> their mouths
> With hideous orifice gaped on us wide,
> Portending hollow truce; at each behind
> A seraph stood, and in his hand a reed
> Stood waving tipped with fire; while we suspense,
> Collected stood within our thoughts amused
> Not long, or sudden all at once their reeds
> Put forth, and to a narrow vent applied
> With nicest touch. Immediate in a flame,
> But soon obscured with smoke, all heaven appeared,
> From those deep throated engines belched, whose roar
> Embowelled with outrageous noise the air,
> And all her entrails tore, disgorging foul
> Their devilish glut.   (6.576–589)

The "disgorging" (or vomiting) and "glut" of the gaping "mouths" and "orifice" of cannon recall the vulgar satirical decorum of Milton's antiprelatical tracts, which associate gluttony, belching, vomiting, and defecation with clerical transgression. Joking reference is made to the hind quarters ("behind," "vent," and "embowelled"). The meticulous application of phallic "reeds" to a "narrow vent" (i.e. a small touch-hole) with "nicest touch" refers literally to the firing of cannon with flaming reeds, but bawdy quibbles add a layer of sexual raillery.[29] Juxtaposition of "her entrails" with sexualized cannonry invites the reader to discover metaphors of polymorphous, debased, and brutal sexuality. The onomatopoetic effects of the belching of "deep throated engines," excretion, and breaking wind recall the problematic puns associated with the "backside of the world," which are at the heart of anticlerical satire in the Paradise of Fools episode.[30]

In sharp contrast to the vulgar humor associated with Satan and the fallen angels, Raphael praises the emergence of Abdiel as a sarcastic counterforce at the outset of rebellion. Calling for loyalty to the Father, his uncompromising defiance of Satan's "argument blasphemous, false and proud" (5.809) makes him a "Protestant angel"[31] who, "Encompassed round with foes," upholds "the cause/Of truth" (5.876; 6.31–32). When the flaming seraph replies to Satan "with retorted scorn" (5.906), he dramatizes identification of satire with casting invective "scorn upon the scorner" according to Milton's *Apology for Smectymnuus* (*CPW* 1: 875). Heavy alliteration intensifies the appropriation of the contemporary idiom of antiformalistic attack on establishmentarian worship in Abdiel's challenge:

> So spake the seraph Abdiel faithful found,
> Among the faithless, faithful only he;
> Among innumerable false, unmoved,
> Unshaken, unseduced, unterrified
> His loyalty he kept, his love, his **zeal**.   (5.896–900)

Abdiel's fervency attests to his distinguishing attribute of **zeal** (5.805, 849), which accords with definition of that trait in *Christian Doctrine* as an "eager desire to sanctify the divine name, together with a feeling of indignation against things which tend to the violation or contempt of religion" (*CPW* 6: 697). Conservative opponents deployed the term **zeal** to stigmatize sectarian enthusiasts. Abdiel's "flame of **zeal** severe" (5.807) recalls St. Peter's jeremiad against "false" pastors in *Lycidas* and

---

[29] In seventeenth-century usage, **vent** meant anus, vulva, or touch-hole of a firearm, in addition to the standard senses of slit or aperture (*OED* "touch-hole"; "vent" n2 II.9.b). On usage of the phallic "reed" in seventeenth-century religious poetry, see Michael C. Schoenfeldt, *Prayer and Power: George Herbert and Renaissance Courtship* (University of Chicago Press, 1991), p. 241. See also Shawcross, *Self*, p. 325, nn. 30–34.

[30] On the use of language related to eating, excretion, and sex to suggest Satanic debasement, see Lieb, *Dialectics*, pp. 118–21, 167–72; Flannagan n. on 6.576–89.

[31] Loewenstein, *Drama*, p. 104.

the sharp words of the antiprelatical pamphlets, which sanction invective satire as a righteous antidote to religious luke-warmness. His words reinscribe "the spirit of seventeenth-century resistance writing and its radical Protestant roots."[32]

Looking like a proleptic type for the Miltonic ideal of an unsalaried volunteer clergy, Abdiel articulates a dissenting credo that opposes his obedient "ministering" to the paradoxical "servitude" of rebel angels (6.178, 182):

> there be who faith
> Prefer, and piety to God, though then
> To thee not visible, when I alone
> Seemed in thy world erroneous to **dissent**
> From all: my **sect** thou seest, now learn too late
> How few sometimes may know, when thousands err. (6.143–48)

Often identified with "Milton's own personal feelings,"[33] Abdiel's words could not be more explicitly contemporaneous, because he advocates sectarian **dissent** as one who has severed all ties with formalistic religious observance. **Dissent** supplanted the term "nonconformity" during the Restoration.[34] Throughout the mid-seventeenth century, royalists employed the other term used by Abdiel in fashioning his identity, **sect**, to stigmatize opponents of episcopalian church polity (*CPW* 3: 348).

Recreating the slippery reversibility of propagandistic language, the accusations and counteraccusations of Satan and Abdiel bring contemporary religious strife to mind. If we interpret the poem in light of Milton's *Of True Religion* and antiformalistic tracts, Abdiel's words suggest a definition of the invisible church made up of the body of Christian believers, as opposed to the visible church tainted by formalism.[35] Seraphic Abdiel defies a gathering of rebels who meet "in **synod**" according to Satan (6.156). Denoting a church council attended by bishops or elders, that ecclesiastical term recalls the original gathering of rebel angels in "close recess and secret conclave" (see Chapter 3). Abdiel plays the role of a "true" dissenter who attacks the imposition of innovative "worship" because it constitutes servile obedience to satanic tyranny. Militant Protestants accused the Churches of Rome and

[32] David Loewenstein, " 'An Ambiguous Monster': Representing Rebellion in Milton's Polemics and *Paradise Lost*," *HLQ* 55 (1992), pp. 297, 307, 310. See also Kranidas, "Rhetoric," pp. 423–32; Guillory, *Authority*, pp. 101, 108.   [33] Hill, *MER*, p. 370; see *ME* 1:11.
[34] Keeble, *Culture*, pp. 41–45. See also Lieb, *Poetics*, p. 290; Radzinowicz, "Politics," p. 221.
[35] Prynne, *Canterbury's Doom* (1664), B2ᵛ.

England of introducing religious innovations that lacked scriptural warrant.

Abdiel's defiant obedience to the Father amidst a multitude that far outnumbers him constitutes an open testimonial of faith that accords with evangelical practice. The dynamic recalls the New Testament model for martyrdom, St. Stephen, whose defense of newborn Christianity in a speech before the Sanhedrin, the council of Jewish leaders, led to his stoning to death, according to Acts 7. The term "martyr" is derived from μάρτυς (Greek for "witness"), which acquired the sense of one who is willing to undergo suffering to the point of death after testifying to faith before a public tribunal. Abdiel's stance recalls the account in *Defensio Secunda* of Milton's insistence upon attesting to his religious convictions at Rome, despite a rumored Jesuit plot against his life:

What I was, if any man inquired, I concealed from no one. For almost two more months, in the very stronghold of the Pope, if anyone attacked the orthodox religion, I openly, as before, defended it. (*CPW* 4: 619)

The rebels' ultimate defeat elicits the Father's "smiling" scorn when he shares with the Son a mocking jest. The Eye of Providence witnesses the Son's victory, which marks a generic shift from satire to tragedy of damnation contained within the overarching pattern of divine comedy. The Son leads the final charge:

> forth rushed with whirlwind sound
> The chariot of paternal deity,
> Flashing thick flames, wheel within wheel undrawn,
> It self instinct with spirit, but convoyed
> By four cherubic shapes, four faces each
> Had wondrous, as with stars their bodies all
> And wings were set with eyes, with eyes the wheels.   (6.749–55)

Ezekiel 1 is the scriptural source for decoration of the chariot with eyes symbolic of providential vision. In a poem engaged with the polemical rhetoric of revolutionary pamphlets and broadsheets, however, that passage also recalls one of the most memorable tropes in Milton's polemical prose. According to *An Apology for Smectymnuus*, Jesus Christ drives the Chariot of Zeal as an "invincible warrior" who, "shaking loosely the slack reins drives over the heads of scarlet prelates, and such as are insolent to maintain traditions, bruising their stiff necks under his flaming wheels" (*CPW* 1: 900–901).

Raphael's seriocomic narration of the abject defeat of Satan and the rebel angels adds a layer of irony to the episode in Book 4 where cherubim apprehend Satan as they patrol Eden by night. Ithuriel and Zephon arrest him crouching in a ridiculously toad-like posture at the ear of Eve.[36] The simile attached to Satan's capture combines a farcical recollection of flatulence at the Paradise of Fools with anticipation of the nationalistic conviction that the Jesuitical Devil invented the Gunpowder Plot:

> As when a spark
> Lights on a heap of nitrous powder, laid
> Fit for the tun some magazine to store
> Against a rumoured war, the smutty grain
> With sudden blaze diffused, inflames the air:
> So started up in his own shape the fiend.   (4.814–19)

Satan's resumption of his usual appearance is akin to the explosion of a magazine crammed with gunpowder, like the powder store built by the rebels on the ground of heaven. On a more grandiose scale, the effect recalls the dramatic use of "magic dust," presumably an explosive powder, in *Comus* (line 165). The scene recalls satirical engravings such as the frontispiece of John Vicars's *The Quintessence of Cruelty*, which portrays Guy Fawkes accompanied by the Devil alongside tuns (i.e. barrels) of gunpowder. They remain unexploded, however, beneath parliament because of "Heaven's all-seeing-eye, which deepest pits espies" (Figure 21).[37] We should recall the epic narrator's insistence that only divine providence can see through hypocritical disguisings.

The ensuing scene takes on the character of a farcical morality play in which Satan undergoes an involuntary costume change to play the role of a melodramatic Vice in conflict with sober angelic Virtues. Aided by internal stage directions, the interrogation proceeds by means of highly ironic dialogue that satirizes Satan's continuing self-deception, which leads him to assume a variety of indefensible positions. The angels' debasement of Satanic claims to heroic stature complements the reverberation of laughter in heaven at demonic intrigue.

That the cherubim are only "half amazed" indicates that they feign surprise at their apprehension of "the grisly king" (4.820–21), who has lost his unfallen grandeur. In tune with his prideful character, Satan delivers bombastic words "filled with scorn" to lowly cherubim over whom he once lorded as an archangel in heaven:

---

[36] See the conclusion of Chapter 5, above. Present discussion of Satan's arrest builds upon conversation with Stephen R. Honeygosky.

[37] Notice the close proximity of hell mouth at the base of Fig. 7 to the inset portrayals of Guy Fawkes's emplacement of gunpowder in the next-to-last level.

> Know ye not me? Ye knew me once no mate
> For you, there sitting where ye durst not soar;
> Not to know me argues yourselves unknown,
> The lowest of your throng. (4.828–31)

Countering "scorn with scorn," Zephon's "grave rebuke" (4.844) mocks the loss of Satan's resplendent "glory":

> Think not, revolted spirit, thy shape the same,
> Or undiminished brightness, to be known
> As when thou stood'st in heaven upright and pure.
>
> (4.835–37)

Satan's dumbfounded silence offers insight into the old debate concerning his heroic stature or lack thereof. The Devil's "abashed" response to his interrogators' sarcastic "scorn" demonstrates his own painful recognition that incapacity to outwit them diminishes his stature (4.846).

Although Satan claims that he willingly submits to capture because it is beneath his dignity to fight with low-ranking cherubim, he feigns an "undaunted" demeanor and desire to battle their commander:

> "If I must contend," said he,
> "Best with the best, the sender not the sent,
> Or all at once; more glory will be won,
> Or less be lost."

Articulating willingness to engage in single combat, a cherubic riposte exposes Satanic cowardice:

> "Thy fear," said Zephon bold,
> "Will save us trial what the least can do
> Single against thee wicked, and thence weak."

The butt of a cosmic joke, Satan mutely undergoes arrest and interrogation: "The fiend replied not, overcome with rage" (4.851–57).

Brought before Gabriel, the commander of the angelic guards who was once his peer, Satan continues his melodramatic delivery "with contemptuous brow" and "frowning stern" (4.885, 924). By contrast, the archangel delivers a cooly sarcastic rebuke, "disdainfully half smiling" (4.903), that punctures Satan's lying confession that he deserted his followers to flee from torment in hell:

> Courageous chief,
> The first in flight from pain, hadst thou alleged
> To thy deserted host this cause of flight,
> Thou surely hadst not come sole fugitive. (4.920–23)

When Satan shifts to an explanation that he was a "faithful leader" in volunteering to come alone as a solitary spy, Gabriel shows greater perception than Uriel in attacking his opponent as a "sly hypocrite" (4.933, 957):

> To say and straight unsay, pretending first
> Wise to fly pain, professing next the spy,
> Argues no leader but a liar traced,
> Satan, and couldst thou faithful add? O name,
> A sacred name of faithfulness profaned.   (4.947–51)

Angelic mockery supplies a reductio ad absurdum that destroys the last vestiges of pretence to Satanic heroism. Like laughter in heaven, angelic mirth calls into question belief that Satan is never ridiculous. In a final hypocritical deception, the fallen angel puffs himself up in preparation for battle with the loyal angels:

> On the other side Satan alarmed
> Collecting all his might dilated stood,
> Like Teneriff or Atlas unremoved:
> His stature reached the sky, and on his crest
> Sat horror plumed.   (4.985–89)

When the Father gauges the respective merits of peace versus fighting in "his golden scales" in heaven, however, Gabriel faithfully defers to the weightier claim of the former. In accordance with providential design, the loyal angels permit Satan to flee "Murmuring, and with him fled the shades of night" (4.1015). That is his last appearance prior to Book 9. If the reader were to recall his previous appearance, it would add a darkly ironic tinge to his final temptation of Eve. Angelic amusement at Satan distances the reader from the imminent Fall of Eve and Adam and highlights the centrality of divine comedy within the satirical design of *Paradise Lost*.[38]

Through the unfolding of divine judgment following the Fall, the Father has the last laugh at Satan and his cohorts when they undergo serpentine metamorphosis. Despite Satan's expectation of "high applause" when he reports to his followers upon return to hell, they welcome his final dramatic performance with a "dismal universal hiss, the sound/of public scorn" (10.505; 508–509). In an amusing inversion of divine laughter, sibilant puns resound in Pandaemonium: "But hiss for hiss returned with forked tongue/To forked tongue, for now were all transformed/Alike, to serpents" (10.518–20). In what may imply parody

---

[38] See Lewalski, *Rhetoric*, pp. 119–20, 222–23.

of the calendar of ecclesiastical holy days that dissenters despised, the serpentine transformation is "yearly enjoined, some say" in an "annual humbling" that serves to "dash their pride" (10.575–77).

Demonic hissing forces Satan off stage in a manner that parallels Milton's youthful satirization of Laudian religion and the monarch who authorized it. Readers of the antiprelatical tracts might recall the meta-theatrical attack in *Animadversions* on "ceremonies, liturgies, and tyrannies which God and man are now ready to explode and hiss out of the land." In a similarly sardonic vein, *Eikonoklastes* applauds the bloody exit of a player king, Charles I, to the accompaniment of "the general voice of the people almost hissing him and his ill-acted regality off the stage" (*CPW* 1: 662; 3: 355). Regardless of whether Satan exits as a farcical comic or melodramatic tragedian, the reader never again encounters him in *Paradise Lost*.

William Empson has highlighted tensions, ambiguities, and contradictions built into anthropomorphic tropes that express derisory mockery of Satan and his allies by the Father and the Son. An understanding of contemporary religious polemics enriches, and complicates, our understanding of that deeply problematic aspect of *Paradise Lost*. Laughter in heaven conveyed polemical immediacy to many seventeenth-century readers. That trope corresponds to contemporary Gunpowder Plot tracts and visual satires, which represent Guy Fawkes and his associates undergoing ironic scrutiny by the Eye of Providence. Possible objects of attack include, but are not limited to, the Gunpowder plotters, Jesuit priests, foreign powers, and crypto-Catholic monarchs. By contrast, the mocking aspect of divine spectatorship is absent from the account of prelapsarian Eden, where the Eye of Providence witnesses the domestic existence of Adam and Eve in which actions ranging from eating to lovemaking are charged with numinous significance. Nonetheless, intense dramatic irony infuses divine vision of the temptation of Eve and Adam and their discovery of idolatry in Eden.

CHAPTER 7

Miltonic transubstantiation

Archangel Raphael's **transubstantiation** of the meal served by Eve, which he shares with Adam at a grassy table in Eden, contributes both to a previously unrecognized layer of religious controversy and to a rather surprising theology of Holy Communion and marriage in *Paradise Lost*. Critics have reduced the subtlety of a range of highly mediated, and often parodic, scriptural allusions in an effort to recover straightforward liturgical references in the text.[1] The meal is a profound instance of "true" feeding that precedes Adam and Eve's disobedience, when they eat forbidden fruit from the Tree of Knowledge. Affording an opportunity for partisan attack on the Roman-rite Mass and related liturgical practices in the Church of England, alimentary concerns ramify into a network of biblical connections concerning Holy Communion and wedlock; eating and marital relations; and the union of Christ the Bridegroom with his Spouse, who may represent the church or the individual soul. Within this complicated figural scheme, angelic **transubstantiation** plays a fundamental role in the Miltonic definition of "true" communion. Drawing upon the overlooked engagement of *Paradise Lost* with sacramental celebration, the present chapter clarifies our understanding of the poem's participation in the violent strife that religious communities engaged in during the mid-seventeenth century.

Although Milton's position on the Eucharist is distant from Trent and relatively close to Geneva and Zurich, it does not correspond to any particular liturgy. The poem's supposed liturgical allusions actually involve scriptural texts used to describe unconstrained modes of prelapsarian worship from which devotional practices of the latter-day church represent a deviation. Making light of **transubstantiation**, presenta-

[1] E.g. Thomas B. Stroup, *Religious Rite and Ceremony in Milton's Poetry* (Lexington, KY: University of Kentucky Press, 1968), p. 64, and passim. He ignores Milton's hostility to set prayer and liturgical ceremonialism, by contrast to Honeygosky, *Milton's House of God*, pp. 201–12, 222–28; and Guibbory, *Ceremony and Community*, pp. 191–92, 205.

tion of the Edenic meal specifically undermines the declaration of *The Canons and Decrees of the Council of Trent*:

And because that Christ, our Redeemer, declared that which he offered under the species of bread to be truly his own body, therefore has it ever been a firm belief in the Church of God, and this holy Synod doth now declare it anew, that, by the consecration of the bread and of the wine, a conversion is made of the whole substance of the bread into the substance of the body of Christ our Lord, and of the whole substance of the wine into the substance of his blood; which conversion is, by the holy Catholic Church, suitably and properly called **Transubstantiation**.[2]

Among Protestant ideologues, belief in the transformation of bread and wine into the body and blood of Christ was a profound theological "error." Milton follows Calvin and Arminius on sacraments: for all three, sacraments are signs or seals, which do not, as in Catholic belief, directly confer grace. He viewed the Catholic position as idolatrous.

Eucharistic parody in *Paradise Lost* is deeply engaged with contemporary religion and politics, notably Milton's own proposition in *Of True Religion*: "But first we must remove their [i.e. recusants'] idolatry, and all the furniture thereof, whether idols, or the Mass wherein they adore their God under bread and wine" (*CPW* 8: 431–32). That wording recalls Milton's youthful mockery of "gods, made of bread" (*Panifici Dei*) in *In Quintum Novembris* (line 56). Contemporary Protestant pamphlets equated **transubstantiation** and idolatry.[3] The uncompromising zeal of Milton's 1673 tract suggests that revisions in the second edition of *Paradise Lost* (1674) allude in a way not previously recognized to the contemporary controversy over **transubstantiation** triggered by the 1669 announcement of the conversion to Roman Catholicism of James, Duke of York. Four years later his betrothal to Mary of Modena triggered the passage of the Test Act, which required all office holders and members of the royal establishment to receive Holy Communion according to the rite of the Church of England, to take the Oath of Supremacy, and to subscribe to a formal declaration that they "believe that in the sacrament of the Lord's Supper there is not any **transubstantiation** of the elements of bread and wine into the body and blood of Christ at or after the consecration thereof."[4] The Duke's refusal to

---

[2] Session 13 (11 October 1551), Chapter 4, in Philip Schaff, ed. and trans., *The Creeds of Christendom*, 3 vols. (New York: Harper & Bros., 1905), vol. II, p. 130. For an identical definition, see Thomas Aquinas, *Summa Theologica*, 3a, 75.4. Apparently coined by Hildebert of Tours (c. 1080), **transubstantiation** came into widespread use in the twelfth century. See Grossman, *Authors*, pp. 104–12.

[3] E.g. Edward Stillingfleet, *Discourse Concerning Idolatry* (1671); Henry More, "An Antidote Against Idolatry," pt. 2 of *An Exposition of the Seven Epistles to the Seven Churches Together with a Brief Discourse of Idolatry, with Application to the Church of Rome* (1669). See *CPW* 8: 432, n. 60.

[4] Quoted from *OED* "transubstantiation" 2. See Keeble, *Culture*, p. 57.

subscribe to the Test Act and his institution of the Mass within the Chapel Royal after his accession as James II were contributory factors in the chain of events that culminated in the Revolution of 1688.

Eve's preparation of a meal "to please/True appetite" (5.304–305) with Adam appears to encapsulate polemical issues that remained alive into the Restoration. Engaging in implicit theological debate, the narrator takes an unorthodox stance that assigns corporeality and appetite to angels:

> So down they sat,
> And to their viands fell, nor seemingly
> The angel, nor in mist, the common gloss
> Of theologians, but with keen despatch
> Of real hunger, and concoctive heat
> To **transubstantiate**; what redounds, transpires
> Through spirits with ease   (5.433–39)

Disclaiming the use of metaphor, the narrator propounds that angels, despite their superior spirituality, are material in nature. That passage hinges upon Milton's monistic materialism, whereby matter and spirit do not undergo separation as they do in Plato's theory of forms or the theology of St. Paul. Milton grounds his metaphysics upon belief that the whole of creation *de deo* (not *ex nihilo*) constitutes a mixture, in varying degrees of purity or corruption, of spiritual and material being. For Milton, it appears that both God and angels have a corporeal nature. Raphael eats earthly food and "transpires" into air what remains after digestion. Although they are normally masculine (10.890), angels can change sex at will (1.424) and, as Raphael informs Adam, enjoy corporeal lovemaking in "eminence, and obstacle find none/Of membrane, joint or limb, exclusive bars" (8.624–25).[5]

Eve's serving of an uncooked fruitarian meal—"No fear lest dinner cool" – and unfermented grape juice anticipates the Lord's Supper as a memorial ceremony that eliminates reference to **transubstantiation** of the elements of bread and wine:

> fruit of all kinds, in coat,
> Rough, or smooth rined, or bearded husk, or shell
> She gathers, tribute large, and on the board
> Heaps with unsparing hand; for drink the grape
> She crushes, inoffensive must, and meaths

---

[5] *CD* 1.7 and 13; *CPW* 6: 305–10, 319, 408. See *ME* 5: 122–23; Fallon, *Milton among the Philosophers*, ch. 5; John Rogers, *The Matter of Revolution: Science, Poetry, and Politics in the Age of Milton* (Ithaca, NY: Cornell University Press, 1996), pp. 125–26, 129, 173–74; William Kolbrener, *Milton's Warring Angels: A Study of Critical Engagements* (Cambridge University Press, 1997), pp. 86–93.

From many a berry, and from sweet kernels pressed
She tempers dulcet creams, nor these to hold
Wants her fit vessels pure, then strews the ground
With rose and odours from the shrub unfumed.   (5.341–49)[6]

Mention of the **board** on which Eve prepares food suggests a possible reference to the Communion table as "the Lord's board." Incense, the chalice, and other instruments of the Mass afford a conspicuous contrast to the "fit vessels pure" with which Eve prepares the meal. She refills vessels reminiscent of the simple wide-mouthed beakers (or wooden cups) used in the administration of Communion in Puritan parishes, as opposed to the smaller, decorative chalices restricted to priestly use in the Mass, where communicants received one species only (the wafer):

Mean while at **table** Eve
Ministered naked, and their flowing cups
With pleasant liquors crowned.   (5.443–45)

The purity of her vessels inverts the poisonousness of the "baneful cup" of Comus and the "charmed cup" of his mother, Circe. The reputation of his father, Bacchus, as the first to crush "the sweet poison of misused wine" from "out the purple grape," further hints at an earlier parody of transubstantiation. Moreover, Protestant commentators conflated Circe's golden cup with the Whore of Babylon's "cup of gold . . . full of abominations, and filthiness of her fornication" (Rev. 17:4; compare Figure 15).[7]

Scholars have never noted how the positioning of **tables** both in Eden, where a hungry angel **transubstantiates** food, and in heaven corresponds to long-standing contention over the celebration of the Lord's Supper. Previously unnoticed repetition of the word **table** focuses attention upon religious controversy.[8] After all, Milton's lifelong attack on "idolatry" affirmed that the Lord's Supper is a communal meal shared at the Lord's **Table**, rather than a Eucharistic celebration at a high **altar**.

[6] Compare the parody of Catholic sacramentalism in Edmund Spenser's Temple of Isis in *FQ* 5.7.4–17. See *SPART*, pp. 106–107.

[7] *Comus*, lines 46–47, 53, 524. The "charmed cup" of Comus (line 51) associates him further with both Duessa, who carries a cup filled with "secret poison" as she rides the Seven-headed Beast (*FQ* 1.8.6, 14), and Acrasia, whose "charmd" cup transforms men into beasts (2.1.55). See also Fletcher's *The Locusts* 2.29–32. John Gee links the enchanted chalice of heathenish drugs and Lamian superstition of the Mass with Circe's power "to metamorphose men into bears and asses" in *The Foot out of the Snare* (1624), p. 36.

[8] In addition to many references in the poem itself, the Argument to *PL* 5 added in the fourth issue of 1668 calls attention to Raphael's joining Adam in "discourse at **table**." The single reference to **tables** in *PR* involves a satirical barb against the Mass (4.114–19).

In line with many references to **tables** in sixteenth- and seventeenth-century anti-Mass tracts, we may interpret Edenic and heavenly **tables** as "pure" originals that underwent displacement when Archbishop Laud restored the high **altar** enclosed with railings in the elevated chancel, the eastern end of a church reserved for use by the clergy. After his deposition, the House of Commons immediately ordered authorities to remove "the Communion **table** from the east end of the church, chapel, or chancel . . . [and] take away the rails, and level the chancels, as heretofore they were, before the late innovations."[9] The accessibility of **tables** in *Paradise Lost* offers a non-ironic counterpart to the savage satire on the Laudian **altar** in *Of Reformation*:

The **table** of Communion now become a **table** of separation [that] stands like an exalted platform upon the brow of the choir, fortified with bulwark, and barricade, to keep off the profane touch of the laicks, whilst the obscene, and surfeited priest scruples not to paw, and mammock the sacramental bread, as familiarly as his tavern basket.[10]

Recalling Milton's antiprelatical tracts, the many references to **tables** in *Paradise Lost* appear to reinscribe accusations that High Church sacramentalism or the Roman Catholic Mass objectify spiritual truths that the Protestant Communion service renders internal and subjective. When he ordered the replacement of communion tables with high altars (see Figure 24), Archbishop Laud overturned a worship service imposed under Elizabeth I in a form substantially the same as that in the second prayer book of Edward VI (1552). Aside from the momentous shift of translating the order of divine service from Latin into English, the first *Book of Common Prayer* (1549) had introduced few changes in the Sarum Use, the medieval liturgy used in the diocese of Salisbury, other than deletion of the prayer of oblation at which the priest withdrew into the chancel and turned his back to the congregation in order to utter the words of consecration ("hoc est enim corpus meum") at the elevation of the host in a reenactment of the Crucifixion as a repeated sacrifice.[11]

That rite of **transubstantiation** had taken place before a high **altar** overshadowed by a theatrical image of Jesus hanging from a cross at the east end of each church. Although the first English prayer book

---

[9] *Die Mercurii 8 September 1641* (1641). See also Hill, *MER*, pp. 82–83.
[10] *CPW* 1: 547–48. It was Calvinistic practice to "fence" the table *figuratively* by usage and ministerial precept against notorious sinners. See the Middleburg Liturgy (1586), ed. Bard Thompson in *Liturgies of the Western Church* (Cleveland: World Publishing 1962), pp. 335–36. See also *OED* "altar" 2a; and Corns, *Uncloistered Virtue*, pp. 121–22.   [11] *Liturgies*, ed. Thompson, p. 74.

eliminated elevation of the host and instituted the sacrament in two species, it retained other elements of the medieval rite such as the kneeling of communicants at **altar** rails that excluded them from the "holy" space of the chancel. Revised in response to the outrage of proto-Puritan radicals, the 1552 prayer book and its Elizabethan and Jacobean successors moved closer to a Zwinglian model by altering the axis of worship through substitution of an unenclosed Communion **table** in the nave (main body of the church) for newly demolished **altars**. The stipulation that the minister stand on the north side of the Communion **table** ensured that he face the surrounding congregation and preside over a communal meal on the model of what militant Protestants understood as the practice of the primitive church (Figure 23). The bishops did retain kneeling at Communion despite radical objections that it implied adoration or **transubstantiation**.[12]

The Elizabethan worship service remained in place until the implementation of Caroline "innovations" in religion, which provide an immediate context for the polemical cast of the Edenic meal in *Paradise Lost*. Puritan resistance to the Laudian restoration of "idolatrous" crucifixes, images of the Virgin Mary and saints, and stained-glass windows was dwarfed by the outcry against the replacement of the Communion table with an altar (Figure 24). Those externals were accompanied by priestly genuflections toward the altar, which included crossing, kneeling, and prostration.[13] Laud's return to liturgical practices banned nearly a century earlier fueled exaggerated fears among Milton and his fellow antiformalists that England was returning to Roman Catholicism. Two orders of worship were in use during the period when Milton composed *Paradise Lost*: the Westminster Assembly's *Directory for the Public Worship of God* (1644) and the *Book of Common Prayer* restored in 1660. Consisting of liturgical prohibitions and instructions to ministers, the *Directory* is not a prayer book per se. It institutes rules for a simple Communion service in which the minister and communicants, seated around a **table**, share bread and drink wine from large cups.[14] The *Directory* articulates "a consistently high doctrine of the real spiritual presence of Christ in the action mediated by the Holy Spirit, and a true means of grace." The prayer book of Charles II, on the other hand,

---

[12] Douglas Harrison, ed., *The First and Second Prayer Books of King Edward VI* (London: Dent, 1968), p. 377. See *ERL*, pp. 30, 134–38.

[13] Davies, *Worship and Theology in England* (Grand Rapids, MI: W. B. Eerdmans, 1996), vol. II, p. 287.

[14] *The Westminster Directory Being a Directory for the Public Worship of God in the Three Kingdoms*, ed. Ian Breward (Bramcote, Notts.: Grove, 1980), Grove Liturgical Studies, vol. XXI, pp. 21–23.

Figure 23   Celebration of the Lord's Supper at a Communion Table in the Nave.
A Course of Catechizing (1674).

ST. PAUL'S CATHEDRAL.

Figure 24   Laudian Restoration of the High Altar Separated from the Nave by a Railing. *St. Paul's Cathedral*, from J. D. Chambers, *Divine Worship in England*.

reestablished controversial elements of Laudian worship, notably railed-off altars and chancel screens, and the use of sacerdotal gestures, crucifixes, religious images, candlesticks, and organ music. Despite the official doctrine of the True Presence, which accords with Calvin's view that the real spiritual presence of Christ's body and blood does not entail Roman Catholic transubstantiation, ritualistic practices suggested adoration.[15]

By contrast to the predominantly vernacular vocabulary used to describe Eve's preparation of the Edenic meal, the Medieval Latin derivation of **transubstantiate** and other words pertaining to digestive and excretory processes parody Scholastic theology and medieval sacramentalism. Indeed, Patrick Hume defines **transubstantiate** and **transubstantiation** as "barbarous Latin words that have much disturbed the world" (n. on 5.438).[16] Raphael's explanation of angelic corporeality and alimentation involves a corresponding lexical shift from vernacular sensation to Latinate digestion:

> both contain
> Within them every lower faculty
> Of sense, whereby they hear, see, smell, touch, taste,
> Tasting concoct, digest, assimilate,
> And corporeal to incorporeal turn. (5.409–413)

The flatulence puns of the Paradise of Fools and War in Heaven constitute inversions of the pure alimentation of Raphael and Adam, and the service of Holy Communion that it anticipates. The narrator insists upon the blamelessness of alimentation per se because Raphael's concoction corresponds to Communion without **transubstantiation** in its latter-day theological sense. The text draws a distinction between "true" spiritual **transubstantiation** and the alleged confusion of Catholic theology. Raphael's body thus transmits a satirical message without being implicated in or tainted by it. The dynamic recalls Moloch's status at the head of the pagan idols, where the middle term of the associative chain of Moloch–St. Peter–Pope escapes contamination (Chapter 3).

Focusing attention on Eve's placement of food atop an earthen **table,** verbal repetition in Raphael's salutation highlights its engagement with linguistic practices of religious propaganda:

[15] Davies, *Worship*, vol. II, pp. 319, 386–92. As a Commonwealth censor, Milton approved the *Racovian Catechism* (1652), which asserts that the Lord's Supper observes a purely commemorative function (C6ᵛ, H6ᵛ). See *OER* 2: 78; 4: 170.

[16] On Eucharistic parody in *Gargantua and Pantagruel*, see Bakhtin, *Rabelais and His World*, p. 379.

> Hail mother of mankind, whose fruitful womb
> Shall fill the world more numerous with thy sons
> Than with these various fruits the trees of God
> Have heaped this **table**. Raised of grassy turf
> Their **table** was, and mossy seats had round,
> And on her ample square from side to side
> All autumn piled, though spring and autumn here
> Danced hand in hand.   (5.388–95)

Humbly domestic language masks a dense web of theological issues associated with the Incarnation (the embodiment of divinity in Jesus' human form). Raphael's greeting to Eve, "Hail mother of mankind," prefigures that event. His salutation is proleptic of the *Ave Maria* (Luke 1:28), Archangel Gabriel's greeting to the Virgin Mary, later used as a Roman-Catholic devotional formula (see Flannagan n. on 5.387). Although Protestants oppose any diversion to Mary of praise that they accord to Jesus Christ as the sole intercessor between the human and divine orders, Catholics and Protestants agree that Eve's motherhood anticipates that of the Virgin Mary and that the Incarnation involves the virtue of humility. It is difficult to conceive of a more palpable link between the Edenic dinner and commemoration of Christ's sacrifice in Holy Communion than the typology of Jesus as the second Adam born of Mary as the second Eve.

Even the seated position of Adam and Raphael hints at one of two postures acceptable to Puritans for receiving Communion under both kinds, bread and wine. Although they also accepted Communion while standing, kneeling suggested "idolatrous" adoration.[17] Puritan hostility to kneeling was a polemical issue during the revolutionary era. Furthermore, in an ironic reversal of Satan's predilection for disguises, Eve's naked ministry may afford a wry glance at the doctrine of the priesthood of all believers and Puritan hostility to a vested clergy. Public nudity carried a polemical charge during the mid-seventeenth century, when critics claimed that the Adamites went naked in order to assert recovery of unfallen innocence and thinkers such as John Hall and John Bunyan advocated feminine nakedness as a lesser provocation than wearing clothing.[18] Such views may echo in the Miltonic narrator's claim that the first couple's nakedness "eased the putting off/These troublesome **disguises** which we wear" (4.739–40).

The grassy **table** in Eden corresponds to the placement of **tables** in

---

[17] See Davies, *Worship*, vol. II, pp. 189–94, 200–210, 305–308, 322; and *TRI*, p. 119, fig. 32.
[18] Christopher Hill, *The World Turned Upside Down: Radical Ideas During the English Revolution* (New York: Viking, 1973), p. 253.

heaven according to Raphael's narration of the War in Heaven, when he describes the banqueting of angels in celebration of the Father's exaltation of the Son:

> Forthwith from dance to sweet repast they turn
> Desirous; all in circles as they stood,
> **Tables** are set, and on a sudden piled
> With angels' food, and rubied nectar flows
> In pearl, in diamond, and massy gold,
> Fruit of delicious vines, the growth of heaven.
> On flowers reposed, and with fresh flowerets crowned,
> They eat, they drink, and with refection sweet
> Are filled, before the all bounteous king, who showered
> With copious hand, rejoicing in their joy.   (5.630–39)

Hume annotates an allusion to Jesus' words to his disciples during the Last Supper, which afford the proto-liturgy for Holy Communion: "These celestial vines seem to allude to that of our Savior, I will not drink henceforth of the fruit of the vine, until the day when I drink it new with you in my Father's kingdom" (Matt. 26:29).

   An important revision in the second edition of *Paradise Lost* highlights an engagement with topical controversy concerning celebration of the Lord's Supper. Milton's revision coincided roughly with the 1673 publication of *Of True Religion* during the controversy over the Test Act, with its anti-transubstantiation oath. The 1674 edition of *Paradise Lost* substitutes the following passage for the above-quoted wording of 5.637–39 in the first edition:

> They eat, they drink, and **in communion** sweet
> **Quaff immortality and joy, secure**
> **Of surfeit where full measure only bounds**
> **Excess,** before the all bounteous king, who showered
> With copious hand, rejoicing in their joy.   (5.637–41)

The shift from **refection** to **communion** renders explicit the topical allusion. The revision praises Holy Communion as a worldly analogue to angelic dining, in particular Raphael's **transubstantiation** of his Edenic meal.

   The revision reflects a strikingly complicated concern with **surfeit** or **excess**. Surely the loyal angels may not eat all that they want on the ground that "full measure only bounds / Excess." The text instead indicates that they are secure against surfeiting because "full measure" (i.e. moderation) does no more than bound excess. By contrast, the rebel

angels refuse to govern unruly appetites. The passage recalls Adam and
Eve's general anxiety about excess (especially in the growth of the
garden) in all of the Edenic books of *Paradise Lost*. The loyal angels share
their concern. Because taste is a figure for knowledge (the poem contains
many puns on "sapience," a word derived from Lat. *sapere*, "to taste or
know"), moderation in eating invokes the core issue of obedience versus
sin.

In Milton's time, the range of meanings for **surfeit** included transgression or fault (words that may refer to sin) in addition to excess,
gluttonous indulgence, indigestion, nausea, and disease brought on by
gluttony.[19] During after dinner dialogue, Raphael's temperate counsel
that Adam and Eve seek "knowledge within bounds" is thus connected
to both Edenic and heavenly meals:

> But knowledge is as food, and needs no less
> Her temperance over appetite, to know
> In **measure** what the mind may well contain,
> Oppresses else with **surfeit**, and soon turns
> Wisdom to folly, as nourishment to wind.
>
> (7.120, 126–30)

Recalling the flatulent windiness of *Lycidas*, the Paradise of Fools, and
the War in Heaven, that speech echoes Raphael's concern with
measure versus **surfeit** in describing the heavenly banquet. The
poem's third and final instance of **surfeit** is in Michael's attack on the
immoderation of those "In triumph and luxurious wealth." A topical
stab at the royal and ecclesiastical establishment of Restoration England
appears to inform the archangel's disdain for indulgence in "pleasure,
ease, and sloth, / **Surfeit**, and lust" by those who have achieved "Fame
in the world, high titles, and rich prey" (11.788, 793–95).

Allusion to priestly ministration at the high **altar** of the Restoration
Church of England is conspicuously absent when angels stand and eat
during the heavenly banquet, thus assuming the only posture acceptable
to antiformalists during the Communion service other than that taken
by Raphael and Adam upon their "mossy seats." The approximation
between the angelic diet of "ambrosial fruitage" (5.427) and vinous
nectar, on the one hand, and Edenic fare of uncooked fruit and unfermented grape juice, on the other hand, affords a further indication that

---

[19] *OED* "surfeit" sb. *Of Reformation* lodges an attack on the "**surfeited** priest [who] scruples not to
paw, and mammock the sacramental bread" (*CPW* 1: 548).

Adam and Eve enjoy "true" communion with the gods before the Fall. Prelapsarian digestion represents the starting point of a process that should lead through higher spiritual understanding to the "immortality and joy" of the textual revision in the second edition. The stark contrast between the heavenly banquet and the cannibalistic gnawing of the hell-dogs, who surfeit themselves upon the body and blood of their mother, Sin (2.798–800), pinpoints implicit reference to Eucharistic controversy. Angelic abstention from eating meat and blood looks like an inversion of the doctrine of **transubstantiation**. By contrast, *Of True Religion* explicitly attacks **transubstantiation** as "idolatry."

Previously unnoticed allusions to familiar sacramental practices of eating, drinking, and sitting infiltrate Milton's account of alimentation in Eden (and heaven). They align the text with pronouncements in *Christian Doctrine* that "the church has no need of a liturgy" and that "internal or spiritual involvement" are necessary in devotion, without which one encounters "hypocritical worship, where the external forms are duly observed" (*CPW* 6: 667, 670). According to that treatise, "true" communion involves not the ingestion of Christ's body, but the believer's mystical "participation, through the spirit, in all of Christ's gifts and merits." Such union involves communion "with the Father in Christ, the Son, and glorification in Christ's image." Furthermore, communion with Christ leads to "communion of his members which, in the Apostles' Creed, is called THE COMMUNION OF SAINTS" (*CPW* 6: 498-99). As such, the sacrament constitutes an external seal of "saving grace . . . by means of a visible sign which he [God] has instituted for the sake of us believers. At the same time we testify our faith and obedience to God with sincerity and gratitude" (*CPW* 6: 542).

The epic narrator's insistence that Raphael engages in digestion and excretion, if only via transpiration into the air, may entail a jarring reinscription of scatological abuse that Protestant polemicists had long directed against the Roman-rite Mass. At the same time alimentation *per se* remains blameless, in a manner analogous to Zwingli's Eucharistic belief that "'eating' is believing" (*OER* 2: 73). An exegesis of a Pauline dictum, "Unto the pure are all things pure" (Titus 1:15), in Milton's *Areopagitica* resonates: ". . . not only meats and drinks, but all kind of knowledge whether of good or evil; the knowledge cannot defile, nor consequently the books, if the will and conscience be not defiled" (*CPW* 2: 512). A related undertone pervades the flatulent simile attached to Raphael's admonition that seeking forbidden knowledge "turns / Wisdom to folly, as nourishment to wind" (7.126–30).[20] "True" **transubstantiation** involves mystical or spiritual communion, as opposed to the alleged Catholic "confusion between sign and thing signified."[21]

Milton's apparent association of Satan with Roman Catholicism involves scatological language associated with Protestant attack on the Mass. That stance may bear out the argument of a Freudian analyst who posits that the inauguration of the Protestant Reformation at the moment when Luther's bowels loosened at the privy suggests that a fundamental connection exists "between Protestantism and anality." Indeed, Luther's belief in the "scatological devil" manifested itself visually when Satan, the Father Superior of the Pope in the view of militant Protestants, assailed him with a hindmost attack. In turn, the father of the Reformation engaged in scatological counterattack, a staple of Reformation polemics.[22] In railing against "worshipping of bread and of wine," for example, John Bale cites Christ himself as an authority for scatological abuse:

... for when they have done their office, being sacraments of Christ's body and blood ... they ascend not into heaven, but being eaten and digested, they are immediately resolved into corruption. Yea, Christ saith that they descend down into the belly and are cast out.[23]

The contemporaneity of such rhetoric may be noted in an innuendo lodged by Lord Russell against "such a ridiculous and nonsensical religion" during debate in the House of Commons concerning the Popish Plot. Milton concurred with Russell's crude insinuation: "A piece of wafer, broken betwixt a priest's fingers, to be our Saviour! And what becomes of it when eaten, and taken down, you know."[24] In more subtly mediated ways, sacramental language in *Paradise Lost* corresponds

---

[20] Because angelic "excretion" is sweating, William Kerrigan rightly notes that angels enjoy the "pleasure of eating" without "the embarrassment of evacuation" in *The Sacred Complex*, p. 210. A concurring note on *PL* 5.438 is in Jonathan Richardson's *Explanatory Remarks on Paradise Lost*(1734): "This artfully avoids the indecent idea, which would else have been apt to have arisen on the angels' feeding, and ... finally distinguishes them from us in one of the most humbling circumstances relating to our bodies."   [21] Norbrook, *Poetry*, pp. 35–36.

[22] Norman O. Brown, *Life Against Death: The Psychoanalytical Meaning of History* (New York: Vintage, 1959), pp. 203, 205, 208–09. See Kerrigan, *Sacred Complex*, p. 240. The lurid language of Thomas More's riposte to Luther's *Contra Henricum Regem Angliae* (1522) indicates that neither Roman Catholics nor Protestants dissociated scatological innuendo from godliness. See *The Complete Works of St. Thomas More*, 10 vols. in 15, ed. and trans. Richard Sylvester, et al. (New Haven: Yale University Press, 1961–), vol. V, pt. i, p. 181.

[23] Bale, *Vocation*, lines 378–89. William Tyndale's *Supper of the Lord* proclaims the normative Protestant view that "Christ's glorified body is not in this world but in heaven,'" in *Whole Works*, ed. Foxe, 2D6.

[24] Anchitel Grey, *Debates of the House of Commons*, 10 vols. (1769) vol. VII, p. 148 (27 April 1679); as quoted in John Kenyon, *The Popish Plot* (London: Heinemann, 1972), p. 1.

to the iconography of *Behold Rome's Monster on his Monstrous Beast!* (1643), an anti-Laudian caricature contemporaneous with his own antiprelatical pamphlets. Verses by John Vicars accompany an engraving by Wenceslaus Hollar that visualizes the anality of the papal Antichrist mounted upon the Seven-headed Beast, which excretes skulls and bones in a travesty of the Roman Mass (Fig. 16). The broadsheet vilifies the Pope (the "child of wickedness") as the Whore of Babylon riding upon the Seven-headed Beast. Alliterative plosives and fricatives simulate alimentary and anal aggression in that lurid attack on the Church of Rome and travesty of the Roman-rite Mass. The "barrel-bellied beast" walks on stilts mockingly appropriate to the Pope's "supreme seat." The "dregs and lees / Of Rome's all-rotten relics, dear decrees" flow from the bunghole at the hind end. "Babel's bishops, Jesuits, friars base" crowd around the "Beast's posteriors" to "fill full-cups of Romish fornication," that is, the Mass.

Milton similarly libels the Catholic Eucharist in *Christian Doctrine*, where he cites a commonplace from late medieval Scholastic disputation:

The papists hold that it is Christ's actual flesh which is eaten by all in the Mass. But if this were so, even the most wicked of the communicants, not to mention the mice and worms which often eat the Eucharist, would attain eternal life by virtue of that heavenly bread. (*CPW* 6: 553)

That gibe was widespread in sixteenth- and seventeenth-century Protestant anti-Mass satire.[25] Similarly objecting that the Mass has virtually turned "the Lord's Supper into a cannibal feast," Milton declares: "Whereas if we eat his flesh it will not remain in us, but, to speak candidly, after being digested in the stomach, it will be at length exuded." In opposition to degradation of "Christ's holy body" by the Mass, he declaims: "Then, when it has been driven through all the stomach's filthy channels, it shoots it out — one shudders even to mention it — into the latrine."[26]

Valorization of "true" communion undergoes both a domestic and an erotic swerve in Adam's account to Raphael of his request to the Father for a mate:

> In solitude
> What happiness, who can enjoy alone,
> Or all enjoying, what contentment find?
> . . .

---

[25] See Miri Rubin, *Corpus Christi: The Eucharist in Late Medieval Culture* (Cambridge University Press, 1991), p. 68.   [26] *CPW* 6: 554, 560.

> Thou in thy secrecy although alone,
> Best with thy self accompanied, seek'st not
> Social communication, yet so pleased,
> Canst raise thy creature to what highth thou wilt
> Of union or communion, deified;
> I by conversing cannot these [the beasts] erect
> From prone, nor in their ways complacence find.
>
> (8.364–66, 427–33)

Even though **union** and **communion** denote "degrees of separateness or plurality in the relationship," reference to "mystical union and Holy Communion" is palpable (Fowler n. on 8.431). Reversal of the transgressiveness of demonic appetite supports Bakhtin's belief in the ambivalence of the lower body, which preserves an "essential link with birth, fertility, renewal, welfare."[27]

The disingenuous response of the smiling deity, as a stratagem within a divine trial of Adam's free will, suggests that irony is an essential attribute of the Father's relationship with human "children," as it is with angels. Nonetheless, his teasing is devoid of the derision that characterizes laughter in heaven at the predicament of the rebel angels. When Adam declines to withdraw his request, the Father acknowledges: "I, ere thou spakest, / Knew it not good for man to be alone" (8.444–45). Like eating, sex is related to knowledge as an ethical function that "can be engaged in either obediently and in moderation, or to excess."[28] The creation of Eve and union of the first couple in "nuptial sanctity and marriage rites" (8.487) was a foreseen part of the divine plan.

Despite the Protestant denial of sacramental status to marriage (one of seven Roman Catholic sacraments) on the ground that only baptism and the Lord's Supper possess scriptural warrant, Adam's request for **communion** with a mate suggests that Edenic wedlock has a sacred character aligned with the Lord's Supper. That position runs counter to the influential opinion of St. Augustine, whose views on the Edenic state exclude the generally accepted place of sexual relations within marriage.[29] Furthermore, the English *Book of Common Prayer* concurs with Calvin in employing human marriage as a figure for Holy Communion based upon Ephesians 5:28–33.[30] The intuitive, non-liturgical union of

---

[27] Bakhtin, *Rabelais and His World*, p. 148. See Chapter 6.

[28] Fowler n. on 5.468. Proper sexual pleasure is a function of "rational delight" (8.391).

[29] Augustine, *City of God*, 14.10–11. James Grantham Turner concludes that Milton is "virtually unique in ascribing active eroticism, not only to the unfallen Adam and Eve, but to angels both fallen and unfallen," in *One Flesh: Paradisal Marriage and Sexual Relations in the Age of Milton* (Oxford: Clarendon Press, 1987), p. 53.   [30] *BCP*, p. 296; *OER* 2: 77.

Adam and Eve into "one flesh," the first deed following her creation, possesses scriptural warrant (*PL* 8.499; Gen. 2:24) and takes on the character of a quite public and universally celebrated act of worship — holy communion, as it were.[31] Indeed, innocent gazing is a key element in the reader's initial encounter with Adam and Eve, one shared with the narrator, angels, the Father, and the Son, an element that undergoes reversal in the impotently voyeuristic desire of cormorant-like Satan,[32] as he perches in the Tree of Life:

> Two of far nobler shape erect and tall,
> Godlike erect, with native honour clad
> In naked majesty . . .
> Nor those **mysterious** parts were then concealed,
> Then was not guilty shame, dishonest shame
> Of nature's works, honour dishonourable,
> Sin-bred . . .
> So passed they naked on, nor shunned the sight
> Of God or angel, for they thought no ill.
>
> (4.288–90; 312–15; 319–20)

Just as "naked" Adam's shoulder-length hair furnishes no concealment, Eve's "unadorned golden tresses" stop short of her "slender waist." Yet they afford a spiritual "veil" that suggests a chaste spirit while her loins remain exposed. Just as Adam and Eve's "naked majesty" reverses Satan's innate habit of disguising, Eve's chaste modesty constitutes an antithesis to the fulsome sexuality associated with the "scaly fold / Voluminous and vast" beneath the waist of Satan's parthenogenetic daughter, Sin (2.651–52).

Editors have misunderstood the prelapsarian state of the genitals by obscuring a link between Holy Communion and the "**mysterious** parts" of Adam and Eve. That adjective has been glossed erroneously as "both secret and sacred, as in a religious **mystery**" or not only "'puzzling because not often seen,' but 'having a religious significance.'"[33] C. S. Lewis's decorous view of **mysterious** as a synonym for "unimaginable," whereby Milton "seems to think that by twice using the word *mysterious* in this connection . . . he excuses his very un-mysterious

---

[31] On Gen. 2–3 as a fundamental text concerning gendered relations throughout Christian tradition and in *PL*, see Turner, *One Flesh*.

[32] Antiprelatical tracts as disparate as *The Protestation of Martin Marprelate* (1589) and *The Dreadful, and Terrible, Day of the Lord God, to Overtake this Generation Suddenly: Once More Proclaimed* (1665) by William Bayly, the Quaker, liken English and Roman prelates respectively to "such cormorants as gape for their downfalls, thereby only to enrich themselves" (p. 19) and "unclean birds of prey" (A1ᵛ).

[33] Nn. on *PL* 4.312 in Orgel and Goldberg; and Flannagan.

pictures,"[34] is also mistaken. The text declares that male and female organs were wholly visible before the Fall. "True" secrecy is an attribute of the deity according to Raphael, who counsels Adam that the Father "Did wisely to conceal, and not divulge / His secrets to be scanned by them who ought / Rather admire" (8.73–75). Adam intuitively understands divine "secrecy," moreover, as the antithesis of his desire for "communion" with a mate (8.427, 431).[35]

Mysterious is a loaded term that suggests the existence of both a window to the divine and an avenue to spiritual communion. Although Protestants denied sacramental status to marriage, it joined the Lord's Supper as one of the seven rites defined as μυστήριον in the Greek New Testament or *sacramentum* in the Vulgate Bible. The functioning of Adam and Eve's "**mysterious** parts" is a witty reconfiguration of Milton's understanding of "the rites of the marriage bed" as a figure for the "spiritual **mystery**" of the "union of Christ and his Church" according to *Tetrachordon*. That significance is present not in "every ungodly and miswedded marriage, but then only **mysterious,** when it is a holy, happy, and peaceful match" (*CPW* 2: 606–07). The reference is to Pauline theology, according to which **mystery** denotes spiritual truth concerning resurrection (1 Cor. 15:51), Holy Communion, and marriage. The reader encounters highly suggestive allusions both to the wedding ceremony in the *Book of Common Prayer*, which declares "the state of matrimony to [be] such an excellent **mystery**, that in it is signified and represented the spiritual marriage and unity betwixt Christ and his Church,"[36] and to the pseudo-Pauline midrash upon Genesis 2:24, which interprets the union of Adam and Eve, the etiological basis for wedlock, with reference to the spiritual union of Christ with the Church:

For this cause shall a man leave father and mother, and shall cleave to his wife, and they twain shall be one flesh. This is a great secret [μυστήριον], but I speak concerning the Church. Therefore every one of you, do ye so: let every one love his wife, even as himself, and let the wife see that she fear her husband. (Eph. 5:31–33)

Christian Doctrine deploys a text from Revelation, "the marriage of the

---

[34] Lewis, *Preface to "Paradise Lost"*, p. 124.

[35] See Lieb, *Poetics*, pp. 62, 74, 356–57 n. 6. For fallen pretenses to secrecy, see *PL* 4.7; 5.672; and 9.810–11. In an inept recognition of the problematic sense of **mysterious**, Richard Bentley's 1732 edition proposes the emendation of *law* to *league* in "Hail wedded love, **mysterious** law" (4.750): "This cannot be from the author. A law, that's supposed **mysterious**, is no law at all; which word in its very notion implies publication and general knowledge."

[36] *BCP*, p. 296.

Lamb is come, and his wife hath made herself ready" (19:7), as the basis for figuring "Christ's love for this invisible and immaculate church of his" in terms of "the love of husband for wife." Coming under the heading "Of Union and Communion with Christ and his Members; also of the Mystic or Invisible Church," discussion in *Christian Doctrine* builds upon figurative representations of the **mystery** of Holy Communion in terms of wedlock (*CPW* 6: 498, 500).

The **mysterious** character of the lovemaking of Adam and Eve and of the angels indicates that human sexuality affords a sanctified and sanctifying means for spiritual **communion** whereby the Edenic couple may ascend "to heavenly love" (8.592).[37] The **mystery** includes both the function and functioning of those "parts." Like their unceremonious marriage, Adam and Eve's worshipful lovemaking in the Edenic bower with "other rites/Observing none, but adoration pure" (4.736–37) constitutes a veiled barb against the ecclesiastical wedding ceremony. Warned by Raphael against overvaluation of coital pleasure, Adam insists that he approaches the nuptial bed "with **mysterious** reverence" (8.599), thus yoking purely sexual and purely prayerful behavior. In turn, Raphael blushes "Celestial rosy red, love's proper hue" as he affirms that angels enjoy sexual union: "nor restrained conveyance need/As flesh to mix with flesh, or soul with soul" (8.619, 628–29).[38] Eve also blushes before intercourse (8.511).

It would be difficult for the secrecy and horrific sexuality associated with the incestuous parentage of Death by Satan and Sin (2.763–67), in a "parody of divine generation," to afford a more pronounced contrast to the **mysterious** rites observed by Adam and Eve before the Fall.[39] The lineage of the "hell-hounds" through Sin's incestuous rape by Death represents a Miltonic expansion of James 1:15 ("Then when lust hath conceived, it bringeth forth sin, and sin when it is finished, bringeth forth death"), but their cannibalistic retreat within her womb to "gnaw" upon their mother's "bowels" (2.799–800) constitutes a lurid Spenserian inversion of the wholesome meal that Eve prepares for Adam and Raphael.

The engagement of *Paradise Lost* with sixteenth- and seventeenth-

---

[37] *Tetrachordon* links wedlock further to gospel texts concerning "the eating of our Savior's flesh, the drinking of his blood" (*CPW* 2: 606).

[38] For a sacramental application of "conveyance," see Hooker's *Laws of Ecclesiastical Polity*, 5.47.4; cited in Fowler n. on 8.628.

[39] Fowler n. on 2.764. The Son employs "**mysterious** terms" in his judgment upon Adam, Eve, and the serpent (10.173). See also Turner, *One Flesh*, pp. 24–27; and Peter Lindenbaum, "Lovemaking in Milton's Paradise," *MiltonS* 6 (1974), pp. 277–306.

century Eucharistic theology has received virtually no attention. Given Milton's general hostility to the sacramental system articulated by medieval Scholasticism, recognition of theological parody opens up an unexplored avenue of investigation. It should enable the reader to recover not only a surprising involvement with anti-Mass satire, but also a sequence of profound imaginative interconnections among eating, digestion, Holy Communion, and theology of marriage. By ignoring Milton's use of irony, inversion, and burlesque, critics have misread parodic allusions as straightforward references to rites and ceremonies in the *Book of Common Prayer* and other liturgies. Indeed, use of the word **transubstantiate** has been misread as a non-ironic sign of the secularization of "the sacred mystery of the Mass" and a corresponding exaltation of "the ordinary physical process of digestion into a sacramental act."[40]

Critics have rightly denied the presence of orthodox sacramentalism in Milton's verse.[41] Reference to **transubstantiation** in an unusual poetic context parodies Roman Catholic Eucharistic doctrine during the Edenic meal where Raphael displays "real hunger, and concoctive heat/To **transubstantiate**" his "viands" (*PL* 5.434; 437–48). (Milton's irony brings to mind Donne's "Twicknam Garden," where "The spider love . . . transubstantiates all.") That theological term contributes parodically to the definition of the "true" sacrament in terms of a commemorative meal,[42] at the same time that Miltonic scurrility satirizes the Roman-rite Mass by means of indelicate scatological implication.

[40] John C. Ulreich, Jr., "Milton on the Eucharist: Some Second Thoughts about Sacramentalism," in *Milton and the Middle Ages*, ed. John Mulryan (Lewisburg, PA: Bucknell University Press, 1982), p. 43. Honeygosky posits that Miltonic **transubstantiation** occurs "not through the visible elements of bread and wine, but through the verbal elements of Scripture" in *House*, p. 223; see also Georgia Christopher, *Milton and the Science of the Saints* (Princeton University Press, 1982), pp. 11–16, 121–22, passim.

[41] E.g. Malcolm M. Ross, *Poetry and Dogma: The Transfiguration of Eucharistic Symbols in Seventeenth-Century English Poetry* (New Brunswick: Rutgers University Press, 1954), p. 157; Madsen, *From Shadowy Types to Truth*, p. 70.

[42] Denying that Holy Communion functions as a conduit for heavenly grace, *CD* states that the "Lord's Supper commemorates the death of Christ by the breaking of bread and the pouring out of wine: both are tasted by all present, and the benefits of his death are thus sealed to believers" (*CPW* 6: 552). See *ME* 7: 133–34.

CHAPTER 8

Idolatry in Eden

Until the Fall, proleptic parodies of transubstantiation and the Mass are associated with the insatiable appetites of the satanic family, which undergo reversal in "true" communion associated with the blameless alimentation and sexuality that Adam and Eve share with the angels. By contrast, the disclosure of idolatry in Eden at the time of the Fall recalls the truculent rhetoric of Milton's antiprelatical tracts.[1] It seems that dramatization of the Fall participates in Protestant misrepresentation of the Mass as a demonic distortion of Jesus' sacrifice as the redemptive act at the center of Christian history. As the intensity of religious conflict subsided over the centuries, however, readers have understandably lost sight of a highly topical concern with sacramentalism and devotional practices. Rediscovery of polemicism in *Paradise Lost*, a text often taken as an outstanding instance of poetic sublimity, invites reconsideration of the temptation and fall of Adam and Eve.

In the early books of *Paradise Lost*, hypocrisy, sophistry, and dramatic role-playing are uniquely demonic attributes. After the tragic turn marked by the fourth invocation (9.1–47), however, the burden of anti-Catholic parody moves to Eve in particular, who takes on satanic modes of speech and self-fashioning in addition to iconographical attributes and formulaic praise from the cult of the Virgin Mary. Given Milton's conception of satire as an elevated offshoot from tragedy, that mode is appropriate to the momentous events in Book 9. The narrator figures the shift to tragedy in terms of Adam's exclusion from "communion" with Raphael at the prelapsarian table, a transition that negates manifold poetic and religious senses of pastoral:

> No more of talk where God or angel guest
> With man, as with his friend, familiar used

---

[1] See Guibbory, *Ceremony and Community*, pp. 195, 210. She demonstrates how *Comus* and Milton's pamphlets are driven by his "obsession with idolatry," p. 147, et seq.

> To sit indulgent, and with him partake
> Rural repast, permitting him the while
> Venial discourse unblamed: I now must change
> Those notes to tragic.   (9.1–6)

Through Satan's temptation of Eve and the Fall, idolatry invades Eden in the form of anticipations of allegedly corrupt worship practices. Long-forgotten allusions to religious controversy and parodic echoes of Medieval Latin hymnody constitute an intrinsic component of the tragedy of the Fall.

Satan's preparation for the temptation of Eve by metamorphosis into serpentine form functions as a preamble to the construction of the Fall, at a topical level that complicates issues concerning conscience and free will, with reference to bestial carnality and engorgement:

> O foul descent! That I who erst contended
> With gods to sit the highest, am now constrained
> Into a beast, and mixed with bestial slime,
> This essence to incarnate and imbrute,
> That to the highth of deity aspired.   (9.163–67)

His grotesque carnality summons up charges that the doctrine of transubstantiation and the Mass presuppose belief in carnal sacrifice and materialistic feeding upon the body and blood of Christ. The travesty of the Incarnation is appropriate to Satan's status as a demonic double of the Son. The satanic soliloquy recalls *Comus*, in which the Elder Brother identifies sin with unchastity that "Embodies, and **imbrutes**" the soul (line 467). That echo suggests that we may transfer Thomas Warton's alignment of the bestializing effect of sin with "carnal ceremonies of popery" (Milton, *Poems*. ed. Warton, p. 192) from Comus to Satan. Warton's reading cites parallels between the words of the Elder Brother and the rhetoric of Milton's antiprelatical tracts.

Tropes of false feeding and alimentary aggression, which inform both *Lycidas* and the antiprelatical pamphlets, pervade Satan's reversal of "true" pastoral feeding in his testimony to Eve concerning his personal experience of eating the forbidden **fruit**:

> Tempting so nigh, to pluck and eat my fill
> I spared not, for such pleasure till that hour
> At feed or fountain never had I found.   (9.595–97)

The orgiastic gorging parallels the defamation of the Mass as "the new-vomited paganism of sensual idolatry" and the attendant collapsing together of Roman church and the Laudian Church of England in *Of Reformation* (*CPW* 1: 520). We may hear an echo of the anti-Catholic catalogue of "the **fruits**/Of painful superstition and blind zeal" at the Paradise of Fools (3.451–52), just as Satan's gluttony anticipates the fulsome dining of Death after it scents "carnage, prey innumerable, and taste/The savour of death from all [living] things" (10.268–69). Following his final metamorphosis into the great dragon (Rev. 12:9), Satan will preside over a Black Mass when the devils seek out a parodic Eden "laden with fair fruit," only to end up chewing on "bitter ashes" (10.550, 566). Featuring a fruit-laden tree and vegetation that is "direfull deadly blacke both leafe and bloom," Spenser's Garden of Proserpina affords a vernacular model for Miltonic parody (*FQ* 2.7.51–56).[2]

Adam's discovery of a threatened breakdown in marital communion ("this sweet intercourse/Of looks and smiles") marks the beginning of the temptation sequence when he accedes to Eve's desire to engage in solitary gardening, an action that leaves her vulnerable to the "malicious foe" whose presence her spouse rightly intuits "somewhere nigh at hand" (9.238–56). Their decision to part company for the first time invites theological interpretation because Eve's choice is the exercise of free will that proves that providence (or predestination as defined by the Father in Book 3) does not constitute necessitarian foreordination. Her exercise of free will unwittingly prepares the way for the eventual repentance and spontaneous prayer for forgiveness of Adam and Eve.

Eve's actions accord further with misogynistic stereotypes that women in general were prone to idolatry and that a series of Catholic queens strove to restore "papistry" in England. In William Prynne's account of the trial of Archbishop Laud, for example, we find the highly charged claim that Roman Catholic plotters

fixed at last of latter times upon a more prevalent and successful means than any of the former; to wit, a project of mating us to the Whore of Rome by matching the heir of the Crown of England to a Romanist. They found many precedents, texts in scripture, and ecclesiastical [hi]story ascertaining them, that **idolatrous** queens and wives were a most infallible prevailing means to draw kings and whole kingdoms to **idolatry**, for which very reason God expressly enjoined the Israelites to make no marriages with the Canaanites.[3]

The epic narrator likens Eve to a **queen** more than once, including the point when solitary Adam weaves for her a floral crown "As reapers oft are wont their harvest queen" (9.842). At the very least, that epithet is

---

[2] According to Grossman, *Authors*, p. 223 n. 36, the annual cycle of temptation undergone by the fallen angels parodies the "ritual of Holy Communion practiced in the Mass." See also *SPART*, p. 119.

[3] Prynne, *Hidden Works of Darkness Brought to Public Light* (1645), p. 1. I am grateful to Katherine Narveson for this citation.

unflattering to monarchy. Profound irony enfolds Adam's pastoral homage because it coincides with Eve's fall and idolatrous propitiation of the Tree of Knowledge in preparation for her temptation of Adam.

At the close of the temptation sequence, Eve's gaze upon the Tree recalls "idolatrous" adoration of images and shrines:

> Fixed on the fruit she gazed, which to behold
> Might tempt alone, and in her ears the sound
> Yet rung of his persuasive words, impregned
> With reason, to her seeming, and with truth.   (9.735–38)

The aural persuasion of serpentine Satan furthermore reconfigures his initial toad-like approach when the cherubim arrested him at Eve's **ear**. The figurative sense that Eve is "impregned" through her ears is akin to belief that the impregnation of Mary, the second Eve, via the ear allowed for the Virgin Birth.[4]

After succumbing to Satanic temptation, Eve's eating of the forbidden fruit seems to take on the character of a parodic Mass that recalls insatiable clerical appetites condemned in Milton's antiprelatical tracts and the gluttony of the hell-dogs, who feast upon the entrails of their mother, Sin. Eve's gorging reverses the dynamic of "true" communion at both the Edenic meal shared by Adam with Raphael and the angels' heavenly repast of "ambrosial fruit" and "rubied nectar":

> Greedily she engorged without restraint
> And knew not eating death: satiate at length,
> And heightened as with wine, jocund and boon.   (9.791–93)

Surely the representation of Eve's sin in terms of intoxication "as with wine" is analogous to misuse of sacramental **wine**, in pronounced contrast to the sobriety of Adam and Raphael when they drank "inoffensive must" (unfermented grape juice) at their "table" of "grassy turf" (5.345, 391).

Eve's idolatrous worship of the altar-like Tree contributes to the text's pervasive concern with "false" religion. It accords with the definition of idolatry in *Christian Doctrine* as the "making or owning an idol for religious purposes, or worshipping it, whether it be a representation of the true God or of some false god" (*CPW* 6: 690–91). Recalling the proleptic cults of the heathen gods recounted at the outset of *Paradise Lost*, her idolatrous hymn is more closely akin to Belial's ubiquitous presence "In temples and at altars" (1.494) than her own naked ministry at the Edenic meal:

---

[4] Le Comte, *Dictionary of Puns*, p. 92.

> O sovereign, virtuous, precious of all trees
> In Paradise, of operation blest
> To sapience, hitherto obscured, infamed,
> And thy fair **fruit** let hang, as to no end
> Created; but henceforth my early care,
> Not without song, each morning, and due praise
> Shall tend thee, and the fertile burden ease
> Of thy full branches offered free to all.   (9.795–802)

Denoting spiritual illumination, **sapience** derives from *sapientia* (Latin "wisdom"), but the root *sapere* (Latin "to taste or know") affords a painful pun on her eating of forbidden fruit. The moment recalls Raphael's counsel concerning **measure** versus **surfeit** in warning that "knowledge is as food, and needs no less/Her temperance over appetite" (7.126–27). Eve's vow to venerate the Tree each morning as part of her ritualistic cult observances cancels her spontaneous morning prayer in company with Adam. That prayer had supplied a proleptic parody of matins, the liturgical office of morning prayer that Milton despised:

> each morning duly paid
> In various style, for neither various style
> Nor holy rapture wanted they to praise
> Their maker, in fit strains pronounced or sung
> Unmediated.   (5.145–49)[5]

It may be that Eve's emulation of Satan as a "false" priest conjures up thinly veiled travesty of the moment when priestly elevation of the consecrated host signals the sacerdotal reenactment of the Passion at a high altar overshadowed by Christ's body hung visibly upon a tree-like cross. (Medieval and early modern poems often call the Cross a "tree.") Her action recalls a declaration in a recusant catechism that proclaims that the church altar "hath a particular signification: as that which supplieth the place in our holy sacrifice, which the Holy Cross supplied, when Christ was crucified on the same."[6] Her belief in the magical power of forbidden fruit upon an altar-like tree invites the reader to discover satire on Roman Catholic and Laudian doctrine that the sacraments function as external aids to salvation, in opposition to the

---

[5] Echoes of Psalm 148 and *Benedicite, omnia opera* function not as "quasi-liturgical" prayer (Fowler nn. on 5.145–208), but rather as a proleptic rendering of scriptural texts cast into liturgical formulae that Milton attacks in *Eikonoklastes* and *Christian Doctrine*. Eve's idolatry contradicts the following examples of "true" worship in *PL*: hymn (3.365–71, 3.410–17, 4.680–84, 7.598–99); sacred music (7.594–98); canticles (7.182–91, 7.557–74); and matins (7.450). See Grossman, *Authors*, pp. 105, 191; Stroup, *Rite*, pp. 30–36; Hill, *MER*, p. 394.

[6] Laurence Vaux, *Catechism or Christian Doctrine, Necessary for Children and Ignorant People* (St. Omer, c. 1670), N10. Falsely dated 1620, it was originally published in Louvain in 1568).

doctrine of justification by faith alone. Eve's idolatrous invocation of the Tree inverts Raphael's preprandial application to Eve of

> the holy salutation used
> Long after to blest Marie, second Eve.
> Hail mother of mankind, whose **fruitful** womb
> Shall fill the world more numerous with thy sons
> Than with these various **fruits** the trees of God
> Have heaped this table.   (5.386–91)

Punning on **fruit** suggests that Eve's veneration of the **fruit** hanging upon the Tree of Knowledge is a proleptic travesty of Jesus' status as descendent of Eve and offspring of the second Eve. Puns frame the Fall from the moment when Eve, with flippancy in character with her vulnerability to temptation, chides Satan for leading her to the Tree: "Serpent, we might have spared our coming hither,/**Fruitless** to me, though **fruit** be here to excess" (9.647–48). When Book 9 concludes abruptly in marital bickering and the refusal of Adam and Eve to shoulder responsibility for their predicament, the narrator echoes her own words:

> Thus they in mutual accusation spent
> The **fruitless** hours, but neither self-condemning,
> And of their vain contest appeared no end.   (9.1187–89)

At that moment, when the emptiness of their "vain" words recalls the Limbo of Vanity, the tragedy of the Fall has eclipsed the jollity that marked Eve's earlier ambiguous response to temptation.[7]

Eve's idolatrous hymn to the Tree may parody its function in Medieval Latin hymnody as a figure for the Cross, the Roman Catholic and Laudian veneration of which struck Puritans as a violation of the prohibition against "graven images" in the Second Commandment. The mockery reverses the widespread monastic habit of imitating Christian hymns and prayers without implying dishonor to the original versions.[8] Her ministration is akin to the language of *Vexilla regis* by Venantius Fortunatus, for example, which dedicates formulaic praise to "the Tree as an altar and its Fruit as a sacrificial victim, '*Salva ara, salve victima.*'" Satan's temptation of Eve with "godlike food" and her acceptance of "fruit divine," which nurtures "at once both body and mind" (9.717; 776; 779), suggests mockery of the language of Eucharistic hymns such as *Pange lingua gloriosi* and *Panis angelicus* by Thomas Aquinas.

---

[7] Ricks, *Grand Style*, p. 73.   [8] See Bakhtin, *Rabelais and His World*, p. 85.

Eve's invocation of the Tree's "sapience" invites discovery of an intertwining set of multilayered parodies of liturgical and iconographical formulae from the cult of the Blessed Virgin. It may be that the wording twists the Roman Catholic litany, which honors Mary as both Mother and the *Sedes Sapientiae* ("Seat of Wisdom, or Science").[9] Furthermore, Eve's propitiation of the "sacred" Tree as "Mother of science" and "Queen of this universe" recalls Satan's salutation of Eve herself as "sovereign mistress," a "goddess among gods, adored and served/By angels numberless," and "Empress of this fair world" (9.532, 547–48, 568, 680, 684). The wording corresponds to William Prynne's attack on "idolatrous queens and wives."[10]

Although one may question whether the text sustains subtle liturgical satire, we should recall that until maturity Milton frequently heard the services in the *Book of Common Prayer*. Dispute concerning the liturgy flared up before and during the Civil Wars. Milton's prose works demonstrate familiarity with Roman Catholic liturgy and hymnody. *Areopagitica* ridicules the *imprimatur* by association with newly discredited hymns: "These are the dear antiphonies that so bewitched of late our prelates, and their chaplains with the goodly echo they made." *Animadversions* denies that Justin Martyr affords a patristic precedent for antiphonal song. Furthermore, critique of Mariology occupied an important place in Reformation thought, notably the theology of Luther, Zwingli, and Calvin. Following the lead of Luther, Protestants rejected recitations and intercessory prayers including the *Salve Regina*, *Ave Maria*, and praise of Mary as Queen of Heaven.[11]

Despite official prohibitions, centuries-old titles such as *Regina Angelorum* ("Queen of Angels") and *Regina Coeli* ("Queen of Heaven") remained in use during the Restoration among recusants who sang hymns in missals and other Catholic prayer books. It may be that *Paradise Lost* links such epithets to proleptic praise of Astoreth (or Astarte) as a Canaanite lunar goddess: "queen of heaven, with crescent horns" (1.439). That phrasing comes from texts such as Jeremiah 7:18 and 44:17–20. Because the crescent moon also symbolizes the Virgin Mary, the association of ritual prostitution with the cult of Astoreth suggests a critique of Mariological devotion. Parody of that kind would mock Catholic veneration of the Virgin Mary as a miracle-working interces-

---

[9] See Anne B. Gardiner, "Milton's Parody of Catholic Hymns in Eve's Temptation and Fall: Original Sin as a Paradigm of 'Secret Idolatries'," *Studies in Philology* 91 (1994), pp. 216–31: esp. 222–23, 226–28; and Lewalski, *Rhetoric*, p. 238.   [10] Prynne, *Hidden Works*, p. 1.
[11] *CPW* 1: 683, 2: 504; *OER*, 3: 10–14.

sor, rather than her place in Christian history as Christ's mother.[12]

Printing presses at St. Omer, site of a Jesuit seminary in Normandy that served the English recusant community, and other Continental locales produced an array of vernacular missals.[13] Smuggled into England, they contained antiphons like *O Gloriosa Virginam*, *Ave Maris Stella*, *Alma Redemptoris Mater*, and *Ave Regina Caelorum*. *The Primer or Office of the Blessed Virgin Mary in English* (St. Omer, 1651) contains a version of *Pange lingua gloriosi* analogous to Eve's supplication of the Tree:

> O blessed fruit of noblest womb!
> On us bestow'd, did us by birth
> He from a Virgin did proceed,
> And being conversant on earth,
> Till he had sown the Gospel's seed   (R7[r–v])

The construction of Eve's temptation and fall as the first instance of human idolatry may mock employment of antiphons to the Virgin Mary in secret rites observed by recusants. By extension, it hints at a covert attack on the reestablishment of the Caroline order of worship during the Restoration. Satan's claim to enlightenment through eating the fruit of the Tree (a type for the Cross) corresponds, furthermore, to a literalization of Jesus' words during the Last Supper, "This is my body," which allows for a centuries-old satirical slur against the dogma of transubstantiation on the ground that it would allow beasts like mice, or serpents, to digest the body of Christ.[14]

Satan's serpentine temptation of Eve "on his rear,/Circular base of rising folds, that towered/Fold above fold a surging maze" (9.497–99) affords an analogy to the *Reason of Church Government*, which states that "Lucifer before Adam was the first prelate angel." The tract derides the office of bishop by likening it to "a great python" and "dragon" (*CPW* i: 762, 857–58). Possible interpretation of Satan and Eve as covert figures for royalist reactionaries and "idolaters" of Restoration England[15] would support recent claims that Milton's late writings are actively engaged with Restoration politics.[16] Parody of Catholic ritual would correspond not to the guarded acceptance of secret Catholic rites in

---

[12] Fowler n. on 9.64–66 cites a further connection between Satan and Marian iconography.
[13] *The Primer More Ample, in a New Order, Containing the Three Offices of the Blessed Virgin Mary, in Latin and English* (Rouen, 1669) is an example of a recusant prayer book available to Milton (Gardiner, p. 220 n. 13).   [14] See *CPW* 6: 553; and Chapter 7, above.
[15] Gardiner, "Parody," pp. 217–19, 221–23, 230–31.
[16] E.g., Blair Worden, "Milton, *Samson Agonistes*, and the Restoration," in *Culture and Society in the Stuart Restoration: Literature, Drama, History* (Cambridge University Press, 1995), ed. Gerald MacLean, pp. 111–36.

Milton's *Treatise of Civil Power in Ecclesiastical Causes* but to the blanket rejection of recusancy in *Of True Religion*.

Parting from the Tree with an idolatrous gesture of "low reverence," Eve's decision to secure Adam's replication of her sin as a travesty of love finds an external counterpart in the rose garland he has woven during her absence. The scene suggests a delicate parody of Mariological iconography. Allusion of that kind would have been accessible to Milton's immediate circle, the coterie audience for whom parts of *Paradise Lost* circulated in manuscript. Its members included Andrew Marvell, a figure well versed in Jesuit emblem books that contained a variety of rose symbols. Formulaic praise of Mary includes both the crown of glory that she wears as *Regina Coeli*, the enthroned Queen of Heaven, and the *hortus rosarum* ("rose garden") that constitutes an extension of the *hortus conclusus* ("enclosed garden") of the Song of Songs (4:12), a symbol for her intact state as the Blessed Virgin. Catholic devotion also pays homage to Mary as *rosa sine spina* (the "rose without thorns"). A recusant tract dedicated to Queen Henrietta Maria expounds the *Rosa Mystica* as a figure for Mary, "the rose which is sprung from thorns . . . and hath filled all things with sweet odors . . . the more reason, in regard of the sweet fragrancy [i.e. Christ] proceeding from her."[17]

Such connections may seem arcane, but we should recall the centrality of roses sacred and profane in both the *Commedia* and *The Faerie Queene*, two important antecedents of *Paradise Lost*. After all, Dante experiences a beatific vision of the celestial rose at the edge of which he beholds the Blessed Virgin as Queen of Heaven (*Paradiso* 30–31). The Edenic scene also corresponds to ironic reversals of Mariological praise in Spenser's Bower of Bliss,[18] where Acrasia, who is anything but a virgin, takes her pleasure to the accompaniment of a deeply ironic *carpe florem* song that celebrates "the Virgin Rose": "Gather therefore the Rose, whilest yet is prime,/For soone comes age, that will her pride deflowre" (2.12.74–75). That Spenser imitates the rose song heard in the magic garden of Armida in *Gerusalemme liberata* (16.14–15) would render any Miltonic parody even more sardonic, given the status of Tasso's work as the great Counter-Reformation epic.

Once again, Milton adopts a transumptive pose as Spenser's grandfather. Before the Fall, Eve is like an unplucked rose, "Her self, though fairest unsupported flower" (9.432). The "blissful bower" or "shady bower" (4.690, 705) where she shares with Adam the fruits of prelapsar-

---

[17] *Maria Triumphans, Being a Discourse Wherein . . . the Blessed Virgin is Defended and Vindicated* (St. Omer, 1635), F6. [18] Greenblatt, *Self-Fashioning*, p. 189; *SPART*, pp. 179–81.

ian love constitutes a proleptic model for ironic inversions in Acrasia's Bower of Bliss (see *FQ* 2.12.52).[19] Milton's reconfiguration of many Spenserian elements (the garden setting, lovers' bower, nudity, and bed of roses), some of which are shared with European hexameral verse, establishes that Spenserian setting as an anti-Eden, which perverts a lost paradise. Nakedness, a key element in the Spenserian and Miltonic bowers, can accordingly symbolize either the presence or absence of virtue. Thus Adam and Eve's nighttime sharing of a blanket of rose petals, despite the innocence of their prelapsarian nakedness, corrects the lewdness of Acrasia's posture "upon a bed of Roses" (*FQ* 2.12.77):

> And on their naked limbs the flowery roof
> Showered roses, which the morn repaired.   (4.772–73)

It may be that a tissue of Mariological parodies enfolds the postlapsarian withering of Eve's floral crown, when "all the faded roses shed." It affords a sign of her loss of innocence, which Adam's stunned response figures as a metaphorical rape: "How art thou lost, how on a sudden lost,/Defaced, deflowered, and now to death devote" (9.893; 900–901). His thought constitutes an inversion of the moment when Satan perceives solitary Eve in her rose garden and pauses oxymoronically "with rapine sweet bereaved/His fierceness of the fierce intent it brought" (9.461–62). **Rapine** conveys the double sense of both "plunder" and "rape," just as **deflower** affords a pun on the deprivation of blossoms, of innocence, of virginity, and of spiritual integrity. Unlike the Lady of *Comus*, who steadfastly resists temptation by Comus, a prototype for Milton's Satan, Eve's sanctity of spirit has undergone rape-like **defloration**. Although **devote** denotes accursedness, the term implies a correlation between disobedience to the Father and ironically idolatrous **devotion** to Death. "Impregnated" by Satan's words, Eve has surrendered her spiritual virginity. Antiprelatical pamphleteers had employed rape as a conventional figure for Laudian ecclesiastical innovations (see conclusion to Chapter 4).

Following the completion of the Fall through Adam's temptation by Eve, the discovery of lust perverts the "mysterious" rites of sexual love that had once served as an essential component of the couple's spiritual "communion." Matching Eve's jollity, Adam cracks a bawdy joke symptomatic of both his fallen reason and the loss of the quasi-sacramental status of their love:

---

[19] For a complete formulation of the present argument, see John N. King, "Milton's Bower of Bliss: A Rewriting of Spenser's Art of Married Love," *Renaissance and Reformation* NS 10 (1986), pp. 289–299.

> if such pleasures be
> In things to us forbidden, it might be wished,
> For this one tree had been forbidden ten. (9.1024–26)

A scriptural allusion woven into his coarse proposition that they engage in crude sex devoid of "amorous intent" highlights their fall into idolatry: "But come, so well refreshed, now let us **play**/As meet is, after such delicious fare" (9.1027–28, 1035). That invitation recalls the archetypal instance of idolatry when, during Moses' ascent of Mount Sinai to receive the Ten Commandments, Aaron led the Israelites in crafting a golden calf and worshipping it as an idol: "So they rose up the next day in the morning, and offered burnt offerings, and brought peace offerings; also the people sat them down to eat and drink, and rose up to **play**" (Exod. 32:6). St. Paul cites the incident as a warning against idolatry (1 Cor. 10:7).[20]

The engagement of Adam and Eve in profanely recreational sex recalls the denunciation of Canaanite idolatry as "harlotry" by Hosea, Jeremiah, and other Hebrew prophets. After all, by destroying the "mysterious reverence" of their "nuptial sanctity" the couple has committed idolatry in the formal sense of substituting devotion to an idol of their own making for worship of the Father, which infused their every action before the Fall. The distinctively sexual manifestation of the idolatry of Adam and Eve may correspond to widespread identification of an allegedly idolatrous Church of Rome as the Whore of Babylon, whereby Protestants like Milton misrepresented the Mass as a fulfillment of prophetic denunciations of "whoring after false gods." The Homily on Idolatry in the *Book of Homilies* accordingly declares:

Doth not the Word of God call idolatry spiritual fornication? Doth it not call a gilt or painted idol or image a strumpet with a painted face? Be not the spiritual wickedness of an idol's enticing like the flatteries of a wanton harlot? Be not men and women as prone to spiritual fornication (I mean idolatry) as to carnal fornication.[21]

Although copulation per se has nothing to do with original sin, it does function as its external "seal,/The solace of their sin" (9.1043–44).

Adam and Eve have entered the covert groves of a fallen Bower of Bliss, where the closest approximation to the once-innocent bower is the site of first fallen sex:

[20] James H. Sims, *The Bible in Milton's Epics* (Gainesville: University of Florida Press, 1962), p. 208.
[21] *Certain Sermons or Homilies Appointed to Be Read in Churches* (1633; *STC* 13660), 2F1; personal copy. See *SPART*, pp. 210–11.

> to a shady bank,
> Thick overhead with **verdant** roof **embowered**
> He led her nothing loth; flowers were the couch,
> Pansies, and violets, and asphodel,
> And hyacinth, earth's freshest softest lap.   (9.1037–41)

In this perverse epithalamium, the floral bed and "verdant roof" evoke both the "blissful bower" where "showered roses" had once blanketed Adam and Eve (4.690, 773) and its postlapsarian reversal in the Bower of Bliss, where Spenser's allegorical mode dictates that Acrasia's enervated lover, Verdant, function at one level as a personification of the color green. In describing the postcoital ennui of Adam and Eve, who now anticipate the clouded reason of Acrasia and her sleeping companion, the Miltonic narrator laments their loss of

> innocence, that as a veil
> Had shadowed them from knowing ill, was gone,
> Just confidence, and native righteousness
> And honor from about them, naked left
> To guilty shame he covered, but his robe
> Uncovered more   (9.1054–59)

Vanished upon the flight of innocence, the absent **veil** recalls by contrast the diaphanous "vele of silke and siluer thin" that enhances, rather than conceals, Acrasia's disorderly nakedness (*FQ* 2.12.77).

As a sign of disobedience, the "carnal desire" and unconcealed lovemaking of Adam and Eve render "obnoxious" the mysterious "parts" whose function had once testified to the interconnection between sexual intercourse and spiritual communion among humans and divine beings (9.1013, 1093–94). Wordplay conflates the English sense of **obnoxious** ("odious") with the Latin root (*obnoxius*, "exposed to harm or evil"), which attests that only now, after the Fall, are Adam and Eve stripped of their innocence in a way that leaves their "parts" **exposed** in shameful nakedness. They decide to clothe "Those middle parts, that this new comer shame,/There sit not, and reproach us as unclean" (1097–98). Personifying their embarrassment, Shame is the allegorical offspring of Sin.

A countermovement follows the strict paraphrase of the Protevangelium (Gen. 3:15) in the Son's curse of the serpent:

> Between thee and the woman I will put
> Enmity, and between thine and her seed;
> Her seed shall bruise thy head, thou bruise his heel.   (10.179–81)

The narrator's framing explanation that "Jesus son of Mary second Eve" would fulfill that prophetic "oracle" weaves scriptural exegesis into the fabric of Milton's poem (10.182–83). By interpreting the Prot-evangelium as the earliest affirmation of justification by faith, Protes-tants like Milton read the ecclesiastical disputes of the sixteenth and seventeenth centuries into the Genesis account of creation. Like *Paradise Regained*, the poem honors Mary as the mother of Jesus in accordance with her sketchy history in the Gospels. Like his co-religionists, Milton rejects the extrascriptural elaboration of Catholic Mariology. Repeated reference to the Eve-Mary typology stresses Eve's role as the conduit of grace in accordance with the Son's messianic prophecy concerning "her seed" (10.180). In accordance with Protestant thinking, however, honor accorded to both Eve and Mary excludes Mariological adoration.

Satirization of Roman Catholic devotion to the Virgin Mary during the temptation sequence undergoes reversal following the Protevan-gelium. Adam's postlapsarian application to his spouse of Raphael's original salutation therefore functions not as a straightforward allusion to the *Ave Maria*,[22] but as an ironic formula that reminds the reader that Eve's role in salvation is contingent upon her status as a type of Mary: "Whence hail to thee,/Eve rightly called, Mother of all Mankind" (11.158–59). Under tutelage by Michael at the close of *Paradise Lost*, Adam achieves his point of highest illumination when he comprehends Eve's role as a type of Mary, whereby the Protevangelium prophesies not worldly conflict between Christ and Satan, but Christ's tragic suffering in accordance with Christian heroism of obedience:

> Now clear I understand
> What oft my steadiest thoughts have searched in vain,
> Why our great expectation should be called
> The seed of woman: virgin Mother, hail,
> High in the love of heaven, yet from my loins
> Thou shalt proceed, and from thy womb the Son
> Of God most high; so God with man unites.
> Needs must the serpent now his capital bruise
> Expect with mortal pain: say where and when
> Their fight, what stroke shall bruise the victor's heel.   (12.376–85)

Near the end of the epic, Adam delivers a postlapsarian hymn to "goodness infinite, goodness immense" (12.469). In its worshipful dedi-cation to divine praise, it constitutes a restoration of a genre perverted in Eve's idolatrous hymn to the Tree of Knowledge.[23]

[22] For a contrary reading, see Flannagan n. on 11.158.   [23] Lewalski, *Rhetoric*, pp. 272, 276.

Milton's parodic configuration and reconfiguration of scriptural typology colors *Paradise Lost* with religio-political concerns. With the waning of sacramental and liturgical disputes that flared up during the sixteenth and seventeenth centuries, later readers have had every reason to forget how hints concerning religious controversy pervade the poem. From Satan's initial gathering of the fallen angels in "close recess and secret conclave," proleptic parodies identify Sin, Death, and the rebellion of the fallen angels with rancorous innuendoes that identify transubstantiation and the Mass with English churchmen and with the appetites, sexuality, and crypto-Catholic policies of Charles I and Charles II. The pure alimentation and blameless sexuality that Adam and Eve shared with the angels before the Fall constitute paradigms that undergo reversal when the disobedience first of Eve and then Adam results in idolatrous worship and sexual transgression. Less accessible to the modern reader are possible applications of scriptural typology to insult both the Mass and reverence accorded to Mariological praise in Roman Catholic devotion. Initiating a movement away from the tragic suffering of the Fall, however, the Protevangelium shifts emphasis away from idolatry in Eden and toward the harshly comforting prophecies that Archangel Michael unfolds concerning the pervasive history of "true" versus "false" churches in the final books of *Paradise Lost*.

CHAPTER 9

The image of both churches

In ways previously unrecognized, the prophecies of Archangel Michael in Books 11 and 12 of *Paradise Lost* culminate the critique of religious "transgression" found in the earlier books. Indeed, we may read his lessons as a consolatory response to the post-Restoration situation of antiformalists and dissenters. Michael's bluntly straightforward delivery, although devoid of parody, taunting gibes, or scoffing puns, attacks "idolatrous" worship practices engaged in by Adam and his descendents. At the same time, the archangel educates Adam concerning "true" worship in a way that accords with Bakhtin's position that degrading laughter coexists with an affirmative and productive side.[1] Michael's status as patron saint of the Church Militant enhances the didacticism of his preachments against religious "error." Scholars have located intermittent examples of political satire in the closing books of *Paradise Lost*,[2] but their sermonic engagement with religious dispute has gone without notice until now. In grounding a new reading of Books 11 and 12 in Restoration church politics, the present chapter demonstrates how they bring to a close the poem's engagement with ritualism, worship, the altar, the temple, justification by faith, and so forth. The archangel's prophecies concerning future conflict between "true" and "false" churches articulate a program of corrective instruction that complements the punitiveness of divine mirth at satanic folly.

Although widespread distaste for Michael's prophecies has endured ever since the publication of Addison's *Spectator* essays, the recovery of

---

[1] Bakhtin, *Rabelais and His World*, pp. 19–21. I borrow the title of this chapter from John Bale's *Image of Both Churches* (c. 1545), the first full-length English Protestant commentary on Revelation. *PL* 11–12 recall Bale's interpretation of universal history in terms of conflict between the "true" church, whose teachings are based upon the preachings of Jesus, and the "false" church, whose headship by the Pope results from alleged subversion by Antichrist. On Bale's *Image* as an enduring model for sixteenth- and seventeenth-century British apocalypticism, see Christianson, *Reformers*, pp. 36–40, 244, and passim; *ERL*, pp. 61–64, et seq.

[2] See Hill, *MER*, pp. 380–90; Broadbent, *Subject*, ch. 11.

scriptural typology as a "tool of *literary* analysis" has contributed to the "rehabilitation" of Books 11 and 12 since the 1950s.[3] Defense of their structural integrity hinges upon Christian interpretation of the Old Testament as a collection of incomplete or shadowy **prefigurations** or **types** of persons, events, and institutions in the New Testament (**anti-types**).[4] At present, it is hard to conceive of a consideration of the final books that could scant the importance of scriptural typology, in line with Michael's distinction between the incompleteness of "types/And shadows" of ritual sacrifice under the Old Law versus their fulfillment through the New Law of Jesus' redemptive sacrifice (12.232–33).

Milton and his contemporaries associate typology not only with Pauline exegeses of Jewish scriptures, but also with "correlative types," that is, contemporary fulfillments of Old Testamental antecedents.[5] Drawing analogies between present-day events and biblical events "belonged to the everyday vocabulary of Puritan politics."[6] Thus the antiprelatical tracts vilify Laudian bishops for Pharisaism. The typological opposition in Books 11 and 12 between external, carnal corruption under the Old Law and the inward operation of faith under the New correlates with polemical innuendoes in the poem's earlier books concerning the formalistic doctrine, ritual, and polity of the Churches of Rome and England, in addition to the practices of Presbyterian and other groupings. Of course, alleged failures of seventeenth-century religion represent only the most recent manifestation of ecclesiastical corruption said by Luther and others to date from the time of Adam and Eve.[7]

Michael's unvarnished prophecies concerning "the state of the Church" until the Second Coming (Argument to Book 12) correspond to the dissenting manifesto in *Of True Religion* (1673), Milton's last word on the state of Christianity. Published at roughly the same time as the revised second edition of *Paradise Lost*, that tract labels Milton not as a

---

[3] Stanley Fish, "Transmuting the Lump: *Paradise Lost*, 1942–79," in *Doing what Comes Naturally: Change, Rhetoric, and the Practice of Theory in Literary and Legal Studies*, Post-Contemporary Interventions (Durham, NC: Duke University Press, 1989), p. 275. Fish exposes institutional reasons for the sea change between C. S. Lewis's 1942 condemnation of "an untransmuted lump of futurity" as "a grave structural flaw" (*Preface*, p. 128) and the 1979 consensus in favor of *PL* 11–12, which is grounded upon the inseparability of Miltonic theology and poetics (pp. 250–51, 263, 275–76).

[4] Barbara K. Lewalski, "Structure and Symbolism of Vision in Michael's Prophecy, *Paradise Lost*, Books XI-XII," *Philological Quarterly* 42 (1963), pp. 25–35.

[5] Lewalski, *Protestant Poetics*, pp. 130–31.

[6] Worden, "Milton, *Samson Agonistes*, and the Restoration," p. 116.

[7] Howard Schultz claims that Michael's historical précis is directed largely against the Church of England in *Milton and Forbidden Knowledge* (New York: MLA, 1955), p. 127.

subscriber to any particular sect, but as an antiformalistic believer for whom inward faith supplies the foundation for meaningful worship. The tract combines rejection of "popish thralldom," religious images, and the "idolatrous" doctrine of transubstantiation, on the one hand, with a radically inward credo grounded upon Protestant doctrines of scripture alone, faith alone, and grace alone, on the other. The pamphlet extols "true worship and service of God [as taught] in the holy scriptures by inspired ministers" and insists upon rejection of "all other traditions or additions whatsoever" (*CPW* 8: 417, 419).

In opposition to official state religion, Milton's pamphlet pleads for liberty of conscience across a broad Protestant spectrum that includes Lutherans and Calvinists (despite Milton's heterodox reconciliation of predestination and free will) in addition to Anabaptists, Arians, Socinians, and "true" Arminians, who do not oppose "free will against free grace" (p. 425). Despite Milton's friendship with members of the Society of Friends such as Thomas Ellwood and Isaac Penington, Quakers go without mention in all of the late tracts, including *Likeliest Means to Remove Hirelings from the Church*, even though its argument resembles theirs.[8] Radically libertarian Friends insisted upon the primacy of the light within, but their guidance by the inward spirit was far from unique in dissenting circles.[9] Although individual sects may err on sacramental or theological questions, according to Milton, their positions fall within permissible limits of dissent from the established Church of England. He excludes recusancy on grounds of heresy.

Michael's training of Adam to reject the "idolatry" of formalistic devotion in favor of inward faith mirrors the dissenting credo in *Of True Religion*. The archangel's delicately ironic response to Adam's effort to physicalize the holy is geared to building up the confidence of his charge. In an aligned response to Eve's grief for the loss of her "native **soil**," Michael constructs a radically inward definition of paradise: "Where he abides, think there thy native **soil**" (11.270, 292). (The phrasing affords a bittersweet pun on the Hebrew word for **soil** in Genesis 2:7, the likely etymology of Adam.)

Adam's poignant lamentation on the imminent loss of Eden manifests a search for a postlapsarian model of worship for himself, Eve, and their

[8] Stephen Marx claims that an antimilitaristic ethos in *PL* parallels Quaker ideology in "The Prophet Disarmed: Milton and the Quakers," *Studies in English Literature 1500–1900* 32 (1992), pp. 111–28, esp. p. 112. David Loewenstein situates *PR* with reference to Quaker interiority and perseverance in "The Kingdom Within: Radical Religious Culture and the Politics of *Paradise Regained*," *L&H* 3rd series 3, no. 2 (1994), pp. 63–89.
[9] See Hill, *World Turned Upside Down*, pp. 186–207, passim.

descendents. If we read the text in accordance with Luther's interpretation of Genesis, Adam engages in an arduous task of differentiating
between "true" and "false" churches:

> This most afflicts me, that departing hence,
> As from his [God's] face I shall be hid, deprived
> His blessed countenance; here I could frequent,
> With worship, place by place where he vouchsafed
> Presence divine, and to my sons relate.   (11.315–19)

Mourning the loss of his unmediated relationship with the Father,
Adam laments his inability to erect **altars** at ostensibly holy sites where
he had worshipped before the Fall:

> So many grateful **altars** I would rear
> Of **grassy turf**, and pile up every stone
> Of lustre from the brook, in memory,
> Or monument to ages, and thereon
> Offer sweet smelling gums and fruits and flowers.   (11.323–27)

Adam's belief in the sanctity of **altars** is wrongheaded, but the
impulse is not wrong. Uncorrected by Michael's preachments, it might
generate kinds of sacramental practices mocked throughout the antiprelatical tracts and earlier books of the epic. Adam's clouded intellect
affords an index of his fallen condition because extemporaneous worship in prelapsarian Eden had required neither **altar** nor liturgy. His
ill-conceived invention of a devotional practice anticipates antiformalistic allegations concerning human "innovations" and "unwritten traditions" of Roman Catholicism and other creeds. In typological terms,
latter-day traditions manifest religious "error" that originated with the
Fall. Before the Fall Adam prayed with Eve in the open air, in the
manner of dissenters contemporary to Milton, and dined with Raphael
at a **table** of **grassy turf** associated with the Lord's Supper as a
communal meal (5.391). Repetition of the phrase **grassy turf** in
Adam's discourse with Michael stresses the point that postlapsarian
altars bear no relation to the unmediated operation of divine **grace**
associated with the prelapsarian **table**.[10]

Although the narrator does posit "a divine presence enclosed within
sanctified boundaries,"[11] that accommodated belief pertains to the
heavenly sanctum where a "golden **altar**" fumes beside the Father's
throne (11.18) rather than to human worship. Demystifying Adam's
belief in physical holiness, Michael leads him to a Pauline-Protestant

---

[10] George Herbert's "Grace" puns on **grace** and **grass**.   [11] Lieb, *Poetics*, pp. 119–20.

understanding that the "true" **altar**, like the "true" temple, lies within. That iconoclastic position recalls Milton's *Reason of Church Government*, which decries the exclusion of the laity from a "perimeter of holy ground about" the **altar** or "wooden table" by means of railings instituted by Archbishop Laud (compare Figures 23–24). The archangel's stand accords with Luther's view that Jacob's altar at Schechem "was not erected for pomp or show, nor for the sacrifices of the Mass."[12] Michael's proto-Protestant attack on the holiness of **altars** takes their establishment at theophanic sites as an external ritualistic practice that will undergo internalization under the New Law. During the Christian dispensation, altar ritual would become "idolatrous." Old Testament holiness anticipates religious ritualism as opposed to the Pauline advocacy of devotion within the inward temple of "the upright heart and pure" (1.18).[13]

Adam's untutored habit of mind stops short of the "superstition and blind zeal" of the Paradise of Fools, where proleptic "pilgrims roam, that strayed so far to seek/In Golgotha him dead, who lives in heaven" (3.452, 476–77). As a counterpart to Michael's correction of Adam's intuitive theological error, the archangel offers instruction concerning the inwardness of "true" devotion by warning against formalistic belief in the sanctity of holy places, pilgrimages, or altars. Affirming that the Father's "omnipresence fills/Land, sea, and air," Michael directs Adam to "surmise not then/His presence to these narrow bounds confined/Of Paradise or Eden" (11.336–37, 340–42). Michael's positive formulation concerning the unmediated nature of devotion supplants his delicate irony concerning Adam's initial belief in holy shrines and altars:

> Yet doubt not but in valley and in plain
> God is as here, and will be found alike
> Present, and of his presence many a sign
> Still following thee, still compassing thee round
> With goodness and paternal love, his face
> Express, and of his steps the track divine.   (11.349–54)

The contrast with future monastics who will inhabit the Paradise of Fools is profound.

In time Adam understands that "God attributes to place/No sanc-

[12] *CPW* I: 843; Luther, *Works*, ed. Jaroslav Pelikan, et al., 55 vols. (St. Louis: Concordia Publ. House, 1959) VI, 185–86 (on Gen. 33:20). See also Pelikan, *Luther the Expositor: Introduction to the Reformer's Exegetical Writings*, the companion vol. to Luther's *Works*, p. 95.
[13] See Jason P. Rosenblatt, *Torah and Law in "Paradise Lost"* (Princeton University Press, 1994), p. 233; Honeygosky, *House*, pp. 174–75.

tity" (11.836–37) when Michael teaches him that the Garden of Eden itself will be swept away by Noah's Flood, the prototypical act of Protestant iconoclasm. Paradise will undergo displacement as a "divine enclosure,"[14] but assurance of redemption will enable it to assume the interiorized form of "A Paradise within thee, happier far" (12.587):

> then shall this mount
> Of Paradise by might of waves be moved
> Out of his place, pushed by the horned flood,
> With all his verdure spoiled.   (11.829–32)

Michael instructs Adam in human history that "only imperfectly reflects the traditional breakdown of the six ages—Creation to Flood, Noah to Abraham, Abraham to David, David to the Babylonian Captivity, the Captivity to the Birth of Christ, the Birth of Christ to Doomsday, and finally the Eternal Sabbath or Millennium." That long-standing scheme undergoes modification by reference to Hebrews 11, which reinterprets Abel, Enoch, Noah, Abraham, Moses, whom Michael reveals to Adam as exemplars of faith, as prefigurations of Christ.[15] Attesting to membership in the invisible church that predates the origin of the visible church at Pentecost, their testimonials of faith accord with the Augustinian allegory concerning the primeval origin of "two cities . . . or societies of human beings, one of which is predestined to reign with God for all eternity, the other doomed to undergo eternal punishment with the Devil" (*City of God*, 15.1). Michael's prophecies further bear out Luther's view that instances of conflict in Genesis exemplify the origination of enduring conflict between "true" and "false" churches.[16]

Although any attempt to impose a reductive, one-to-one allegory of church history upon Books 11 and 12 would fail, given the malleability of scriptural typology, Archangel Michael's prophecies supply paradigms for spiritual obedience that counter instances of "false" ecclesiology throughout *Paradise Lost*. His line of spiritual worthies accords with Milton's own definition of the invisible church in *Christian Doctrine* as the "mystic body" derived from "union and communion with the Father and with Christ, and among the members of Christ's body themselves." Defining "Abel, Noah, Abraham, etc." as "ordinary minister[s]" who anticipate Christian clerical vocation, that text explains that the "marks of the visible church are pure doctrine [i.e. preaching], the true external

---

[14] Lieb, *Poetics*, pp. 136–37, et seq. See also Loewenstein, *Drama*, pp. 108–109.
[15] Lewalski, "Structure," p. 29. See also MacCallum, "History," pp. 150–51.
[16] Luther, *Works*, 6: 32 (on Gen. 31:19). See also Jaroslav Pelikan, *Luther the Expositor*, p. 95.

worship of God, true evangelical charity, insofar as it can be distinguished by man, and the correct administration of the seals" or sacraments. *Christian Doctrine* considers both churches, even though Milton concerns himself chiefly with the invisible.[17] Of course, the visible church errs when it is not coterminous with the invisible.

The contemporaneity of Miltonic typology is apparent from a broadsheet published during the Protectorate, *The Fruits of Faith in these Five Famous Men, Scripture Worthies Heb. XI* (Figure 25). The engraving portrays Joseph instead of Abel, but Enoch, Noah, Abraham, and Moses are present. Inclusion of Abel in Michael's line of worthies accords with the views of dissenters who perceived Abel as the first victim of religious persecution. The broadsheet applies those types of Christ as models for the spiritual experience of "A Newborn Christian," including the "inward" and "outward" person, conscience, and patience. Those are among the virtues in which Michael, as "a consummate typologist,"[18] instructs Adam.

The rectitude of Abel and his successors recalls the zeal of Abdiel, the "Protestant" angel of the War in Heaven. The seraph's obedience to the Father in solitary defiance of Satan affords a prototype for the motif of "the one just man alive" (11.818) associated with the worthies of Hebrews 11. Abdiel's status as a faithful witness accords with his presentation as an antiformalistic hero whose dissent undergoes replication in the defiance of Abel, Enoch, Noah, Abraham, and Moses against the idolatry of their respective generations. Offering a model for "true" heroism of Christian obedience, Abdiel's loyalty anticipates testimonials of faith by members of the antiformalist minority whose religious enthusiasm triggered persecution during the Restoration era.[19]

Abel's murder by Cain (11.429–49) warrants careful attention, because it establishes a typological connection to dissenting interpretation of the faithful son as a model for antiformalistic self-identity. It is the first vision in the series shown by Michael to enable Adam and Eve "to learn/True patience, and to temper joy with fear/And pious sorrow" (11.360–62). Abel's obedience affords a sharp contrast to sinful failures throughout *Paradise Lost*. Although he goes unmentioned in Old Testament considerations of faith, he receives honor in Jesus' prophecy that Christian martyrs will inherit "the blood of Abel the righteous" (Matt. 23:35).

---

[17] *CPW* 6: 499, 563, 570–71. See Honeygosky, *House*, p. 164, et passim).
[18] Regina Schwartz, "From Shadowy Types to Shadowy Types: The Unendings of *Paradise Lost*," *MiltonS* 24 (1988): p. 126.   [19] Steadman, *Hero*, pp. 66–67.

Figure 25   The Line of Faithful Worthies. *The Fruits of Faith in these Five Famous Men, Scripture Worthies Heb. XI* (1656).

Early in the Christian era Cain and Abel underwent allegorization as types for the Old and New Covenants. According to St. Augustine, opposition between the "cities" (i.e. societies) of God and Satan originated in the two brothers.[20] During the Reformation, Protestant theologians such as Luther and Tyndale viewed Cain's slaughter of Abel as the archetype for the age-old conflict between "true" and "false" churches. Luther, in particular, declares that Roman Catholicism originated with Cain, but we need not seek for so specific an identification in Book 11.[21] A Geneva Bible gloss on Hebrews 11:4 associates Abel with the doctrine of predestination because God "imputed him righteous." His sacrificial offering therefore functions as the first testimonial of faith. A companion gloss on Genesis 4:10 speaks of him as a **saint**, an epithet claimed by antiformalists as a token of election: "God revengeth the wrongs of his saints, though none complain."

Paying homage to Abel as a spiritual forebear who underwent persecution as "the proto-martyr of the world,"[22] antiformalists such as Milton viewed him as a model for persecution attendant upon the Restoration. According to the Quaker author, John Crooke, the suffering of "righteous Abel" anticipates oppression under the Clarendon Code because Cain murdered him "for no other cause than the worshipping of God according to his conscience, in the faith and power of God, which was not consistent with Cain's hypocrisy and formality."[23] In Leveling pamphlets published during the Interregnum, Gerrard Winstanley worked out a socioeconomic variation that anticipates Quaker thought. It handles the Bible story more loosely than Milton's more literalistic vision. In tracts such as *The True Leveler's Standard* (1649) and *Watch-Word to the City of London* (1649), Winstanley allegorizes the conflict between Cain and Abel in terms of the pervasive oppression of the meek by wealthy and covetous property owners. The latter text thus attacks "the oppression of lords of manors, hindering the poor from the use of the common land" as an example of "Cain killing Abel to this very day."[24]

Evidence does not indicate that Milton belonged to the Society of

[20] Augustine, *City of God*, 15.1–8. See also St. Ambrose, *Concerning Cain and Abel*, 1.1.5.

[21] Luther, *Works*, 42: 192; Pelikan, *Luther*, pp. 95–106; William Tyndale, *An Answer to Sir Thomas More's Dialogue, The Supper of the Lord*, ed. Henry Walter, vol. XLIV, Parker Society (Cambridge University Press, 1850), p. 107.

[22] *The Brownists' Conventicle: Or an Assembly of Brownists, Separatists, and Nonconformists* (1641), A1ᵛ.

[23] Crooke, *The Cry of the Innocent* (1662), A2; as quoted in Keeble, *Culture*, p. 189.

[24] Gerrard Winstanley, *Works, with an Appendix of Documents Relating to the Digger Movement*, ed. George H. Sabine (New York: Russell & Russell, 1965), p. 323. See also pp. 215, 254, 256, 289, 290, 425–26.

Friends, but a set of tracts by a Quaker contemporary, William Bayly, clarifies our understanding of Abel's stature as a dissenting hero and prototype for antiformalistic spirituality of the kind that we encounter in Books 11 and 12. Taking the conflict between Cain and Abel as a prefiguration of the apocalyptic "battle betwixt Michael and the Dragon, in which the seed of the woman is bruising the serpent's head" (A2), Bayly's *Life of Enoch Again Revived, in Which Abel's Offering is Accepted* (1662) corresponds to the final books of *Paradise Lost* in its breathless movement from the Creation to the Last Judgment. That pamphlet represents Cain and Abel respectively as types for the "outward or fleshly birth" of carnal corruption as opposed to "the inward invisible life" of the spirit (A3ᵛ–B1). Bayly's *The Blood of the Righteous Abel* (1659) and *An Epistle General Containing Wholesome Exhortations and Good Counsel from the Spirit of Truth* (1664) further identify Abel as an antiformalistic forebear. In language that recalls the Protevangelium, Bayly's *Jacob Is Become a Flame and the House of Esau Stubble* (1662) claims that Abel exemplifies the persecution of the "seed of the Woman, which is Christ (in his people)," that is, adherents of the "true" church (A3ᵛ, B2).[25]

In itself, the vision of Cain and Abel is devoid of controversial associations. Michael accordingly explains the slaughter in terms of conflict between faithlessness and the sufficiency of faith:

> the unjust the just hath slain,
> For envy that his brother's offering found
> From heaven acceptance; but the bloody fact
> Will be avenged, and the other's faith approved.   (11.455–58)

Nevertheless, Protestant apologists imposed polemical applications on the story. In one of many Old Testamental examples of divine election of a younger brother over his elder, typology that Protestants used to mock Catholicism as the "old" religion, Cain travesties Abel's spirituality. Milton's representation of Cain accords with mockery of his "seed, stock, or offspring," that is, "popes, emperors, bishops, kings, priests, princes, dukes, earls, or councils of ungodly men," in William Bayly's *Jacob Is Become a Flame* (A2ᵛ–3).

Sharing of an **altar** by Cain and Abel indicates that the physical site per se lacks spiritual significance. Abel's sacrifice of "the firstlings of his

---

[25] Bayly's fifth extant pamphlet is *The Dreadful, and Terrible, Day of the Lord God, to Overtake this Generation Suddenly* (1665). A one time Baptist minister, he was a Dorset shipmaster who served as a Quaker missionary in North America after conversion by George Fox. See Hugh Barbour, *The Quakers in Puritan England* (New Haven: Yale University Press, 1964), p. 52.

flock" with "incense strewed" in genuine "piety thus and pure devotion" betokens divine election and justification by faith (11.437, 439, 452).
The Father rejects Cain's agrarian offering, by contrast, because "his
was not sincere" (11.443). Hebrews 12:24 explains that Abel is a type of
Christ, the Good Shepherd, even though the "sprinkling" of the latter's
blood "speaketh better things than that of Abel." As the first shepherd,
he affords a clerical model for pastoral care.[26] The younger brother's
offering of sacrificial lambs on "cleft wood," with "all due rites per-
formed," typifies Christ's sacrifice on the Cross[27] both as "the lamb of
God, which taketh away the sin of the world" (John 1:29) and as "a
sheep [led] to the slaughter" (Acts 8:32).

Emphasis upon Abel's "sheep-walks and **folds**" (11.431) would seem
to suggest a controversial undertone if we recall that Milton very often
associates **fold** with ecclesiastical conflict. Examples include wolfish
clerics of *Lycidas*, who "Creep and intrude, and climb into the **fold**" (line
115), and Satan's entry into Eden like "a prowling wolf" who steals into
"God's **fold**" (4.183, 192). Those passages allude to St. Paul's prophecy
concerning the corruption of the Pentecostal church: "After my departing shall grievous wolves enter in among you, not sparing the **flock**"
(Acts 20:29). Unlike Satan, whose wolf-like predation affords a demonic
precedent for the "lewd hirelings" who will intrude "into his [God's]
church" (4.193), Abel recalls the Miltonic ideal of an unsalaried antiformalistic ministry. The livelihood of such ministers came from hard work
sincerely undertaken, rather than enforced payment of tithes.[28]

Cain's presentation incorporates a previously unrecognized concern
with transubstantiation and the Mass. Just as Abel is a type of Jesus as
the second Adam, Cain as a "sweaty reaper" falls heir to the curse that
associates **sweat** with original sin. In accordance with the Protevangelium, the first Adam must **sweat** to produce food: "In the **sweat** of
thy face shalt thou eat **bread**" (10.205).[29] Bearing the stamp of Satan,

[26] This ancient view recurs in texts ranging from Spenser's *Shepheardes Calender* to Thomas Fuller's *Abel Redivivus, Or the Dead Yet Speaking* (1651). Thus the narrator of Spenser's July Eclogue cites "the first shepheard" as the prototype for proper clerical meekness, simplicity, and humility (lines 125–31). E. K. provides this gloss: "The firste shepheard was Abell the righteous, who (as scripture sayth) bent his mind to keeping of sheepe, as did hys brother Cain to tilling the grownde."

[27] *PL* 11.440; Hugh R. MacCallum, "Milton and Sacred History: Books XI and XII of Paradise Lost," in *Essays in English Literature from the Renaissance to the Victorian Age Presented to A.S.P. Woodhouse*, ed. Millar Maclure and F.W. Watt (University of Toronto Press, 1964), p. 154.

[28] See Chapter 2; Matt. 7:15, 9:36, 10:6, 15:24; Knott, *Discourses of Martyrdom in English Literature, 1563–1694* (Cambridge University Press, 1993), pp. 165–67.

Sin, and Death, the sweaty brother's making of insincere offerings at a sacrificial **altar**, his growing of wheat for the baking of **bread**, and his slaughter of Abel, who "Groaned out his soul with gushing **blood**" (11.447), suggest an unflattering glance at belief in the transubstantiation of **bread and wine** into Christ's **body and blood** before a high **altar**. Analogy between the Roman-rite Mass and the elder brother's crime of manslaughter thus parallels an anti-Mass satire by Luke Shepherd, *The Upcheering of the Mass* (c. 1547), which connects the Roman-rite sacrament to the crime of Cain: "Some call her [the Mass] pope's daughter/Some say she made [i.e., created] manslaughter" (A4).

By contrast to Abel's spirituality, Cain recalls the physicality of Adam's postlapsarian belief in shrines and **altars** as holy places. The elder brother's sacrilege corresponds to William Bayly's claim that he is the forebear of "superstitious and idolatrous priests, bishops, and hirelings."[30] Death by stoning further suggests a typological relationship between Abel and St. Stephen as the Christian proto-martyr who died from stoning following his polemical sermon before the Sanhedrin (Acts 7).[31] Because Abel was the first martyr (Matt. 23:35, Luke 11:51), Stephen succeeded him as a scriptural prototype for testimony of faith to the point of death.

Even Cain's insincere failure to cull out the chaff in the first fruits of his "tillage," by contrast to Abel's faithful offering of "the firstlings of his flock/Choicest and best" (11.434–38), suggests a possible stab against the offering of tithes as **first fruits**. Christians believe that the New Law abrogates Hebrew tithing in the form of ritual sacrifice of the initial produce of the agricultural year. Milton went so far as to believe that it abrogates tithing altogether. Prefiguring the Crucifixion, Abel's offering of better sacrifices recalls prayers offered by Adam and Eve as "first fruits" that earned divine favor as a sign of "implanted grace" (11.22–23). By contrast, Cain's offering of first fruits recalls the narrator's invective against wolf-like Satan's invasion of Eden: "So since into his church lewd hirelings climb" (4.193). *Likeliest Means to Remove Hirelings* similarly attacks the installation of salaried clergy, who received payment out of tithes. Other pamphlets attack the maintenance of ecclesiastical "wolves" who are "stuffed with tithes." It was customary for

---

[29] According to Virginia R. Mollenkott, Cain's sin parallels its satanic archetype: "The Cycle of Sins in *Paradise Lost*, Book XI," *Modern Language Quarterly* 27 (1966), p. 34. On Adamic typology, see Raymond B. Waddington, "The Death of Adam: Vision and Voice in Books XI and XII of *Paradise Lost*," *Modern Philology* 70 (1972), pp. 19–21.

[30] Bayly, *Jacob is Become a Flame and the House of Esau Stubble* (1662), A4.

[31] Frye, *Imagery*, p. 303.

bishops and other holders of church benefices to seek lay appropriations, over and above tithes, in order to pay the **first fruits** that generally amounted to the entire income of their first year, which they owed to the donor of their living.[32]

Following the vision of Death's "grim cave," the sequel to Cain's murder of Abel, intimations of religious strife infiltrate the vision of the men of apparent faith who unite with a "bevy of fair women" (11.582). Like Archangel Uriel, Adam is taken in by external appearances: "Just men they seemed, and all their study bent/To worship God aright" (11.577–78). Despite their appearance as a "sober race of men, whose lives/Religious titled them the sons of God," the men who dwell in "the tents/Of wickedness" are descendents of Cain. Their skillful production of sophisticated artifice, "Unmindful of their maker," gives them the appearance of "false" clerics who pursue Satanic contrivance on the model of Comus, Belial, or Mammon (11.607–608, 611, 621–22). The dwellings of Cain's inheritors mirror those of the fallen angels, in line with Abdiel's challenge to Satan: "Yet not for thy advice or threats I fly/These wicked tents devoted" (5.889–90).

Dramatic irony pervades Adam's humorous inclination "to admit delight,/The bent of nature" (11.596–97) when the women arouse erotic desire in his descendants (and in him!) by means of "Soft amorous ditties" and "dance" (11.584):

> then all in heat
> They light the nuptial torch, and bid invoke
> Hymen, then first to marriage rites invoked.
>
> (11.589–91)

True to his own character, Adam fails to perceive lust as a mark of original sin inherited through Cain. That misinterpretation evokes not laughter in heaven, but angelic correction aimed at the inculcation of spiritual values that undergo inversion during the vision. Following the stock pattern of vision, misjudgment, and angelic moralization, Michael couches his correction in terms of the Pauline opposition of inward spirituality versus external "carnal" corruption.[33]

The beguiling women who appeal to Adam's lustful bent are "fair atheists" whose "gems and wanton dress" and "lustful appetance" mark them as seductive offspring of Eve, well versed in temptation (11.583,

---

[32] See Collinson, *Religion*, pp. 68, 72–73, 123; and D. M. Wolfe, *Milton in the Puritan Revolution* (New York, 1941), pp. 107, 109, who cites Milton's *Tenure*, *Defensio Secunda*, and *Christian Doctrine*.

[33] Maus acknowledges the Protestant cast of the early modern rhetoric of inwardness without citing its Pauline origins in *Inwardness*, pp. 4, 8, 10–11, 19–20, 23.

619, 625). Although the prelapsarian lovemaking of Adam and Eve had taken on a quasi-sacramental, albeit non-liturgical cast, the invention of "marriage rites" and invocation of the Roman god Hymen may allude to the Roman-rite liturgy, which included wedlock among the seven sacraments. Protestants recognized only Baptism and the Lord's Supper, in the belief that only two sacraments possessed scriptural warrant. Patrick Hume's 1695 commentary indicates that devotion to Hymen "denotes their forsaking the true God, and setting up abominable idols" (n. on 11.590).

In the fourth vision, Enoch's solitary testimonial of faith as "the only righteous in a world perverse" recalls professions made by Abdiel and Abel (11.664–711):

> till at last
> Of middle age one rising, eminent
> In wise deport, spake much of right and wrong,
> Of justice, of religion, truth and peace,
> And judgment from above.　　　　　　　(11.664–68)

Courting martyrdom on the model of Abel, Enoch is a solitary preacher of religious "truth" whose direct translation to heaven is a sign of divine favor (Heb. 11:5).[34] Indeed, William Bayly's *Life of Enoch* interprets him and the other worthies of Hebrews 11 as types of "the most inward life, which is of God," as opposed to the unrepentant "generation" of Cain (B1ᵛ). Emphasis upon Enoch's interiority must have exerted special appeal to readers who rejected formalistic worship during the Restoration.

Noah's building of the "wondrous ark" as the "one just man alive" exemplifies the antiformalistic ideal of the invisible church made up of the faithful few who emulate the zeal of Abel and Enoch. As one who "preached/Conversion and repentance" in the midst of a sinful generation, Noah resembles a type for evangelical ministry (11.723–24, 818–19).[35] Emphasis upon the Ark as a figure for the Church Triumphant[36] accords with seventeenth-century Protestant iconography. The engraved title page of George Carleton's *A Thankful Remembrance* (Figure 22), for example, aligns that figure for England's providential deliver-

---

[34] See Steadman, *Hero*, pp. 66–67.

[35] See Luther, *Works*, 2: 99 (on Gen. 7:17–24), passim.

[36] See Albert C. Labriola, "The Medieval View of Christian History in *Paradise Lost*," in *Milton and the Middle Ages*, ed. John Mulryan (Lewisburg, PA: Bucknell University Press, 1982), pp. 125–27; Mollenkott, "Cycle," p. 39.

ance with the triumph *Per aquas* ("through waters") of *Ecclesia Vera* ("the true church") over *Ecclesia Malignantium* ("the evil church"), identified with the Devil, the Pope, a cardinal, and a monk. Despite the emptying out of hopes for ecclesiastical restoration, messianic expectations cling to the conclusion of Book 11, according to which all human yearnings undergo apocalyptic deferral "till fire purge all things new,/Both heaven and earth, wherein the just shall dwell" (11.900–901).

Following Michael's shift from vision to narration, which prevents Adam from seeing "later, more spiritual manifestations of the Covenant of Grace,"[37] the archangel's instruction concerning Abraham's exile from his homeland recounts a narrative fundamental to antiformalistic tradition.[38] Dissenters regarded Abraham's "calling" to emigrate from the idol-worshipping land of Mesopotamia as a prototype for inspiration by inward faith and conscience. William Bayly's *Epistle General* therefore cites him as the model for those "under judgment or sentence of banishment for the testimony of Jesus Christ." Like their spiritual forefather, dissenters "wander . . . exposed to the want of a certain dwelling place in the earth" (A1–2). In other tracts, Bayly identifies the "seed of Abraham (which is Christ in us)" with the Quakers, who undergo persecution by "Babylonish" and "Egyptian" bishops.[39] Antiformalists did not originate such exegesis, because Jewish, Christian, and Muslim theologians regard Abraham as the prototype for conversion and faith. For Luther and others, he is a patriarch of the "true" church.[40]

Michael's account of the Exodus, another narrative fundamental to antiformalistic literary tradition,[41] expounds the standard Christian interpretation of the Israelites' flight from Egyptian bondage as a type for the transition from Old to New Law. From the time of Tyndale, English Protestants furthermore regarded Moses' opposition to Pharaoh as a prefiguration of the conflict between the "true" church and the Roman Antichrist. As such, Moses plays a "prophetic, ministerial role."[42] Pharaoh's contrasting status as "lawless tyrant" and "obdurate king" (12.173, 205) identifies him as a spiritual heir of Satan. Eighth among the ten plagues sent by God to win release for the Israelites, the "darksome cloud of locusts" brings the reader full circle to the epic

---

[37] Lewalski, "Structure," pp. 29–31.   [38] Keeble, *Culture*, pp. 263–68.

[39] Bayly, *Jacob is Become a Flame*, A4ᵛ, B3; *The Life of Enoch Again Revived, in which Abel's Offering is Accepted* (1662), A4ᵛ–B1.

[40] Commentary on Gen. 12–20 in Luther, *Works*, II–III: passim; Calvin, *Institutes*, 2.10.11. See Rosenblatt, *Torah*, p. 229.   [41] Keeble, *Culture*, pp. 273–78.   [42] Shawcross, *Self*, p. 268.

simile in Book 1, which likens hovering devils to the "cloud of locusts . . . o'er the realm of impious Pharaoh" (1.341–42). That figure hints at a possible link between the fallen angels and Jesuitry.[43]

The oppression of dissenters under the Clarendon Code affords a contemporary analogue to the Israelites' fear of a "Return . . . back to Egypt, choosing rather/Inglorious life with servitude" (12.219–20). In ironic anticipation of Michael's words, Milton's argument against restoration of monarchy in his final pre-Restoration tract, *The Ready and Easy Way,* had warned against "this noxious humor of returning to bondage" by willing placement of "our necks again under kingship, as was made use of by the Jews to return back to Egypt" (*CPW* 7: 407, 462). By contrast, Puritan tradition declared free choice of the wilderness as a "signal mark of the saint."[44] It may be that the marginal role played by Moses' brother, Aaron, in Michael's account of the Exodus reflects contemporary claims that he offers a precedent for prelacy. Milton argues against that belief in *Reason of Church Government,* which rejects "the priesthood of Aaron [as] a pattern whereas to ground episcopacy." That position agrees with Tyndale's seminal view that Aaron "signifieth every disciple of Christ, and every true preacher of God's word."[45] Nonetheless we remember that Aaron is tainted by the Israelites' construction and worship of the golden calf, to which Milton alludes during the discovery of idolatry in Eden (see Chapter 8).

Moses' transmission of the Law marks him as a more complete type of Christ, "whose high office now/Moses in figure bears" (12.240–41), than the worthies who have gone before: Abel, Enoch, Noah, and Abraham. His prefiguration of Christ's status as the sole mediator between God and humanity feeds into Michael's theological formulation, negations of which undergo mockery elsewhere in Milton's poem. Mosaic prophecy would undergo reversal in sacerdotal arrogation of an intercessory "Mosaic" role in the visible church, just as the replacement of ceremonial law and "works of law" with justification by faith and "works of faith" anticipates antiformalistic rejection of the ritualism of the Churches of Rome and England.[46] Wrongly interpreted, the shedding

---

[43] Tyndale, *Answer,* p. 144. According to Peter Sterry's *England's Deliverance* (1652), papacy and presbytery represent "two spiritual Egypts . . . Twice hath the Lord overwhelmed them in the Red Sea of their own blood" (p. 29).

[44] Keeble, *Culture,* p. 273. See also Hill, *MER,* pp. 206–207.

[45] *CPW* 1: 766; Tyndale, *Treatises,* p. 209.   [46] See Madsen, *Types,* p. 108, and passim.

of blood in Mosaic "rites/Of sacrifice" prefigures transubstantiation and the Mass.[47]

It may be that Michael's abbreviated account of the Babylonian Captivity and the Judaeans' return from exile has a polemical undertone. The desecration of the Temple in Jerusalem and captivity of the Chosen People recall the anguished outcry against "the Babylonian woe" in Milton's "On the Late Massacre in Piedmont," a sonnet that dwells upon Rome as Babylon, the Scarlet Whore of both Old and New Testaments. Puritans such as Cornelius Burges had applied the return from Babylon as a prefiguration of the downfall of the prelates during the early 1640s.[48] Michael's narrative parts from that preacher's forward-looking optimism, however, in describing the return from captivity and the ensuing pollution of the Temple by fractious priests who anticipate clerical corruption under the New Law:

> But first among the priests dissension springs,
> Men who attend the **altar**, and should most
> Endeavour peace.   (12.353–56)

The officiation of Jewish priests at a sacrificial **altar** recalls Belial's presence "at **altars**, when the priest/Turns atheist" (1.494–95), and Cain's shedding of Abel's blood before their archetypal **altar**. Furthermore, the seizure of power by priests of the Asmonean dynasty exemplifies sacerdotalism that would eventually flourish in papal and episcopal claims to both spiritual and temporal power. Michael's attack on discord within the priesthood recalls Milton's antiprelatical pamphlets (see Flannagan n. on 12.353).

After Michael's lesson concerning Christ's death and resurrection leads Adam to his highest point of understanding, the latter's final question feeds into the archangel's concluding prophecy concerning corruption in the visible church (12.480–550). Adam asks:

> what will betide the few
> His faithful, left among the unfaithful herd,
> The enemies of truth; who then shall guide
> His people, who defend?   (12.480–83)

He thus reformulates an earlier question inspired by Abel: "Is piety thus and pure devotion paid?" (11.452). Although Michael acknowledges that martyrs (i.e. faithful witnesses) will suffer persecution, he offers consoling

---

[47] *PL* 12.231–32. MacCallum, "History," p. 157.
[48] Burges, *Sermon Preached to the Honourable House of Commons*, 3rd ed. (1640), p. 36. See Knott, *Discourses*, p. 167.

knowledge concerning the inscription upon their hearts of "the law of faith/Working through love" (12.488–89) by the inward operation of the Holy Spirit.

Michael's final lesson binds together polemical strands that the reader encounters in many episodes of *Paradise Lost*. That densely scriptural paraphrase of the institution of the visible church at Pentecost, when "the Spirit/Poured first on his apostles, whom he sends / To evangelize the nations" (12.487–89), is studded with topoi that echo and reecho in Milton's poem and both *Lycidas* and the antiprelatical tracts. Inspiration of the apostles to "speak all tongues, and do all miracles" (12.501) will reverse the linguistic confusion inflicted upon the builders of the Tower of Babel (12.48–62),[49] whose "vain design" will earn them a place at the Paradise of Fools (3.467). The alert reader might recall that the Pentecostal descent of the Spirit like a great wind undergoes ironic reversal in satire on the friars at the Limbo of Vanity.

Following the Pentecostal age, clerical corruption and belief in apostolic succession will supplant the "true" apostleship of Christian witnesses:

> Wolves shall succeed for teachers, grievous wolves,
> Who all the sacred mysteries of heaven
> To their own vile advantages shall turn
> Of lucre and ambition, and the truth
> With superstitions and traditions taint,
> Left only in those written records pure,
> Though not but by the Spirit understood.   (12.508–14)

Jesus provides the model for invective in the Sermon on the Mount, which prophesies the appearance of "false prophets, which come to you in sheep's clothing, but inwardly they are ravening wolves" (Matt. 7:15). Michael's polemical sermon echoes attacks on clerical "wolves," be they the pope, English prelates, Presbyterians, or "hireling" ministers of all denominations, throughout Milton's career. Although Michael frames his description of the "state of the Church" in general terms, allusion to restoration of the prelatical Church of England as the latest in a pervasive sequence of ecclesiastical failures seems altogether likely.[50]

The parodic Pentecost of the Paradise of Fools, the proleptic residence of Catholic mendicants, is at hand when Michael foresees the advent of a clerical hierarchy that will corrupt spiritual affairs through

---

[49] Loewenstein, *Drama*, p. 116.
[50] See John 10:12; Wilding, *Dragons Teeth*, pp. 243–44. Ignoring the appeal of Matt. 7:15 to dissenters like Milton, Edward Stillingfleet limits his *Sermon Preached November 5, 1673* (1674) to an orthodox application against the Church of Rome.

collaboration with temporal authority:

> Then shall they seek to avail themselves of names,
> Places and titles, and with these to join
> Secular power, though feigning still to act
> By spiritual, to themselves appropriating
> The Spirit of God, promised alike and given
> To all believers; and from that pretence,
> Spiritual laws by carnal power shall force
> On every conscience; laws which none shall find
> Left them enrolled, or what the Spirit within
> Shall on the heart engrave.   (12.515–24)

Patrick Hume's 1695 commentary glosses "names,/Places and titles" with reference to papal offices: "Of Names; Christ Vicar General, Universal Bishop, Successor to St. Peter: Places; Bishop of Rome; Titles; His Holiness, Infallibility, assuming to themselves worldly power, and human authority." That reading seems overly particular, but the claim of the Roman hierarchy to intercede between the "Spirit of God" and individual Christians does contradict Michael's assertion of the priesthood of all believers, whereby lay people may attain spiritual understanding without clerical intercession.

The archangel's invective is not limited to the Roman church hierarchy, because all institutional bodies are included in his critique of organized religion. His language would seem to allude to the persecution of antiformalists during the Restoration under "spiritual laws by carnal power" enforced "on every conscience," but scriptural typology is not limited to any particular historical instance.[51] Michael's position corresponds to Milton's personal toleration of sectarian dissent,[52] but the text does not mention sectarianism by name. Studied vagueness may represent a response to Crown censorship, but it does leave the impression that the poem lauds dissent at the same time that it maintains functional ambiguity.

Turning worship in a radically inward direction, Michael's prophecies complement controversial attack with testimonials of faith by the line of "just men" (Abel, Enoch, Noah, Abraham, and Moses). Grounded upon Pauline texts including Romans 8, Galatians, and Hebrews 11, the archangel's opposition between external corruption of the flesh and inward liberation of the spirit corresponds to the Lutheran doctrine of justification by faith alone and other fundamental Protestant

---

[51] Timothy C. Miller, "Milton's Religion of the Spirit and 'the state of the Church' in Book XII of *Paradise Lost*," *Restoration* 13 (1989): p. 8. See Fowler nn. on 12.507–508, 528–30.

[52] Shawcross, *Self*, pp. 251–52.

tenets.[53] Recurring in Protestant treatises since the time of Tyndale, the dichotomy between flesh and spirit pervades Milton's *Treatise of Civil Power* and other texts:

That the inward man is nothing else but the inward part of man, his understanding and his will, and that his actions thence proceeding, yet not simply thence but from the work of divine grace upon them, are the whole matter of religion under the gospel. (*CPW* 7: 255)

Like Milton, William Bayly consistently opposes "the inward life, of uprightness and Truth" modeled upon Abel and the line of worthies who succeed him to the "outward or fleshly birth" of the descendants of Cain.[54] The broadsheet based upon Hebrews 11, *The Fruits of Faith in these Five Famous Men*, similarly opposes "inward man" to "outward man" among the evangelical categories of its "Picture of a Newborn Christian" (see Figure 25).

In a return to sentiments expressed in the opening invocation of *Paradise Lost*, in which the narrator prays to the "Spirit, that dost prefer/Before all **temples** the upright heart and pure" (1.17–18), Michael articulates the Pauline definition of the faithful believer as a "**temple** of the Holy Ghost" (1 Cor. 6:19) who supplants the edifice of any merely physical church. The inward **temple** is a site for "true" worship that undergoes parody in the idolatrous shrines satirized in earlier books of Milton's poem. The archangel's devotional formulation would have offered consolation to dissenters opposed to the ecclesiastical establishment. In response to Adam's final question, Michael prophesies that "carnal power" will prove incapable of demolishing God's

> living **temples**, built by faith to stand,
> Their own faith not another's: for on earth
> Who against faith and conscience can be heard
> Infallible? Yet many will presume:
> Whence heavy persecution shall arise
> On all who in the worship persevere
> Of spirit and truth; the rest, far greater part,
> Well deem in outward rites and specious forms
> Religion satisfied; truth shall retire
> Bestruck with slanderous darts, and works of faith
> Rarely to be found.　　　　　　　　　　(12.527–37)

---

[53] See Luther, *Works*, 29: 229–41; 35: 347–56. On inwardness v. outwardness in Milton's prose, see Honeygosky, *House*, pp. 139–42, 169–80.

[54] Bayly, *Life of Enoch*, A3–B2ᵛ, quoting B1ʳ⁻ᵛ. See also his *Blood of Righteous Abel Crying from the Ground*, *Jacob Is Become a Flame*, and *An Epistle General Containing Wholesome Exhortations and Good Counsel from the Spirit of Truth* (1664), passim.

Although the suffering of the faithful will begin with persecution and martyrdom under the Roman emperors, worship in "spirit and truth" will endure in the visible church until the introduction of "outward rites and specious forms." Patrick Hume interprets that passage in opposition to Catholicism: "These living temples stand founded in their own faith, (not that of the Church of Rome)." Commenting that "the belief and consciences of Christians" are "independent of Rome's infallible chair" (i.e. the papal see, from Latin *sedem*, "seat"), he discerns polemical attack on the "ceremonies, rituals, gaudy processions, and fair shows" of popes who govern Rome in succession to ancient emperors (n. on 12.534). Nevertheless, Milton never confined attack on sacerdotalism solely to the Church of Rome.

In the manner of St. Peter's prophecy in *Lycidas*, Michael's prophecy extends to the contemporary moment. Articulating ideas that correlate with those of antiformalists such as William Bayly, Archangel Michael delivers what reads like a dissenting sermon concerning freedom of conscience, belief in the indwelling Spirit, fierce anticlericalism, and opposition to institutionalized worship and "hireling" ministers. Those principles align *Paradise Lost* not with any particular sect, but with Milton's position concerning the variety of sects in *Of True Religion*.[55] The poem's tolerationist impulse extends to the apocalyptic readiness with which the archangel concludes:

> so shall the world go on,
> To good malignant, to bad men benign,
> Under her own weight groaning till the day
> Appear of respiration to the just,
> And vengeance to the wicked, at return
> Of him so lately promised to thy aid,
> The woman's seed, obscurely then foretold,
> Now amplier known thy saviour and thy Lord,
> Last in the clouds from heaven to be revealed
> In glory of the Father, to dissolve
> Satan with his perverted world, then raise
> From the conflagrant mass, purged and refined,
> New heavens, new earth, ages of endless date
> Founded in righteousness and peace and love
> To bring forth fruits joy and eternal bliss.   (12.537–51)

At the conclusion of *Paradise Lost*, Adam prepares to leave Eden in company with Eve. Seeming more the father of Abel than Cain, he has

---

[55] See Shawcross, *Self*, pp. 251–52, 255–56; Hill, *World*, pp. 186–207, passim.

absorbed Michael's preachments concerning patient obedience, inward faith, and true heroism of saintly martyrdom. Through increasingly compressed prophecies, the archangel has inculcated in his charges a set of spiritual values that complement and fulfill earlier instances of "controversial merriment" at religious "folly." The archangel's "theology of suffering,"[56] anticipates the experience of members of the "true" church, who ostensibly include antiformalists and dissenters of the Restoration era: "that suffering for truth's sake/Is fortitude to highest victory,/And to the faithful death the gate of life" (12.569–71). Adam's conversion from idolatry, notably his belief in shrines, altars, and holy places, to patient suffering dramatizes a shift away from formalistic ritual. Michael's consolation extends the promise that good works predicated upon faith will enable Adam and Eve to "possess/A paradise within thee, happier far" (12.586–87):

> only add
> Deeds to thy knowledge answerable, add faith,
> Add virtue, patience, temperance, add love,
> By name to come called Charity , the soul
> Of all the rest.   (12.581–85)

[56] Knott, *Discourses*, p. 152.

Conclusion

Published together in 1671, *Paradise Regained* and *Samson Agonistes* afford a reprise of some familiar elements concerning the post-Restoration predicament of antiformalistic believers.[1] Even though those elements hint at a concern with religious satire or polemic in Milton's brief epic and apocalyptic tragedy, that potential remains undeveloped by contrast to *Paradise Lost*. The 1671 publications are devoid of explicit topical outbursts. They fail to match the deeply embedded engagement of *Paradise Lost* with religious polity, "papistry," prelatical governance of the church, clerical celibacy, monasticism, sacramentalism, transubstantiation, substitution of a railed-off high altar for a Communion Table accessible to the laity, or other polemical issues that embroiled seventeenth-century British public life.

Paradise Regained does feature the mid-air gathering of a demonic "consistory" (1.42) and the "conflux issuing forth, or entering in" the Capitol of Imperial Rome (4.62–64), which recall both the "secret conclave" and bee-like swarming of the devils at Pandaemonium, "the high capital/Of Satan and his peers" (1.756–57). The reader also encounters Satan as "an aged man in rural weeds" (1.314), whose disguising recalls his appearance in *Paradise Lost* in the "habit" of a "stripling cherub" who personifies Hypocrisy (*PL* 3.636, 643). The radical inwardness of *Paradise Regained* styles the Son, in many respects, as an antiformalistic hero compatible with the mindset of Quaker brethren, including Milton's friends, Thomas Ellwood and Isaac Penington, and members of other dissenting sects. Having read *Paradise Lost* in manuscript, Ellwood claimed to have inspired composition of its sequel. It may be that the Son's "unobserved" return "Home to his mother's house private" (4.638–39), at the conclusion of *Paradise Regained*, alludes

---

[1] See Schultz, *Forbidden Knowledge*, passim; Hill, *MER*, pp. 415, 419, 421–22. Dispute continues over the date of composition of *Samson Agonistes*.

to religious observances at private homes in violation of the Conventicles Acts of 1664 and 1670, which banned congregational meetings at locations other than established churches.[2]

The Son's dauntless ability to see through satanic disguise is not conducive, however, to the development of intense dramatic irony of the kind that pervades the earlier biblical epic, where cherubic Satan deceives Uriel or eavesdrops upon Adam and Eve in different bestial guises. In place of sardonic wordplay or mocking laughter in heaven, the reader encounters the voice of divine approval: "This is my son beloved, in him am pleased" (1.85; sic). The Son's heroism functions as the austere antitype for the "true" heroism of righteousness, fortitude, and faith celebrated by Archangel Michael. Milton does not follow the lead of William Perkins and Thomas Taylor, Protestant commentators who situate the Temptation of Jesus by Satan within an anti-Catholic polemical context.[3] By contrast to Patrick Hume and Thomas Warton, who offer a richly detailed textual foundation for their detection of religious complaint and satire in *Paradise Lost*, Robert Thyer fails to substantiate his purported discovery of a contradiction between the "youthful meditations of our Savior" and the "superstitious trumpery" and "apocryphal trash" of Catholic tradition.[4]

In *Samson Agonistes*, the Old Testament hero's destruction of the temple of the Philistine fish god, Dagon, recalls the pompous majesty of Pandaemonium.[5] Samson's attack on Philistine "pomp and sacrifice" (line 436) may prefigure iconoclastic attack on seventeenth-century "idolatry," but allusions to ecclesiastical history are not extensive.[6] In the eyes of William Bayly, Dagon is a type for tyrannical religio-political authority (*Epistle General*, B1).[7] Thomas Warton interprets the Public Officer's speech concerning "the well-feasted priest" and popular "holy-days" (lines 1419–21), however, as "a concealed attack on the ritual of the church of England." Warton lodges the further claim that Milton

---

[2] Gary Hamilton, "*Paradise Regained* and the Private Houses," in *Of Poetry and Politics: New Essays on Milton and His World*, ed. P. G. Stanwood, vol. 126, (Binghamton, NY: MRTS, 1995), pp. 239–48, esp. pp. 241, 148.

[3] Perkins, *The Combat between Christ and Devil Displayed* (1606), B4, B6; Taylor, *Christ's Combat and Conquest* (1618), B3ᵛ, V6.

[4] *PR*, ed. Charles Dunster (1795), n. on 1.201.

[5] Gilman, *Iconoclasm*, pp. 170–77, citing p. 175.

[6] Loewenstein, *Drama*, pp. 138, 147; Guibbory, *Ceremony and Community*, pp. 220–26. See also Knoppers, *Historicizing Milton*, pp. 54–63.

[7] See Guibbory, *Ceremony and Community*, pp. 221, 224; Jackie Di Salvo, "The Lord's Battells: *Samson Agonistes* and the Puritan Revolution," MiltonS 4 (1972), 39–62, 44.

expresses his contempt of a nobility and an opulent clergy, that is, lords both temporal and spiritual, who by no means coincided with his leveling and narrow principles of republicanism and Calvinism, and whom he tacitly compares with the lords and priests of the idol Dagon. (Milton, *Poems*, ed. Wharton, p. 51)

Bearing an "enchanted cup" reminiscent of the Whore of Babylon, Dalila recalls Protestant attacks on the Church of Rome as an unholy seductress. A recollection of the serpentine aspect of Miltonic Sin informs the Chorus's declaration that Samson's Philistine lover is "a manifest serpent by her sting/Discovered in the end, till now concealed" (lines 997–98). Blind Samson's regeneration to the point where he embraces spirituality and obedient patience in place of outward valor enables him to destroy the temple of Dagon through heroism predicated upon inward illumination rather than physical strength.[8] Like the very end of *Paradise Lost*, *Paradise Regained* and *Samson Agonistes* dramatize spiritual freedom contingent upon the inward integrity of new-style heroes of faithful obedience.

By contrast to the 1671 publications, *Paradise Lost* demonstrates a deep engagement with religious complaint and satire, one that is fundamental to the interplay among the poem's many literary genres and modes. The text responds to and participates in contemporaneous dispute concerning ecclesiastical governance and worship, which had a profound impact on many aspects of public and private life. The present study has documented this preoccupation with heated religious dispute as an important, but previously unrecognized, component of Milton's great epic of the Fall. The eruption of St. Peter's satirical voice within the pastoral monody in *Lycidas* prepares the way for the broad critique of "false" worship in the biblical epic, one that reformulates contentious issues examined in Milton's antiprelatical tracts. The present study extends to *Paradise Lost* a mode of reading invited by the expanded headnote of the 1645 edition of *Lycidas*, which "by occasion foretells the ruin of our corrupted clergy." The declaration that Archangel Michael's prophecies consider "the state of the Church" until the Second Coming accordingly takes on great importance (*PL* 12. Argument). His history of the Christian church concludes with instruction relevant to the situation of antiformalists during Milton's age and preceding generations.

Critics have misunderstood Milton's commitment to "controversial merriment" ever since Joseph Addison and neoclassical critics whom he

---

[8] For an alternative view, see Loewenstein, "Kingdom," p. 83.

influenced censured the allegory of Sin and Death and antifraternal satire at the Paradise of Fools. *The Spectator* influenced later readers with the declaration that "sentiments which raise laughter can very seldom be admitted with any decency into an heroic poem, whose business is to excite passions of a much nobler nature."[9] Attacking the predominance of wordplay in *Paradise Lost*, Addison, Johnson, and others rejected Miltonic humor, vernacular usages, and technical vocabulary as lowly violations of epic decorum. The imposition of neoclassical canons of taste upon Milton's pre-Enlightenment poetics contributed to an enduring suppression of the poem's polemical and satirical aspect.

Addison's strictures ignore early modern interpretative and cultural practices that accord with Milton's habitual recourse to pun, parody, burlesque, ironic allusion, vernacular usage, learned etymological wordplay, and unflattering scriptural typology to ridicule religious "error." His poetic practice is more closely attuned to anti-Catholic broadsheets, Dryden's satires, and sacramentarian pamphlets than to the neoclassical decorum of Dryden's *The State of Innocence* (a dramatization of *Paradise Lost*), or Addison's *Cato*, or Johnson's *Irene*. Published in 1695 within a generation of Milton's death, Patrick Hume's *Annotations on "Paradise Lost"* (1695) exemplifies older habits of interpretation. Typical of Hume's alertness to religious controversy are annotations in which he elucidates encoded attacks on religious "rites and shows, solemn processions and copes wrought with gold" and "ceremonies, rituals, gaudy processions, and fair shows" at both the beginning and ending of the poem (nn. on 1.371–72, 12.534). Recognizing fully the futility of any attempt to reduce the richness of Milton's artistry to one-to-one religiopolitical allegory, the present study follows the example of Hume, Thomas Warton, and others in looking to Milton's revolutionary pamphlets, over and beyond important precedents in Homeric and Virgilian epic, for analogues to poetic attacks on "corrupt" devotional practices.

Only by coming to terms with Milton's fondness for what Addison and Dr. Johnson would term "false wit," and for polemically charged vernacular diction and theological vocabulary, can we gain access to the polemical dimension of *Paradise Lost*. It is as much a part of the poem as the sublimity discerned by Milton's eighteenth- and nineteenth-century readership. In line with the iconography of seventeenth-century Protestant broadsheets and pamphlets, in which Satan and attendant demons

---

[9] Addison, *The Spectator*, no. 279.

engage in attempt after attempt to undermine the "true" church, religious complaint and satire are appropriate to the representation of Satan and his offspring in the demonic world of hell. From the outset of *Paradise Lost*, the procession of idols and "secret conclave" of demonic lords summon up antipapal innuendoes that accord with attacks in Milton's *Of True Religion*, dissenting tracts, and Hume's annotations. Quibbling wordplay, scriptural travesty, and narrative irony undercut the ostensibly tragic experience and epic stature of Satan and the damned. Ecclesiastical complaint and satire play a crucial role in neutralizing Satan's claim to heroic grandeur and representing the fall of the rebel angels from the sublime to the ridiculous. The absence of controversy in Raphael's account of the divine creation of the world in Book 8 indicates that it is a distinctive feature of the fallen world.

Contrary to widespread belief, Satan and his cohorts are ridiculous in the eyes of the Father, the Son, loyal angels, and the narrator, and satire occupies an important place in the encyclopedic array of literary genres and modes in *Paradise Lost*. The satirical and polemical dimension represents an essential component of the poem, one whose recognition changes our perceptions of the text in a fundamental way. Finding ample precedent in the Bible for scornful mockery of "ungodliness," Milton insists on a close kinship between satire and the elevated genres of tragedy and epic. Indeed, one need look no farther than the sardonic role-playing and wry jests shared by the Father and Son, or members of the angelic patrol who apprehend toad-like Satan in a laughable posture at the ear of Eve, to note the importance of the satiric mode within the generic multiplicity of *Paradise Lost*. Recognition of the poem's controversial and satirical character contributes to the rehabilitation of the highly problematic and unpopular episodes involving Sin and Death, the Paradise of Fools, and the War in Heaven.

Although no one seriously argues that Milton failed to compose those episodes, few present-day readers would claim that they are agreeable or approach the brilliance of the pastoral idyll played out by unfallen Adam and Eve. It is difficult if not impossible, however, to dismiss them from consideration as insignificant, irrelevant, or nonessential. One may echo William Empson's judgment and claim that the episodes at hell gate and Limbo or the primal rebellion in heaven constitute "bad poetry," but it is more important to probe how they afford a basis for the pervasive degradation of Satan and religious corruption whose origin the narrator and Michael, an angelic subnarrator, trace to him. In advance of Death's postlapsarian construction of a "pontifical" bridge from hell to earth, the Spenserian allegory of Sin and Death constitutes a poetic bridge over which Satan approaches the newly created world. The outrageous puns and innuendoes of that episode alert the reader to the advent of religious corruption at the very outset of human history.

More than that, those episodes frame the painfully nostalgic representation of Edenic pastoral as Adam and Eve enjoy their fleeting moments of unfallen bliss. The narrator's response to Satan's covert entry "into God's fold," when he leaps over the wall of Eden, demonstrates how satire infuses prelapsarian pastoral with anticipation of dispute concerning mandatory offering of tithes in support of a salaried ministry: "So since into his church lewd hirelings climb" (4.193). Ecclesiastical satire and polemic thus provide not a filter through which the reader witnesses Satan eavesdropping upon Adam and Eve, but an intrinsic part of the long-anticipated initial encounter with the "happy state" of "our grand parents" (1.29). Sharing the reader's vantage point, the all-seeing Eye of Providence enfolds polemical iconography into the Edenic episodes and, later, Raphael's narration of the War in Heaven. Not only do the epic narrator's topical outbursts against hypocrisy, clerical celibacy, transubstantiation, and the Mass constitute an integral part of Edenic pastoral, they intensify its poignancy. By contrast, opposition between the lewdness of "courts and palaces" where Belial "reigns" (1.497) and the lovemaking of Adam and Eve within their unfallen bower enhances its humbly worshipful aspect.

Ecclesiastical complaint and satire represent an essential component of the transformation of pastoral idyll announced by the fourth and final invocation: "I now must change/These notes to tragic" (9.5–6). Apparent parodies of transubstantiation, the Mass, and Medieval Latin hymnody mark the stages in Eve's tragic descent into disobedience. Ridicule of Satan's claim to heroic grandeur balances Adam and Eve's growing exemplification of "the better fortitude/Of patience and heroic martyrdom/Unsung" (9.31–33). Despite their fallen conversion to satanic "idolatry," heavenly correction supplies a constructive alternative to destructive attack on religious "error." The Father's cynicism toward the fallen angels does not extend to Adam and Eve, to whom he imputes both grace and faith.

Instructed by Archangel Michael, Adam comprehends harsh prophecies concerning human history, which conclude with intense focus on the patient suffering and obedient heroism of persecuted believers among his descendents. Accordingly *Paradise Lost* is immersed in history of the past, the future, and contemporaneous religious conflict of Milton's own age, which occupies an important place in the archangel's education of Adam. With angelic guidance, Adam and Eve pass beyond contrition to share "one faith unanimous though sad,/With cause for evils past, yet much more cheered/With meditation on the happy end" (12.603–05). Knowledge that no worldly place is holy or worthy of pilgrimage or ritual devotion contributes to the mournfully consolatory expulsion from paradise when Adam and Eve depart from Eden guided by indwelling faith.

Appendix

Figure 5

A discovery of the Jesuits' trumpery, Newly Packed Out of England

> If any man shall question what this sack
> Contains, I'll tell him; 'tis a Popish pack,
> A truss of trinkets, holy crosses, beads,
> Religious relics, Ave-Marias, creeds,
> Our lady's image, images of saints,
> That waxen lamb, that the shaved priest depicts
> By the name of Agnus Dei, indulgences,
> Pardons for venial, and for foul offences:
> You have here tradition from a fertile pate,
> And copies, teaching to equivocate:
> Here's supererogation, so much merit
> Stocked up by one, that many may inherit,
> By his good deeds, those everlasting joys,
> That few friars come to, and a thousand toys.
> For him has coin to buy them, here be cowls,
> And the sheep's clothing, they that weary fouls
> Do sometimes walk in, for the man that strips
> Himself, himself to punish; here be whips,
> And right ones, I can tell you: And to quell,
> The pampered body into lust would swell,
> (Instead of hemp or flaxen shirts to wear)
> (To scrub their itches) here be shirts of hair.
> Here's holy water, ashes, holy oil,
> Palm, holy tapers, spittle, and a coil
> With holy salt, and holy bells, I hope,
> Holy hemp twisted; so much for the Pope
> With his blind guides: And last (to stuff it full)
> Here's a nun's bastard, and a roaring bull.

So much for the pack, now to the peddler.

Be trudging with your crosses, in the loss
Of your pretenses; if you love the cross,
There's cross enough, I think, to make you fret
Your crosses now, have with cross carding met.
Your beads, and numbered Ave-Marias take,
And trudge to Rome, there's room enough, to make
Some use and practice of them: here you see,
We have no room for such vain things to be.
And as for images, your selves now go
Like images made up of mess-line Dow;
(For Dow's your cake in England, England knows),
The substance from the shadow: such poor shows
Please fools and mad men: then 'tis fit we part,
You pray by the eye, we by the soul and heart.
Pack, with your Agnus Dei, (goodly knacks)
Balm, holy water, and pure virgin's wax.
(They say 'tis made of pretty things indeed.)
Prick your fine lamb, see if your lamb will bleed
Ours bled for us: that blood, our soul's purgation
Without the purge of your imagination:
You know my mind, and whence the invention came,
Good works be packing with your waxen lamb
Indulgences, from your indulgent Father,
Do not extol so much, be thankful rather:
To England's pity, who (but that his will
Is more to pardon than to punish still)
Might quickly send you (wisely think upon it)
To doctor Story's old three-cornered bonnet,
I marry sir, Equivocation! Fie,
What fools are they to think we cannot lie,
Without their wit to help us? But to swear,
And break that oath, yet have the conscience clear.
Aye, there's the trick: for so equivocation
Leads men to hell in a more stately fashion.
This, says a man, goodness enough may do,
To save his own soul, and half his neighbor too,
'Tis wondrous strange, yet let no man deride it,
For we have friars have been at heaven and tried it,
But striving thus to set these baubles forth,
I lose more time than all the bundle's worth.
Overview the pack at leisure. I forgot
Dags, daggers, pistols, poison, powder-plot:
I know not well where these are in or no,
I hope they are, and ready packed to go
Back to that spotted bosom did invent them,

And 'gainst a pair of spotless bosoms sent them,
Stuffed full with their worse mischief; for that whore
That kings and princes humbly must adore:
(That rides upon that many headed beast),
At king's and kingdom's levels, at the least.
Her workmen too shall bless, maintain and nurse them,
And they who dare not (being sworn to it) curse them,
A holy mother still. Beside these lurches,
(To show her spite) she'll make them fire our churches,
Then is it not time they pack? Pack up, away,
Back devils to your saints: for some men say,
In many places you have many, one
That helps sore eyes; another for the bone
Touched with the morbe of Naples [i.e. syphilis]: one for youth
Troubled with scabs; one for an aching tooth:
Nay you have saints for horses, and for swine,
For dogs, for oxen, for your goat, and kine;
For lambs and geese; so get you gone, your back,
Prepare, good peddler, for your popish pack.
Our land, they know it flows with milk and honey,
Therefore I do suspect there are too many.
Trusting to shifts, by corners and disguises,
Dare venture still to play their popish prizes:
They soon shall know that we have hounds to scent them,
Find out their skulking, strip them and present them,
To the eye of justice; then they know what follows,
Up Newgate first, then after to the Gallows.

FINIS

London, printed for Henry Gosson; dwelling on
London Bridge.

Figure 8

Come, come all you that are with ROME offended,
Come now and hear from whence the Pope descended,
THE LINEAGE OF LOCUSTS
OR
THE POPE'S PEDIGREE
Beginning with his prime ancestor the Devil, plainly set forth to be noted of all good
Christians and true Catholics, for the avoiding of those subtle snares continually laid for them by his insinuating agents.

THE PEDIGREE

1. The Devil begat darkness.
2. And darkness begat ignorance.
3. And ignorance begat error and his brethren.
4. And error and his brethren begat free-will and self-love.
5. And self-love begat merits.
6. And merits begat forgetfulness of God's grace.
7. And forgetfulness of God's grace begat mistrust.
8. And mistrust begat satisfaction.
9. And satisfaction begat sacrifice of the Mass.
10. And sacrifice of the Mass begat Popish priesthood.
11. And Popish priesthood begat prayer for the dead.
12. And prayer for the dead begat sacrilege of souls.
13. And sacrilege of souls begat superstition.
14. And superstition begat hypocrisy the king.

And these are fourteen generations.

1. And hypocrisy the king begat lucre.
2. And lucre begat purgatory.
3. And purgatory begat foundation of irreligious houses.
4. And foundation of irreligious houses begat patrimony of the church.
5. And patrimony of the church begat mammon of iniquity.
6. And mammon of iniquity begat abundance.
7. And abundance begat cruelty.
8. And cruelty begat domination.
9. And domination begat pomp.

10. And pomp begat ambition.
11. And ambition begat intrusion into the church right.
12. And intrusion into the church right begat simony.
13. And simony begat universal superintendency.
14. And universal superintendency begat the Pope, the cardinals, and all his brethren.

> And these are fourteen generations, in the *transfiguration of abomination.*

1. And the Pope begat the mystery of iniquity.
2. And the mystery of iniquity begat divine sophistry.
3. And divine sophistry begat rejection of the Scripture.
4. And rejection of the Scripture begat tyranny.
5. And tyranny begat murder of the saints.
6. And murder of the saints begat the despising of God.
7. And the despising of God begat dispensation.
8. And dispensation begat license to sin.
9. And license to sin begat abomination.
10. And abomination begat confusion.
11. And confusion begat travail in the spirit.
12. And travail in the Spirit begat disputation.
13. And disputation begat matter to write of:
By which writing the son of perdition Antichrist specified in so many places of Scripture was revealed.

The Protestant's Conclusion

The Pope, himself (the simple to beguile)
Servum servorum Dei doth instill,
The servant of God's servants, who (we find)
To seem his master's better is inclined,
Christ humble was, humility requiring,
The Pope is proud to honor still aspiring,
Christ was content to wear a crown of thorns,
But the Pope's head a crown of gold adorns,
A triple crown which hardly him sufficeth
But of his foul ambition what ariseth?
Hunc capit inferum, quem deferit ordo supernum.

Forsaken by the choir supernal,
He's taken by the fiends infernal,
For let false Catholics say what they can
He's neither God nor angel, nor a man,
But prodigious beast or monster fell.
With all his brood hatch'd or begot in hell,
     And so I leave him.

Figure 16

Behold Rome's Monster on His Monstrous Beast!
To fullness of his foulness (now) increased!
How he in papal pride doth ride along,
And how his sons and shavelings thrust and throng
To see his sacred hollow holiness
His Babylonish blasphemies express.
His barrel-bellied beast on stilts doth stalk,
And with seven hideous heads doth proudly walk.
The heads, seven hell-spawned deadly sins do show.
Wherein Rome's rabble rankly rise and grow.
Four faithless feet, Deceit, Debate, and Pride,
With ill got Gain, his steps on stilts do guide:
To raise him up aloft, in supreme seat,
Like Saturn's son, ruling all princes great.
His long cloud-threatening fierce advanced tail
The very stars (God's saints) doth sore assail:
Whereby is shown, Rome's bloody inquisition,
Wasting God's saints, hastening their own perdition,
Then Babel's bishops, Jesuits, friars base,
About the beast's posteriors flock apace,
And from his barrel breech, the dregs and lees
Of Rome's all rotten relics, dear decrees,
They fill full cups of Romish fornication;
Which, by the princes of Rome's domination,
So filled, are swilled, and they made drunk thereby,
And in destruction sleeping, snorting die.
As (thus) proud Babel's bawd doth proudly prance,
In blood and blasphemy herself to advance

Against God and his dear saints; heaven's indignation
Pours down the vials of dire desolation
Upon Rome's whore, and with his nostrils' breath,
Sends his obsequious servant, Sergeant Death,
Her to arrest, with his death wounding dart;
Who shoots his shaft and reaves and cleaves his heart.
Whom (as she in her height of pride did sit)
He, with his rope of wrath, pulls to the pit
Of desolation and destruction dire,
To burn in hell's all ever burning fire.
Thus is proud Babel fallen, and in her fall,
Fallen are her vassals, Satan's vessels all:
Even now, this work begins, for Rome looks sickly,
Even so Lord Jesus come, oh Lord come quickly;
To right the wrongs of thy distressed saints.
To send an end to all their woes and plaints.
Most humbly heartily prayeth,
JOHN VICARS

Imprinted at London, and are to be sold by William Peak at his shop
near Holborn Conduit, next the Sun Tavern, 1643.

Figure 19

The Solemn Mock Procession of the POPE, Cardinals, Jesuits, Friars,
etc. Through the City of London, November the 17th 1679

The EXPLANATION

Such is the just and generous detestation and hatred of the English
nation against the tyranny and superstition of the Popish religion (if it be
lawful to call such a mass of cruelty and nonsense by so sacred a name)
that they have taken all occasions to express their abhorrence thereof;
but more especially since the discovery of that horrid and traitorous
conspiracy against his majesty's person, the Protestant religion and
government established, which they sufficiently testified on the 17th of
November; that being the day on which the unfortunate Queen Mary
died, and that glorious sun, Queen Elizabeth of happy memory, arose in
the English horizon, and thereby dispelled those thick fogs and mists of

Romish blindness, and restored to these kingdoms their just rights both as men and Christians. In commemoration of this great blessing, some honorable and worthy gentlemen, both in London, and at the Temple (remembering the burning of London, and the Temple, by Popish hands) were pleased to be at the charge of an extraordinary triumph upon the day aforesaid, to confront the insolence of the Romish faction, who after all the miraculous discoveries of their cursed contrivances, have still the impudence yet to hope of succeeding in their traitorous designs for enslaving these nations.

Upon the said 17th of November, 1679, the bells began generally to ring at three o'clock in the morning: about five o' clock in the evening, all things being in readiness, the solemn procession began, setting forth from Moorgate, and so proceeding to Bishopsgate, and down Hounds-ditch to Aldgate, and thence through Leadenhall Street, the Royal Exchange, Cheapside, and so to Temple Bar, in the following order; I. Marched six whistlers to clear the way, in pioneer's caps and red waistcoats. II. A bellman ringing, who with a loud and dolesome voice cried all the way, "Remember Justice, Godfrey." III. A dead body representing Sir Edmundbury Godfrey, in the habit he usually wore, the cravat wherewith he was murdered, about his neck, with spots of blood on his wrists, shirt, and white gloves that were on his hands, his face pale and wan, riding on a white horse, and one of his murderers behind him to keep from falling, representing the manner how he was carried from Somerset House to Primrose Hill. IV. A priest in a surplice with a cope embroidered with dead men's bones, skeletons, skulls, etc., giving pardons very freely to those who would murder Protestants, and proclaiming it meritorious. V. A priest alone, in black, with a large silver cross. VI. Four Carmelite Friars in white and black habits. VII. Four gray friars in their proper habits. VIII. Six Jesuits with bloody daggers. IX. A consort of wind music, called the waits. X. Four Popish bishops in purple and lawn sleeves, with golden crosses on their breasts. XI. Four other popish bishops in their *pontificalibus*, with surplices, rich embroidered copes, and golden miters on their heads. XII. Six cardinals in scarlet robes and red caps. XIII. The Pope's chief physician with Jesuit's powder in one hand, and an urinal in the other. XIV. Two priests in surplices, with two golden crosses. Lastly, the Pope in a lofty glorious pageant, representing a chair of state, covered with scarlet, the chair richly embroidered, fringed, and bedecked with golden balls and crosses; at his feet a cushion of state, two boys in surplices, with white silk banners and red crosses, and bloody daggers for murdering heretical kings and princes, painted on them, with an incense pot before them, sat on each side censing his holiness, who was arrayed in a rich scarlet gown, lined through with ermine, and adorned with gold and silver lace; on his head a triple crown of gold, and a glorious collar of gold and precious stones, St. Peter's keys, a number of beads, Agnus Dei's and other Catholic trumpery; at his back stood his holiness's privy councilor, the Devil, frequently caressing, hugging and whispering, and often times instructing him aloud, to destroy his majesty, to forge a Protestant plot, and to fire the city again; to which purpose he held an infernal torch in his hand. The whole procession was attended with 150 flambeaux and torches by order; but so many more came in volunteers as made them up some thousands. Never were the balconies, windows, and houses more numerously filled, nor the streets closer thronged with multitudes of people, all expressing their abhorrence of popery, with continual shouts and acclamations, so that by a modest computation it is judged there could not be fewer than two hundred thousand spectators: thus with a slow and solemn state they proceeded to Temple Bar, where with the innumerable swarms, the houses seemed converted into heaps of men, women, and children; for whose diversion there were provided great variety of excellent fireworks. Temple Bar being since its rebuilding, adorned with four stately statues, those of Queen Elizabeth and King James fronting the city, and of King Charles the first of blessed memory, and our present gracious sovereign, on the other side towards Westminster. The statue of Queen Elizabeth in respect to the day, was adorned with a crown of gilded laurel, in her hand a golden shield, with this motto inscribed, THE PROTESTANT RELIGION, MAGNA CHARTA, and flambeaux placed before it: the Pope being brought near thereunto, the song following was sung in parts, between one who represented the English Cardinal Howard, and another, the people of England.

Cardinal Howard
From York to London town we come
To talk of Popish ire;
To reconcile you all to Rome,
And prevent Smithfield fire.
The People answer.
Cease, cease, thou Norfolk Cardinal,
See yonder stands Queen Bess,
Who saved our souls from Popish thrall

O Queen Bess, Queen Bess, Queen Bess.
Your Popish plot and Smithfield threat
We do not fear at all
For lo! Before Queen Bess's feet
You fall, you fall, you fall.
Now God preserve great Charles our King,
And eke all honest men;
And traitors all to justice bring,
Amen, Amen, Amen.

Thus having entertained the thronging spectators for some time with ingenious fireworks, and a vast bonfire being prepared just over against the Inner Temple gate, his holiness, after some compliment and reluctancy, was decently tumbled from all his grandeur into the impartial flames; the crafty Devil, his chief minister, leaving his infallibilityship in the lurch in his extremity. This justice was attended with a prodigious shout, that might be heard far beyond Somerset House; and the same evening there were large bonfires generally in the streets, with universal acclamations, Long live King Charles, Let popery perish, and papists with their plots and counter-plots as hitherto, be confounded: To which every honest Englishman will readily say, AMEN.

London, printed for Jonathan Wilkins, at the Star in Cheapside next Mercer's Chapel, 1680.

Select Bibliography

PRIMARY SOURCES

Unless otherwise noted, London is the place of publication for primary sources.
Anonymous. *Arminius Between Truth and Heresy*. Amsterdam, 1641.

Book of Homilies. 1548.

The Brownist's Conventicle: Or An Assembly of Brownists, Separatists, and Nonconformists. 1641.

A Course of Catechizing. 1674.

The Devil's Triumph Over Rome's Idol. 1680.

Die Mercurii 8 September 1641. 1641.

Directory For the Public Worship of God. 1645.

A Discovery of the Jesuits' Trumpery, Newly Packed Out of England. 1641.

The Fruits of Faith in these Five Famous Men, Scripture Worthies Heb. XI. 1656.

The Happy Instruments of England's Preservation. 1681.

Lambeth Fair: Wherein You Have All the Bishops' Trinkets Set to Sale. 1641.

The Life and Death of Mistress Rump. 1660.

The Lineage of Locusts. 1641.

Maria Triumphans, Being a Discourse Wherein . . . the Blessed Virgin is Defended and Vindicated. St. Omer, 1635.

Mistress Rump Brought to Bed of a Monster. 1660.

News from Hell: Or the Revelation of a Vision. 1660.

News From Rome. 1680.

Old Rome's New Church of Knaves and Fools. 1689.

The Plowman's Tale. Showing by the Doctrine and Lives of the Romish Clergy, that the Pope is Antichrist and they His Ministers. 1606. Attributed to Geoffrey Chaucer.

The Protestation of Martin Marprelate. 1589.

The Racovian Catechism. Amsterdam, 1652.

The Solemn Mock Procession of the Pope, Cardinals, Jesuits, Friars, Etc. Through the City of London. 1680.

Time Carrying the Pope from England to Rome. 1641.

The Times Dissected, or a Learned Discourse of Several Occurrences Very Worthy of Special Observation to Deter Evil Men, and Encourage Good. 1641.

206

To the Praise of Mistress Cellier the Popish Midwife: On Her Incomparable Book. 1680.

Triple Episcopacy: Or, A Threefold Order of Bishops. 1641.

The True Emblem of Antichrist: Or Schism Displayed. 1651.

Vox Pacifica. 1649. Attributed to George Wither.

Wyclif's Wicket. 1546. Attributed to John Wycliffe.

Addison, Joseph, and Richard Steele. *The Spectator*. Edited by Donald F. Bond. 5 vols. Oxford: Clarendon Press, 1965.

Bale, John. *Acts of English Votaries*. 2 vols. 1560.

    The Complete Plays of John Bale. 2 vols. Edited by Peter Happé. Cambridge: D.S. Brewer, 1985–86.

    The Select Works of Bishop Bale. Edited by Henry Christmas. Vol. XXXVI. Cambridge: Parker Society, 1849.

    The Vocacyon of Johan Bale. Edited by Peter Happé and John N. King. Renaissance English Text Society, vol. XIV (1989). Binghamton, NY: MRTS, 1990.

    Yet a Course at the Romish Fox. Antwerp, 1543.

Bate, George. *Elenchi Motuum Nuperorum in Anglia*. Revised ed. 1663.

Bathurst, Theodore. See Spenser, *Shepherds' Calendar*.

Bayly, William. *The Blood of the Righteous Abel Crying From the Ground*. 1659.

    The Dreadful, and Terrible, Day of the Lord God, to Overtake this Generation Suddenly. 1665.

    An Epistle General Containing Wholesome Exhortations and Good Counsel from the Spirit of Truth. 1664.

    Jacob Is Become a Flame and the House of Esau Stubble. 1662.

    The Life of Enoch Again Revived, in Which Abel's Offering is Accepted. 1662.

Becon, Thomas. *Works*. 1560.

Bedell, William. *A Protestant Memorial: Or, the Shepherd's Tale of the Powder Plot*. 1713.

Booty, John E., ed. *The Book of Common Prayer 1559: The Elizabethan Prayer Book*. Charlottesville: University Press of Virginia, 1976.

Breward, Ian, ed. *The Westminster Directory Being a Directory for the Public Worship of God in the Three Kingdoms*. Bramcote, Notts.: Grove, 1680.

Browne, William. *Poems of William Browne*. Edited by Gordon Goodwin. 2 vols. 1894.

Bunyan, John. *The Pilgrim's Progress*. Edited by Roger Sharrock. Harmondsworth: Penguin, 1965.

Burgess, *A Sermon Preached to the Honourable House of Commons Assembled in Parliament. At Their Public Feast, November 17. 1640*. 3rd ed. 1641.

Carleton, George. *A Thankful Remembrance of God's Mercy*. 3rd ed. 1627.

Chaucer, Geoffrey. See Anon., *The Plowman's Tale*.

Council of Trent. *Decrees of the Council of Trent*. 1543–63.

Dormer, James. *A Sermon Preached Before Their Majesties in Their Chapel at St. James*. 1687.

Dryden, John. *The Best of Dryden*. Edited by Louis I. Bredvold. New York: Ronald Press, 1983.

    The Works of John Dryden. Edited by Edward Niles Hooker, H.T. Swedenberg,

Jr., et al. 20 vols. Berkeley and Los Angeles: University of California Press, 1959–89.

Fletcher, Giles and Phineas. *Poetical Works*. 2 vols. Cambridge University Press, 1908–1909.

Foxe, John, ed. *The Acts and Monuments of These Latter and Perilous Days*. 2nd ed. 1570.

Fuller, Thomas. *Abel Redivivus, Or the Dead Yet Speaking*. 1651.

Gauden, John (attributed to). *Eikon Basilike: The Portraiture of His Sacred Majesty in His Solitudes and Sufferings*. Formerly attributed to Charles I. Edited by Philip Knachel. Ithaca, NY: Cornell University Press for the Folger Shakespeare Library, 1966.

Gee, John. *The Foot Out of the Snare: with a Detection of Sundry Late Practices and Impostures of the Priests and Jesuits in England*. 1624.

Grey, Anchitel. *Debates of the House of Commons*. 10 vols. 1769.

Grey, Lady Jane. *An Epistle of the Lady Jane to a Learned Man of Late Fallen from the Truth of God's Word*. 1554.

Haggar, Henry. *No King But Jesus: Or, The Walls of Tyranny Razed*. 1652.

Harrison, Douglas, ed. *The First and Second Prayer Books of King Edward VI*. London: Dent, 1968.

Herring, Francis. *Mischief's Mystery: Or, Treason's Masterpiece, the Powder-Plot*. Translated by John Vicars. 1617.

Pietas pontificia, seu, conjurationis illius prodigiosae, in Jacobum regem, Novembris quinto. 2 vols. 1605.

November 5, 1605. The Quintessence of Cruelty, or Masterpiece of Treachery, the Popish Powder-Plot, Invented by Hellish Malice, Prevented by Heavenly Mercy. Translated by John Vicars. 1641

H[ume], P[atrick]. *Annotations on Milton's "Paradise Lost"*. 1695.

Johnson, Samuel. "Life of Milton" (1779). In *Johnson's "Lives of the Poets": A Selection*. Edited by J.P. Hardy. Oxford: Clarendon Press, 1971.

Landor, Walter Savage. *The Complete Works of Walter Savage Landor*. Edited by T. Earle Welby. 16 vols. 1927–36.

Leighton, Alexander. *An Appeal to the Parliament; Or, Sion's Appeal Against the Prelacy*. Amsterdam, 1629.

Luther, Martin. *Works*. Edited by Jaroslav Pelikan et al. 55 Vols. St. Louis: Concordia Publishing House, 1959.

Marprelate, Martin (pseudonym). *The Marprelate Tracts* (1588–89). Edited by William Pierce. London: J. Clarke, 1911.

Marvell, Andrew. *Andrew Marvell*. Edited by Frank Kermode and Keith Walker. Oxford University Press, 1990.

Milton, John. *Complete Poems and Major Prose*. Edited by Merritt Y. Hughes. Indianapolis, IN, and New York: Odyssey Press, 1957.

Complete Prose Works of John Milton. Edited by Don M. Wolfe, et al. 8 vols. New Haven: Yale University Press, 1953–1982.

Paradise Lost. 4th ed. 1688.

Paradise Lost. Edited by Thomas Newton. 2nd ed. 1750.

Paradise Lost. Edited by Roy Flannagan. New York: Macmillan, 1993.

Paradise Regained. Edited by Charles Dunster. 1795.

The Poems of John Milton. Edited by John Carey and Alastair Fowler. London and New York: Longman, 1968.

Poems Upon Several Occasions, English, Italian, and Latin, with Translations, by John Milton. Viz. Lycidas, L'Allegro, Il Penseroso, Arcades, Comus, Odes, Sonnets, Miscellanies, English Psalms, Elegiarum Liber, Epigrammatum Liber, Sylvarum Liber. Edited by Thomas Warton. 1785.

Poetical Works. Edited by Thomas Newton. 3 vols. 1749–53.

More, Henry. "An Antidote Against Idolatry." Part 2 of *An Exposition of the Seven Epistles to the Seven Churches Together With a Brief Discourse of Idolatry, with Application to the Church of Rome.* 1669.

More, Thomas. *The Complete Works of St. Thomas More.* Edited and translated by Richard Sylvester, et al. 10 vols in 15. New Haven: Yale University Press, 1961–.

Newcomen, Matthew. *The Craft and Cruelty of the Church's Adversaries.* 1643.

Overton, Richard. *A New Play Called Canterbury, His Change of Diet.* 1641.

Peacham, Henry. *Minerva Britanna, or a Garden of Heroical Devices.* 1612.

Perkins, *The Combat Between Christ and Devil Displayed.* 1606.

Perse, William. *A Sermon Preached. . .on the Fifth Day of November 1689.* York, 1689.

Pordage, Samuel. *Mundumm Explicatio.* 1661.

Prynne, William. *Hidden Works of Darkness Brought to Public Light.* 1645.

A Looking-Glass for all Lordly Prelates. 1636.

Canterbury's Doom. 1644.

Histrio-mastix. 1633.

Puttenham, George. *The Art of English Poesy.* 1589.

Ralegh, Sir Walter. *The History of the World.* 1614.

Robinson, Thomas. *Anatomy of the English Nunnery at Lisbon in Portugal.* 1622.

Ruskin, John. *Notes on the Construction of Sheepfolds.* 1851.

Sandys, George, trans. *Ovid's Metamorphoses Englished, Mythologized, and Represented in Figures.* Oxford, 1632.

Schaff, Philip, ed. and trans. *The Creeds of Christendom.* 3 vols. New York: Harper and Bros., 1905.

Shakespeare, William. *The Norton Shakespeare Based on the Oxford Edition.* Edited by Stephen Greenblatt, et al. New York and London: W. W. Norton, 1997.

Shelley, Percy Bysshe. *Complete Works.* 10 vols. London: Ernest Benn, 1926–30.

Shepherd, Luke. *Pathos, or an Inward Passion of the Pope for the Loss of His Daughter the Mass.* 1548.

The Upcheering of the Mass. 1548.

Smart, Peter. *A Sermon Preached in the Cathedral Church at Durham.* 1640.

Smith, G. Gregory, ed. *Elizabethan Critical Essays.* 2 vols. London: Oxford University Press, 1904.

Smith, Richard. *The Powder Treason Propounded by Satan, Approved by Antichrist, Enterprised by Papists, Practiced by Traitors, Revealed by an Eagle, Expounded by an Oracle, Founded in Hell, Confounded in Heaven.* 1615.

Spenser, Edmund. *The Faerie Queene.* Edited by A.C. Hamilton. London: Longman, 1977.

    The Shepherds' Calendar, Containing Twelve Eclogues, Proportionable to the Twelve Months, by Edmund Spenser Prince of English Poets. With Latin translation by Theodore Bathurst. Edited by William Dillingham. 1653.

    The Yale Edition of the Shorter Poems of Edmund Spenser. Edited by William A. Oram, et al. New Haven and London: Yale University Press, 1989.

Spingarn, J.E., ed. *Critical Essays of the Seventeenth Century.* 2 vols. Oxford: Clarendon Press, 1908–1909.

Stillingfleet, Edward. *Discourse Concerning Idolatry.* 1671.

    Sermon Preached November 5, 1673. 1674.

Stirry, Thomas. *A Rot Amongst the Bishops, or, a Terrible Tempest in the Sea of Canterbury.* 1641.

Thompson, Bard, ed. *Liturgies of the Western Church.* Cleveland: World Publishing, 1962.

Toland, John, ed. *A Complete Collection of the Historical, Political, and Miscellaneous Works of John Milton, Both English and Latin.* 1698.

Turner, William. *The Hunting and Finding Out of the Romish Fox.* Bonn, 1543.

Tyndale, William. *An Answer to Sir Thomas More's Dialogue, The Supper of the Lord.* Edited by Henry Walter. Parker Society, vol. XLIV. Cambridge University Press, 1850.

    Doctrinal Treatises. Edited by Henry Walter. Parker Society, vol. XLII. Cambridge University Press, 1848.

    Whole Works of William Tyndale, John Frith, and Doctor Barnes. Edited by John Foxe. 1573.

    The Works of William Tyndale. Edited by G. E. Duffield. Appleford: Sutton Courtenay Press, 1964.

Vaux, Laurence. *Catechism or Christian Doctrine, Neccessary for Children and Ignorant People.* St. Omer, c. 1670.

Vicars, John. *Babylon's Beauty: Or, the Romish Catholics' Sweetheart.* 1644.

    Behold Rome's Monster on His Monstrous Beast! 1643.

    England's Remembrancer, Or, A Thankful Acknowledgement of Parliamentary Mercies to our English Nation. 1641.

Walpole, Horace. *A Catalogue of the Royal and Noble Authors of England.* Strawberry Hill, 1758.

Ward, Samuel. *To God, In Memory of his Double Deliverance From the Invincible Navy and the Unmatchable Powder Treason.* Amsterdam, 1621.

Willan, Robert. *Conspiracy Against Kings, Heaven's Scorn.* 1622.

Winstanley, Gerrard. *Works, with an Appendix of Documents Relating to the Digger Movement.* Edited by George H. Sabine. New York: Russell and Russell, 1965.

Wither, George. *A Collection of Emblems, Ancient and Modern.* 1635.

SECONDARY SOURCES AND REFERENCE WORKS

Achinstein, Sharon. *Milton and the Revolutionary Reader.* Literature in History.

Princeton University Press, 1994.

Adelman, Janet. "Creation and the Place of the Poet in *Paradise Lost*." In *The Author in His Work: Essays on a Problem in Criticism*, ed. Louis L. Martz, Patricia Meyer Spacks, and Aubrey Williams, pp. 51–69. New Haven: Yale University Press, 1978.

Anselment, Raymond A. *"Betwixt Jest and Earnest": Marprelate, Milton, Marvell, Swift and the Decorum of Religious Ridicule*. University of Toronto Press, 1979.

Armitage, David, et al., eds. *Milton and Republicanism*. Cambridge University Press, 1995.

Bakhtin, Mikhail M. *The Dialogic Imagination: Four Essays*. Edited by Michael Holquist. Translated by Caryl Emerson and Michael Holquist. Austin: University of Texas Press (Slavic Series), 1981.

   Rabelais and His World. Translated by Helene Iswolsky. Bloomington: Indiana University Press, 1984.

Barbour, Hugh. *The Quakers in Puritan England*. New Haven: Yale University Press, 1964.

Barish, Jonas A. *The Antitheatrical Prejudice*. Berkeley and Los Angeles: University of California Press, 1981.

Benet, Diana T. "Hell, Satan, and the New Politician." In *Literary Milton: Text, Pretext, Context*, ed. Diana T. Benet and Michael Lieb, pp. 91–113, 235–37. Duquesne Studies: Language and Literature Series, vol. XVI. Pittsburgh: Duquesne University Press, 1994.

Bennett, Joan S. *Reviving Liberty: Radical Christian Humanism in Milton's Great Poems*. Cambridge, MA: Harvard University Press, 1989.

Blake, William. *Complete Prose and Poetry of William Blake*. Edited by Geoffrey Keynes. London: Nonesuch, 1989.

Bloom, Harold. *A Map of Misreading*. New York: Oxford University Press, 1975.

Boorsch, Suzanne. "The 1688 *Paradise Lost* and Dr. Aldrich." *Metropolitan Museum Journal* 6 (1972), pp. 133–50.

Borris, Kenneth. "Allegory in *Paradise Lost*: Satan's Cosmic Journey." *MiltonS* 26 (1990), pp. 101–33.

   Spenser's Poetics of Prophecy in "The Faerie Queen" V. English Literary Studies Monograph Series, vol. LII. University of Victoria Press, 1991.

Boswell, Jackson C. *Milton's Library: A Catalogue of the Remains of John Milton's Library and an Annotated Reconstruction of Milton's Library and Ancillary Readings*. New York: Garland, 1975.

British Museum, Department of Prints and Drawings. *Catalogue of Political and Personal Satires Preserved in the Department of Prints and Drawings*. Prepared by Frederic G. Stephens and M. Dorothy George. Vols. I–IV (prepared by Stephens) are entitled *Catalogue of Prints and Drawings in the British Museum*. 11 vols. in 12. London: British Museum, 1870–1954.

Broadbent, J.B. *Some Graver Subject: An Essay on "Paradise Lost"*. London: Chatto & Windus, 1960.

Brown, Norman. *Life Against Death: The Psychoanalytic Meaning of History*. Middletown, CT: Wesleyan University Press, 1959.

Browning, Judith E. "Sin, Eve, and Circe: *Paradise Lost* and the Ovidian Circe Tradition." *MiltonS* 26 (1991), pp. 135–57.

Brumbaugh, Barbara. "'Under the Pretty Tale of Wolves and Sheep': Sidney's Ambassadorial Table Talk and Protestant Hunting Dialogues." Forthcoming in *Spenser Studies* 13.

Buhler, Stephen M. "Kingly States: The Politics in *Paradise Lost.*" *MiltonS* 28 (1992), p. 61.

Burke, Peter. *Popular Culture in Early Modern Europe*. New York University Press, 1978.

Cable, Lana. *Carnal Rhetoric: Milton's Iconoclasm and the Poetics of Desire*. Durham, NC: Duke University Press, 1995.

Carey, John. "Milton's Satan." In *The Cambridge Companion to Milton*, ed. Dennis Danielson, pp. 131–45. Cambridge University Press, 1989.

Chambers, J.D. *Divine Worship in England*. London: B. M. Pickering, 1877.

Christianson, Paul. *Reformers and Babylon: English Apocalyptic Visions from the Reformation to the Eve of the Civil War*. University of Toronto Press, 1978.

Christopher, Georgia. *Milton and the Science of the Saints*. Princeton University Press, 1982.

Clifton, Robin. "Fear of Popery." In *The Origins of the English Civil War*, ed. Conrad Russell, pp. 144–67. London: Macmillan, 1973.

Collinson, Patrick. *The Birthpangs of Protestant England: Religion and Cultural Change in the Sixteenth and Seventeenth Centuries*. London: Macmillan, 1988.

The Religion of Protestants: The Church in English Society, 1559–1625. Oxford: Clarendon Press, 1982.

Corbett, Margery and Ronald Lightbown, *The Comedy Frontispiece: The Emblematic Title-page in England 1550–1660*. London: Routledge and Kegan Paul, 1979.

Corns, Thomas N. "Ideology in the *Poemata.*" *MiltonS* 19 (1984), pp. 195–203.

Milton's Language. London: Basil Blackwell, 1990.

"Obscenity, Slang and Indecorum in Milton's English Prose." *Prose Studies* 3 (1980), pp. 5–14.

Uncloistered Virtue: English Political Literature, 1640–1660. Oxford: Clarendon Press, 1992.

Cressy, David. *Bonfires and Bells: National Memory and the Protestant Calendar in Elizabethan and Stuart England*. Berkeley and Los Angeles: University of California Press, 1989.

Cunnar, Eugene R. "Milton's 'Two-Handed Engine': The Visionary Iconography of *Christus in Statera.*" *MiltonQ* 17 (1983), pp. 29–38.

Danielson, Dennis. *Milton's Good God: A Study in Literary Theodicy*. Cambridge University Press, 1982.

Darbishire, Helen, ed. *The Early Lives of Milton*. London: Constable, 1932.

Davies, Horton. *Worship and Theology in England*. Grand Rapids, MI: W.B. Eerdmans, 1996.

Davies, Julian. *The Caroline Captivity of the Church: Charles I and the Remolding of Anglicanism 1625–1641*. Oxford: Clarendon Press, 1992.

Davies, Stevie. *Images of Kingship in "Paradise Lost": Milton's Politics and Christian Liberty*. Columbia, MO: University of Missouri Press, 1983.

Davis, J.C. "Against Formality: One Aspect of the English Revolution." *Transactions of the Royal Historical Society* 6th ser., 3 (1993), pp. 265–88.

"Religion and the Struggle for Freedom in the English Revolution." *Historical Journal* 35 (1992), pp. 526–30.

Di Salvo, Jackie. "The Lord's Battells: *Samson Agonistes* and the Puritan Revolution." *MiltonS* 4 (1972), pp. 39–62.

Dollimore, Jonathan. *Radical Tragedy: Religion, Ideology, and Power in the Drama of Shakespeare and His Contemporaries*. 2nd ed. Durham, NC: Duke University Press, 1993.

Drake, Gertrude C. "Satan's Councils in 'The Christiad,' 'Paradise Lost,' and 'Paradise Regained.'" In *Acta Conventus Neo-Latini Turonensis*, ed. Jean-Claude Margolin, pp. 979–89. Paris: Vrin, 1980.

Empson, William. *Milton's God*. Revised ed. London: Chatto & Windus, 1965.

Erickson, Lee. "Satan's Apostles and the Nature of Faith in *Paradise Lost* Book I." *Studies in Philology* 94 (1997), pp. 382–94.

Fallon, Stephen M. *Milton Among the Philosophers: Poetry and Materialism in Seventeenth Century England*. Ithaca, NY: Cornell University Press, 1991.

"Milton's Sin and Death: The Ontology of Allegory in *Paradise Lost*." *ELR* 17 (1987), pp. 329–50.

Fincham, Kenneth, and Peter Lake. "The Ecclesiastical Policies of James I and Charles I." In *The Early Stuart Church, 1603–1642*, ed. Kenneth Fincham, pp. 23–49. Stanford University Press, 1993.

Fish, Stanley E. "Driving From the Letter: Truth and Indeterminacy in Milton's *Areopagitica*." In *Re-membering Milton: Essays on the Texts and Traditions*, ed. Mary Nyquist and Margaret W. Ferguson, pp. 234–54. New York: Methuen, 1987.

Surprised by Sin: The Reader in "Paradise Lost". Berkeley and Los Angeles: University of California Press, 1971.

"Transmuting the Lump: *Paradise Lost*, 1942–79." In *Doing what Comes Naturally: Change, Rhetoric, and the Practice of Theory in Literary and Legal Studies*, pp. 247–93. Durham, NC: Duke University Press, 1989.

Fowler, Alastair. *Kinds of Literature: An Introduction to the Theory of Genres and Modes*. Cambridge, MA: Harvard University Press, 1982.

French, J. M. "Milton as a Satirist." *PMLA* 51 (1936), pp. 414–29.

Frye, Roland. *Milton's Imagery and the Visual Arts: Iconographic Tradition in the Epic Poems*. Princeton University Press, 1978.

Gardiner, Anne B. "Milton's Parody of Catholic Hymns in Eve's Temptation and Fall: Original Sin as a Paradigm of 'Secret Idolatries.'" *Studies in Philology* 91 (1994) pp. 216–31.

Gilman, Ernest. *Iconoclasm and Poetry in the English Reformation: "Down Went Dagon."* University of Chicago Press, 1986.

Gless, Darryl J. *Interpretation and Theology in Spenser*. Cambridge University Press, 1994.

Goldberg, Jonathan and Stephen Orgel, eds. *John Milton.* Oxford University Press, 1996.

Greenblatt, Stephen. *Renaissance Self-Fashioning: From More to Shakespeare.* University of Chicago Press, 1980.

Gregerson, Linda. *The Reformation of the Subject: Spenser, Milton, and the English Protestant Epic.* Cambridge Studies in Renaissance Literature and Culture, vol. VI. Cambridge University Press, 1995.

et al., ed. *The Norton Shakespeare Based on the Oxford Edition.* New York and London: W. W. Norton, 1997.

Grossman, Marshall. *"Authors to Themselves": Milton and the Revelation of History.* Cambridge University Press, 1987.

Guibbory, Achsah. *Ceremony and Community from Herbert to Milton: Literature, Religion, and Cultural Conflict in Seventeenth-Century England.* Cambridge University Press, 1998.

Guilhamet, Leon. *Satire and the Transformation of Genre.* Philadelphia: University of Pennsylvania Press, 1987.

Guillory, John. *Poetic Authority: Spenser, Milton, and Literary History.* New York: Columbia University Press, 1983.

Hamilton, Gary. *"Paradise Regained* and the Private Houses." In *Of Poetry and Politics: New Essays on Milton and His World.* Edited by P. G. Stanwood. Vol CXXVI. Binghampton, NY: MRTS, 1995.

Helgerson, Richard. *Forms of Nationhood: The Elizabethan Writing of England.* University of Chicago Press, 1992.

"Milton Reads the King's Book: Print, Performance, and the Making of a Bourgeois Idol." *Criticism* 29 (1987), pp. 1–25.

Hibbard, Caroline M. *Charles I and the Popish Plot.* Chapel Hill, NC: University of North Carolina Press, 1983.

Hill, Christopher. *The Collected Essays of Christopher Hill.* 3 vols. Brighton: Harvester, 1985.

"George Wither and John Milton." In *English Renaissance Studies Presented to Dame Helen Gardner in Honour of Her Seventieth Birthday,* pp. 212–27. Oxford: Clarendon Press, 1980.

A Tinker and a Poor Man: John Bunyan and his Church, 1628–1688. New York and London: W. W. Norton, 1988.

Milton and the English Revolution. 2nd. ed. Harmondsworth: Penguin, 1979.

The World Turned Upside Down: Radical Ideas During the English Revolution. New York: Viking, 1973.

Hillerbrand, Hans, et al., ed. *The Oxford Encyclopedia of the Reformation.* 4 vols. Oxford University Press, 1996.

Hind, Arthur M. *Engraving in England in the Sixteenth and Seventeenth Centuries.* 3 vols. Cambridge University Press, 1953–64.

Hirst, Derek. *Authority and Conflict: England, 1603–1658.* Cambridge, MA: Harvard University Press, 1968.

Hodgkins, Christopher. *Authority, Church, and Society in George Herbert: Return to the Middle Way.* Columbia, MO: University of Missouri Press, 1993.

Hollstein, F. W. H. *Dutch and Flemish Etchings, Engravings, and Woodcuts c. 1450–1700.* 43 vols. Amsterdam: Hertzberger, 1949–.

Höltgen, Karl Josef. "The Reformation of Images and Some Jacobean Writers on Art." In *Functions of Literature: Essays Presented to Erwin Wolff on His Sixtieth Birthday*, ed. Ulrick Broich, et. al., pp. 119–46. Tübingen: Max Niemayer Verlag, 1984.

Honeygosky, Stephen R. *Milton's House of God: The Invisible and Visible Church.* Columbia, MO: University of Missouri Press, 1993.

Howard, Jean E. "The New Historicism in Renaissance Studies." *ELR* 16 (1986), pp. 13–43.

Howard, Leon. "'That Two-Handed Engine' Once More." *HLQ* 15 (1952), pp. 173–84.

Hughes, Ann. "The Frustrations of the Godly." In *Revolution and Restoration: England in the 1650s*, ed. John Morrill, pp. 70–90. London: Collins & Brown, 1992.

Hughes, Merrit Y. "Milton's Limbo of Vanity." In *Th'Upright Heart and Pure*, ed. Amadeus Fiore, pp. 7–24. Pittsburgh: Duquesne University Press, 1967.

et al., ed. *A Variorum Commentary on the Poems of John Milton.* 6 vols. New York: Columbia University Press, 1970–.

Hunter, William B., Jr., John T. Shawcross, John M. Steadman, et al., eds. *A Milton Encyclopedia.* 9 vols. Lewisburg: Bucknell University Press, 1978–83.

"The Provenance of the *Christian Doctrine*." *Studies in English Literature 1500–1900* 32 (1992), pp. 129–66.

Jameson, Fredric. "Religion and Ideology: A Political Reading of *Paradise Lost.*" In *Literature, Politics, and Theory*, ed. Francis Barker, et al., pp. 35–56. London: Methuen, 1986.

Jemielity, Thomas. "Divine Derision and Scorn: The Hebrew Prophets and Satirists." *Cithara* 25 (1985), pp. 47–58.

Jones, J. R. *Country and Court: England, 1658–1714.* The New History of England, vol. V. London: Edward Arnold, 1978.

Kahn, Victoria. "Allegory, the Sublime, and the Rhetoric of Things Indifferent in *Paradise Lost.*" In *Creative Imitation: New Essays on Renaissance Literature in Honor of Thomas M. Greene*, ed. David Quint, et al., pp. 127–52. Binghamton, NY: MRTS, 1992.

Kantra, Robert A. *All Things Vain: Religious Satirists and Their Art.* University Park, PA: Pennsylvania State University Press, 1984.

Keeble, N. H. *The Literary Culture of Nonconformity in Later Seventeenth-Century England.* Athens, GA: University of Georgia Press, 1987.

Kenyon, John. *The Popish Plot.* London: Heinemann, 1972.

Kernan, Alvin. *The Cankered Muse: Satire of the English Renaissance.* New Haven: Yale University Press, 1959.

Kerrigan, William. *The Sacred Complex: On the Psychogenesis of "Paradise Lost."* Cambridge, MA: Harvard University Press, 1983.

King, John N. *English Reformation Literature: The Tudor Origins of the Protestant Tradition.* Princeton University Press, 1982.

"Milton's Bower of Bliss: A Rewriting of Spenser's Art of Married Love." *Renaissance and Reformation* n.s. 10 (1986), pp. 289–99.

Spenser's Poetry and the Reformation Tradition. Princeton University Press, 1990.

Tudor Royal Iconography: Literature and Art in an Age of Religious Crisis. Princeton Essays on the Arts. Princeton University Press, 1989.

Klein, Joan L. "The Demonic Bacchus in Spenser and Milton." *MiltonS* 21 (1985), pp. 93–118.

"From Errour to Acrasia." *HLQ* 41 (1977), pp. 173–99.

Knoppers, Laura L. *Historicizing Milton: Spectacle, Power, and Poetry in Restoration England.* Athens, GA: University of Georgia Press, 1994.

Knott, John R. *Discourses of Martyrdom in English Literature, 1563–1694.* Cambridge University Press, 1993.

Kolbrener, William. *Milton's Warring Angels: A Study of Critical Engagements.* Cambridge University Press, 1997.

Kranidas, Thomas, "Milton and the Rhetoric of Zeal." *Texas Studies in Language and Literature* 6 (1965), pp. 452, 432.

Labriola, Albert C. "The Medieval View of Christian History in *Paradise Lost.*" In *Milton and the Middle Ages.* Edited by John Mulryan. Lewisburg, PA: Bucknell University Press, pp. 125–27.

Lake, Peter. "Anti-popery: The Structure of a Prejudice." In *Conflict in Early Stuart England,* ed. R. Cust and Ann Hughes, pp. 72–106. New York: Longman, 1989.

Le Comte, Edward. "Milton as Satirist and Wit." In *Th'Upright Heart and Pure: Essays on John Milton Commemorating the Tercentenary of the Publication of Paradise Lost,* ed. Amadeus P. Fiore. Vol. X, pp. 45–59. Pittsburgh, PA: Duquesne University Press, 1967.

Lee, Sidney and Leslie Stephen, eds. *Dictionary of National Biography.* 63 vols. London: 1885–1900.

Leonard, John. "'Trembling Ear': The Historical Moment of *Lycidas.*" *Journal of Medieval and Renaissance Studies* 21 (1991), pp. 59–81.

Levitan, Alan. "The Parody of Pentecost in Chaucer's Summoner's Tale." *University of Toronto Quarterly* 40 (1970–71), pp. 236–46.

Lewalski, Barbara K. "How Radical Was the Young Milton?" In *Milton and Heresy,* ed. John Rumrich and Steven Dobranski, pp. 49–72. Cambridge University Press, 1998.

"Milton's *Comus* and the Politics of Masquing." (forthcoming)

"Paradise Lost" and the Rhetoric of Literary Forms. Princeton University Press, 1985.

Protestant Poetics and the Seventeenth-Century Religious Lyric. Princeton University Press, 1979.

"Structure and Symbolism of Vision in Michael's Prophecy, *Paradise Lost,* Books XI–XII" *Philological Quarterly* 42 (1963), pp. 25–35.

Lewis, C. S. *A Preface to "Paradise Lost."* London: Oxford University Press, 1942.

The Screwtape Letters. New York: Macmillan, 1948.

Lieb, Michael. *The Dialectics of Creation: Patterns of Birth and Regeneration in "Paradise*

Lost." Amherst, MA: University of Massachusetts Press, 1970.

"Milton among the Monks." In *Milton and the Middle Ages,* ed. John Mulryan, pp. 103–14. Lewisburg, PA: Bucknell University Press, 1982.

Poetics of the Holy: A Reading of Paradise Lost. Chapel Hill, NC: University of North Carolina Press, 1981.

Lindenbaum, Peter. "John Milton and the Republican Mode of Literary Production." *Yearbook of English Studies* 21 (1991), pp. 121–36.

"Lovemaking in Milton's Paradise." *MiltonS* 6 (1974), pp. 277–306.

Loewenstein, David. "'An Ambiguous Monster'; Representing Rebellion in Milton's Polemics and *Paradise Lost.*" *HLQ* 55 (1992), pp. 295–315.

"'Fair Offspring Nurs't in Princely Lore': On the Question of Milton's Early Radicalism." *MiltonS* 28 (1992), pp. 37–48.

'The Kingdom Within: Radical Religious Culture and the Politics of *Paradise Regained.*" *L&H,* 3rd. ser., 3 (1994), pp. 63–89.

Milton and the Drama of History: Historical Vision, Iconoclasm, and the Literary Imagination. Cambridge University Press, 1990.

Lovejoy, Arthur O. "Milton and the Paradox of the Fortunate Fall." In *English Literary History* 4 (1937), pp. 161–79.

Low, Anthony. *The Georgic Revolution.* Princeton University Press, 1985.

MacCallum, Hugh. "Milton and Sacred History: Books XI and XII of *Paradise Lost.*" In *Essays in English Literature from the Renaissance to the Victorian Age Presented to A.S.P. Woodhouse,* ed. Millar Maclure and F.W. Watt, pp. 149–68. University of Toronto Press, 1964.

Milton and the Sons of God: The Divine Image in Milton's Epic Poetry. University of Toronto Press, 1986.

Madsen, William G. *From Shadowy Types to Truth: Studies in Milton's Symbolism.* New Haven: Yale University Press, 1968.

Mager, Donald N. "John Bale and Early Tudor Sodomy Discourse." In *Queering the Renaissance,* ed. Jonathan Goldberg, pp. 141–61. Durham, NC: Duke University Press, 1994.

Marcus, Leah S. *The Politics of Mirth: Jonson, Herrick, Milton, Marvell, and the Defense of Old Holiday Pastimes.* University of Chicago Press, 1986.

Marks, Herbert. "The Twelve Prophets." In *The Literary Guide to the Bible,* ed. Robert Alter and Frank Kermode, pp. 207–33. Cambridge, MA: Harvard University Press, 1987.

Marx, Stephen. "The Prophet Disarmed: Milton and the Quakers." *Studies in English Literature: 1500–1900* 32 (1992), pp. 11–28.

Maus, Katharine E. *Inwardness and Theater in the English Renaissance.* University of Chicago Press, 1995.

McClung, William A. "The Architecture of Pandaemonium." *MiltonQ* 15 (1981), pp. 109–12.

McGuire, Maryann C. *Milton's Puritan Masque.* Athens, GA: University of Georgia Press, 1983.

McLoone, George H. "*Lycidas*: Hurled Bones and the Noble Mind of Reformed Congregations." *MiltonS* 26 (1990), pp. 59–80.

Miller, Timothy C. "Milton's Religion of the Spirit and 'the state of the Church' in Book XII of *Paradise Lost.*" *Restoration* 13 (1989), pp. 7–16.

Mollenkott, Virginia R. "The Cycle of Sins in *"Paradise Lost."* Book XI." *Modern Language Quarterly* 27 (1966), pp. 33–40.

Moore, Leslie E. *Beautiful Sublime: The Making of "Paradise Lost."* 1701–1734. Stanford University Press, 1990.

Morkan, Joel. "Wrath and Laughter: Milton's Ideas on Satire." *Studies in Philology* 69 (1972), pp. 475–95.

Murray, J. A. H., et al. *A New English Dictionary on Historical Principles.* 11 vols. Oxford University Press, 1884–1933.

Nicolson, Marjorie Hope. *John Milton: A Reader's Guide to His Poetry.* New York: Noonday Press, 1963.

Norbrook, David G. *Poetry and Politics in the English Renaissance.* London: Routledge and Kegan Paul, 1984.

Parker, William Riley. *Milton: A Biography.* 2 vols. Oxford: Clarendon Press, 1968.

Patterson, Annabel. *Censorship and Interpretation: The Conditions of Writing and Reading in Early Modern England.* Madison, WI: University of Wisconsin Press, 1984.

    "'Forc'd Fingers': Milton's Early Poems and Ideological Constraint." In *'The muses common-weale": Poetry and Politics in the Seventeenth Century*, ed. Claude Summers and Ted-Larry Pebworth, pp. 9–22. Columbia, MO: University of Missouri Press, 1988.

    Reading Between the Lines. Madison: University of Wisconsin Press, 1993.

    "Still Reading Spenser After All These Years?" *ELR* 25 (1995), pp. 432–44.

Pecheux, Sister Mary Christopher. "The Council Scenes in *Paradise Lost.*" In *Milton and the Scriptural Tradition: The Bible into Poetry*, ed. James H. Sims and Leland Ryken, pp. 82–103. Columbia, MO: University of Missouri Press, 1984.

    "The Second Adam and the Church in *Paradise Lost.*" *English Literary History* 34 (1967), pp. 173–87.

Poole, Kristen E. "Living with Insects, or Living within Sects: Swarming Wasps, the Liberated Conscience, and Thomas Edwards's *Gangraena.*" In *Form and Reform in Renaissance England: Essays in Honor of Barbara Kiefer Lewalski*, ed. Amy Boesky and Mary Crane. Newark: University of Delaware Press, (forthcoming).

Quilligan, Maureen. *Milton's Spenser: The Politics of Reading.* Ithaca, NY: Cornell University Press, 1983.

Quint, David. *Epic and Empire: Politics and Generic Form from Virgil to Milton.* Literature in History. Princeton University Press, 1993.

    "Milton, Fletcher, and the Gunpowder Plot." *Journal of the Warburg and Courtauld Institutes* 54 (1991), pp. 261–68.

Radzinowicz, Mary Ann. "The Politics of *Paradise Lost.*" In *Politics of Discourse: The Literature and History of Seventeenth-Century England*, ed. Kevin Sharpe and Steven N. Zwicker, pp. 204–29. Berkeley and Los Angeles: University of

California Press, 1987.

Revard, Stella Purce. *The War in Heaven: "Paradise Lost" and the Tradition of Satan's Rebellion.* Ithaca, NY: Cornell University Press, 1980.

Richardson, Jonathan. *Explanatory Remarks on "Paradise Lost"* (1734).

Ricks, Christopher. *Milton's Grand Style.* Oxford: Clarendon Press, 1963.

Rogers, John. *The Matter of Revolution: Science, Poetry, and Politics in the Age of Milton.* Ithaca, NY: Cornell University Press, 1996.

Rosenberg, D.M. "Satirical Technique in Milton's Polemical Prose." *Satire Newsletter* 5 (1971), pp. 91–97.

Rosenblatt, Jason. "Sir Edward Dering's Milton." *Modern Philology* 79 (1982), pp. 376–85.

Torah and Law in "Paradise Lost." Princeton University Press, 1994.

Rosenheim, Edward W. *Swift and the Satirist's Art.* University of Chicago Press, 1963.

Ross, Malcolm M. *Poetry and Dogma: The Transfiguration of Eucharistic Symbols in Seventeenth-Century English Poetry.* New Brunswick: Rutgers University Press, 1954.

Rovang, Paul. "Milton's War in Heaven as Apocalyptic Drama: 'The Foes Justly Hast in Derision'." *MiltonQ* 28 (1994), pp. 28–35.

Rubin, Miri. *Corpus Christi: The Eucharist in Late Medieval Culture.* Cambridge University Press, 1991.

Rumrich, John. *Matter of Glory: A New Preface to "Paradise Lost."* University of Pittsburgh Press, 1987.

'Milton's God and the Matter of Chaos." *PMLA* 110 (1995), pp. 1035–46.

Milton Unbound: Controversy and Reinterpretation. Cambridge University Press, 1996.

Samuel, Irene. "Milton on Comedy and Satire." *HLQ* 35 (1972), pp. 107–30.

Schoenberg, Estella. "Seventeenth-Century Propaganda in English Book Illustration." *Mosaic* 252 (Spring 1992), pp. 1–24.

Schoenfeldt, Michael C. *Prayer and Power: George Herbert and Renaissance Courtship.* University of Chicago Press, 1991.

Schultz, Howard. "Christ and Antichrist in *Paradise Regained*." *PMLA* 67 (1952), pp. 790–808.

Milton and Forbidden Knowledge. New York: MLA, 1955.

Schwartz, Regina. "From Shadowy Types to Shadowy Types: The Unendings of *Paradise Lost*." *MiltonS* 24 (1988), pp. 123–39.

Remembering and Repeating: On Milton's Theology and Poetics. Cambridge University Press, 1988.

Scribner, R.W. *For the Sake of the Simple Folk: Popular Propaganda for the German Reformation.* Cambridge University Press, 1981.

Shawcross, John T. "Assumptions and Reading Spenser." *Explorations in Renaissance Culture* 21 (1995), pp. 1–20.

John Milton: The Self and the World. Lexington, KY: University of Kentucky Press, 1993.

Milton: A Bibliography for the Years 1624–1700. Binghamton, NY: MRTS, 1984.

Shuger, Debora K. *Habits of Thought in the English Renaissance: Religion, Politics, and the Dominant Culture*. Berkeley and Los Angeles: University of California Press, 1990.

Sims, James H. *The Bible in Milton's Epics*. Gainesville: University of Florida Press, 1962.

Stallybrass, Peter and Allon White. *The Politics and Poetics of Transgression*. Ithaca, NY: Cornell University Press, 1986.

Steadman, John M. *Milton and the Renaissance Hero*. Oxford: Clarendon Press, 1967.

"'Teeth Will Be Provided': Satire and Religious or Ecclesiastical Humor." *Thalia* 6 (1984), pp. 23–31.

Stein, Arnold. *Answerable Style*. Minneapolis, MN: University of Minnesota Press, 1953.

Stroup, Thomas B. *Religious Rite and Ceremony in Milton's Poetry*. Lexington, KY: University of Kentucky Press, 1968.

Szittya, Penn. *The Antifraternal Tradition in Medieval Literature*. Princeton University Press, 1986.

Teskey, Gordon. "From Allegory to Dialectic: Imagining Error in Spenser and Milton." *PMLA* 101 (1986), pp. 9–23.

Tillyard, E. M. W. *The Elizabethan World Picture*. London: Chatto & Windus, 1943.

Milton. London: Chatto & Windus, 1930.

Studies in Milton. London: Chatto & Windus, 1951.

Treip, Mindele. *Allegorical Poetics and the Epic: The Renaissance Tradition to "Paradise Lost."* Lexington, KY: University of Kentucky Press, 1994.

Turner, James Grantham. *One Flesh: Paradisal and Sexual Relations in the Age of Milton*. Oxford: Clarendon Press, 1987.

Tyacke, Nicholas. *Anti-Calvinists: The Rise of English Arminianism c. 1590–1640*. Oxford: Clarendon Press, 1987.

Ulreich, John C., Jr. "Milton on the Eucharist: Some Second Thoughts about Sacramentalism." In *Milton and the Middle Ages*, ed. John Mulryan, pp. 32–56. Lewisburg, PA: Bucknell University Press, 1982.

"'And By Occasion Foretells': The Prophetic Voice in *Lycidas*." *MiltonS* 18 (1983), pp. 3–23.

Waddington, Raymond B. "The Death of Adam: Vision and Voice in Books XI and XII of *Paradise Lost*." *Modern Philology* 70 (1972), pp. 19–21.

Waters, D. Douglas. "Milton and the 'Mistress-Missa' Tradition." *MiltonQ* 6 (1972), pp. 6–8.

Duessa as Theological Satire. Colombia, MO: University of Missouri Press, 1970.

White, Paul Whitfield. *Theatre and Reformation: Protestantism, Patronage, and Playing in Tudor England*. Cambridge University Press, 1993.

Whiting, George W. "The Satire in *Eikonoklastes*." *Notes and Queries* 170 (1936), pp. 435–38.

Wilding, Michael. *Dragons Teeth: Literature in the English Revolution*. Oxford: Clarendon Press, 1987.

Wind, Edgar. *Pagan Mysteries in the Renaissance*. Revised ed. New York: Norton, 1968.

Wing, Donald. *Short Title Catalogue of Books Printed in England, Scotland, Ireland, Wales, and British America and of English Books Printed in Other Countries 1641–1700*, 2nd ed. revised and enlarged, 3 vols. New York: MLA, 1972.

Wittreich, Joseph A. *Visionary Poetics: Milton's Tradition and his Legacy*. San Marino: Huntington Library, 1979.

Wolfe, D. M. *Milton in the Puritan Revolution*. T. Nelson and Sons: New York, 1941.

Woodhouse, A. S. P. *The Heavenly Muse: A Preface to Milton*. Edited by Hugh MacCallum. University of Toronto Press, 1972.

Wooten, John. "The Comic Milton and Italian Burlesque Poets." *Cithara* 22 (1982), pp. 3–12.

"From Purgatory to the Paradise of Fools." *English Literary History* 49 (1982), pp. 741–50.

"The Metaphysics of Milton's Epic Burlesque." *MiltonS* 13 (1979), pp. 255–73.

"Satan, Satire, and Burlesque Fables." *MiltonQ* 12 (1978), pp. 51–58.

Worden, Blair. "John Milton and Oliver Cromwell." In *Soldiers, Writers, and Statesmen of the English Revolution*, ed. Ian Gentles, Joseph Morrill, and Blair Worden, pp. 243–64. Cambridge University Press, 1988.

"Milton, *Samson Agonistes*, and the Restoration." In *Culture and Society in the Stuart Restoration: Literature, Drama, History*, ed. Gerald MacLean, pp. 111–36. Cambridge University Press, 1995.

Zwicker, Steven N. *Lines of Authority: Politics and English Literary Culture, 1649–1689*. Ithaca, NY: Cornell University Press, 1993.

Index

Abbot, George, 18n.62
Abdiel, 126–28, 173, 180
Abel *see* Cain and Abel
Abraham, 172–73, 181–82
Adam and Eve, 81, 165, 172, 190
    fall of, 114, 121, 131, 134, 170
    matrimonial relationship between, 133,
        149–51, 164
    participation in Edenic "communion,"
        135–36, 141–42, 144–45
    relationship between, 85, 105–106
    temptation of, 108, 133
Addison, Joseph
    and neoclassicism, 2, 94, 123–24, 191–92
    on *PL*, 11–12, 69–70, 84, 90
    on satire, 101, 192
altars, 142
    Edenic, 137, 170
    Laudian, 32, 144, 189
    sacrificial, 158
Aldrich, Henry, 60, 65, 87
Anabaptism, 7, 169
Anglican, Anglicanism *see* England, Church of
antiformalism, 22, 95, 137, 189
    and heroism, 41, 190
    and John Milton, 2–3, 89, 175–76, 182
    and polemic tracts, 89, 102, 126–27
antitrinitarianism, 7
Aquinas, St. Thomas, 158
Arianism, 169
Ariosto, Lodovico
    Orlando furioso, 89–90, 121, 125
Arminianism, 7, 169
Arminius Between Truth and Heresy (broadsheet),
    71–72
Arminius, Jacobus, 71, 134
Atterbury, Francis, 65, 67
Aubrey, John, 10, 31
Augustine, St., 30, 80, 114, 148, 172, 175

Bakhtin, Mikhail,

and the carnivalesque, 16, 80, 167
    on parody or satire, 7, 78, 99, 124, 148
Bale, John, 21, 33, 146, 184
    Acts of English Votaries, 85n.46, 100n.19
    Image of Both Churches, 71, 78
    John Baptist's Preaching, 104
    Three Laws, 103
Bastwick, John, 27–29, 41
Bate, George, 11
Bayly, William, 176, 180–81, 186–87, 190
    Behold Rome's Monster, 100, 147
Belial, 179
    and demonic council, 121–23
    as cultural trope, 54–55
Bentley, Richard (the bookseller), 60, 65
Bentley, Richard (the publisher), 94–95
Bible,
    books of:
        Acts, 37, 99–100, 128, 177–78
        Corinthians, 83, 109, 150, 163, 186
        Corinthians, 103
        Ephesians, 40–41, 148, 150
        Exodus, 44–46, 163, 181
        Ezekiel, 29, 128
        Genesis, 100, 106, 149, 164, 169, 175
        Hebrews, 175, 177, 180, 185–86
        James, 77, 87, 151
        John, 29, 117
        Luke, 142, 178
        Matthew, 14, 30, 33, 53, 82, 95, 103, 173,
            178, 184
        Philippians, 77
        Proverbs, 14, 113–14, 116
        Psalms, 113–14, 120
        Revelation, 41, 47, 78, 82, 136, 155
        Song of Solomon, 161
    in English, 33, 40
bishop(s),
    anti-prelatism, 3
    see also episcopacy, Laud, prelacy
Blake, William, 111